e-Business

book 1

John Goymer

Endorsed by Edexcel

www.heinemann.co.uk
✓ Free online support
✓ Useful weblinks
✓ 24 hour online ordering

01865 888058

Heinemann

Inspiring generations

Heinemann Educational Publishers
Halley Court, Jordan Hill, Oxford OX2 8EJ
Part of Harcourt Education

Heinemann is the registered trademark of
Harcourt Education Limited

First published 2004

09 08 07 06 05 04
10 9 8 7 6 5 4 3 2 1

British Library Cataloguing in Publication Data is available
from the British Library on request.

ISBN 0 435 45447 1

Edited by Mick Watson
Designed by Artistix
Typeset by Tech-Set Ltd, Gateshead
Original illustrations © Harcourt Education Limited, 2004
Printed by Scotprint Ltd.

Websites
There are links to relevant websites in this book. In order to ensure that the links are up-to-date, that the links work
and that the sites aren't inadvertently linked to sites that could be considered offensive, we have made the links
available on the Heinemann website at www.heinemann.co.uk/hotlinks.
When you access the site, the Express Code is **4471P**.

Please note that the examples of websites suggested in this book were up to date at the time of writing. It is essential
for tutors to preview each site before using it to ensure that the URL is still accurate and the content is appropriate.
We suggest that tutors bookmark useful sites and consider enabling students to access them through the school or
college intranet.

Contents

For Philippa and Sophie

Acknowledgements

A wide range of experienced professionals have assisted with this book, as one might expect with such a diverse range of issues. My gratitude is extended to all those who have helped me. I especially wish to record my thanks to my colleague Denise Daniels, e-business course leader at South Tyneside College, whose original commitment to the e-business cause prompted and stimulated this work and whose ongoing intelligent advice and support for it have been immeasurable. Many of my colleagues have tolerated my regular distraction and sometime hysteria, with patience and good humour – I extend my thanks and gratitude to them all.

Beyond my own college, I owe a great deal to many active business professionals. Paul Callaghan, Chairman of Leighton Media, represents that rare phenomenon; a very successful e-business entrepreneur with his heart still in part rooted in his teaching origins. I owe a good deal to his friendly, encouraging advice and expert guidance. Other busy people in private industry have included Peter Merrie, Tom Wakefield and Phil Mordey of B & Q, who were always positive and supportive; as were Martin and Dave Robson of Save and Drive. Others spared me their valuable business time, often in unannounced *ad hoc* phone conversations and e-mails – people like Tom Prendergast of attoAbrasives in Ireland – again I extend my sincere thanks to them all.

I would like to thank commissioning editor Anna Fabrizio and senior editor Camilla Thomas of Heinemann for their strong encouragement and support from the very beginning of the work and latterly Mick Watson for his constructive assistance in producing the final text. Finally, thanks to my wife Susan for her tolerance and personal support during the work.

John Goymer, May 2004

The authors and publishers would like to thank the following individuals and organisations for permission to reproduce material and photographs:

Alamy Cover;
Corbis/Harcourt Education page 60 (right);
Harcourt Education/Gareth Boden page 32;
Macromedia pages 97 and 98;
Nokia page 33;
Powergen/Peter Richardson page 60 (left) and
Sainsbury's page 82.

Every effort has been made to contact copyright holders of material reproduced in this book. Any omissions will be rectified in subsequent printings if notice is given to the publishers.

Introduction

About e-business

e-business is a fascinating blend of two disciplines, Information Communications Technology (ICT) and Business studies – reflecting the reality of doing business in the 21st century. Because of e-business, ICT is being given extra meaning and substance, while business study is given added new twists and issues. There's nothing to fear in this and much to be gained as a student (*and* a teacher).

Your own personal strengths may veer towards technical ICT, (you might be a 'techy') or they might be more comfortable with general business topics (you are a 'suit'). Either way, there is enough content in this textbook to guide you enjoyably through this challenging variety of topics.

Why study e-business?

Save and Drive, a motor accessories retailer based in the city of Sunderland, sold *one* car roof box in the whole of 2003. By 5 o'clock on Thursday March 18th 2004, they had sold *seventeen* since the start of that day. How did they do this? By giving away free gifts? With offers of holidays, scooters or bikes? No, they did it by being *online* with a transactional website (one they could sell from) that was well presented and by having the background internal business processes to support their quality web presence. Check the business out at www.saveanddrive.co.uk.

Recent research from *The Computer Bulletin* has identified that a top company has *saved* on its transaction (buying and selling) costs by eighty-five percent. A medium sized company has *increased* its international sales and developed new markets. A small retailer has gone online and established a niche international market. Acme Whistles (see www.acmewhistles.co.uk) has successfully entered new global markets selling whistles all over the world. Then there's Save and Drive. The message is that businesses of all shapes and sizes are taking up e-business.

About this book

This book is designed to meet the needs of the six unit BTEC National (Applied) Award in e-business. Units 1 and 2 are assessed by an Integrated Vocational Assignment (IVA) that is internally assessed and externally reviewed; the remaining units are all internally assessed.

Assignment tasks within this text are presented in such a way that you can clearly see what you have to do to meet the basic pass requirements and what additional work you can do to build up to higher grades. You can choose your level and build up to top grades in your strongest areas.

The units covered in this book are:

- Unit 1 – Introduction to the internet & e-business
- Unit 2 – Internet marketing
- Unit 3 – Website design and construction
- Unit 5 – e-Business project
- Unit 6 – Government, e-business & society
- Unit 7 – Database systems
- Unit 13 – e-Business planning
- Unit 14 – e-Business implementation

Features of the book

Over to you   Thought-provoking questions for you to consider and respond to individually.

Chat room   Topics and issues generating discussions with class colleagues or teachers.

Connect   Invitations for you to connect to the internet and conduct research or investigations into e-business topics.

Outcome Activity   Tasks that are directly related to the assessment criteria for your course.

There is a glossary of terms and an index at the end of the book to give you further help. Terms that are included in the glossary are shown in **bold** where they first appear in the book. In the index, page numbers in **bold** indicate a glossary entry.

The study of business is rapidly changing because its subject matter, real business, has been – and remains – on a steep learning curve. We'd all best get used to e-business because it is here to stay!

Good luck with your e-business studies and congratulations on choosing such a forward facing programme.

John Goymer, May 2004

Unit 1 — Introduction to the internet & e-business

After completing Unit 1 you will be able to:

- describe the *range of business* organisations that use the internet
- show how various *aims and objectives* of businesses can be met via the internet
- describe how 'doing e-business' *impacts* (affects) customers
- illustrate possible *internet opportunities* for e-businesses.

> ***Your understanding of this unit will be tested via an externally marked Integrated Vocational Assignment (IVA).***

This unit will introduce you to the variety of ways in which modern business organisations are increasingly using the internet for e-business. You will learn about the range of business activities that now take place 'online' and consider the reasons why a business might choose to establish itself on the World Wide Web (www).

Notice the terms internet and World Wide Web are often used to refer to the same thing. In fact the term 'internet' refers to the network of linked computers around the world and the 'web' is formed by the software and applications that run across it. They are therefore two different things.

The ability to 'inter-network' computers has existed since around 1969. However, the web of software allowing information exchange has only taken off in the last ten years or so, thanks to the original work of Tim Berners-Lee at CERN.

Using the railway network as an illustration, the internet is the rails and carriages and the web is the 'content' sitting on it being transported. Unit 3 deals with this more fully. 'Being online' usually means that your computer is connected to the internet and you can use the web.

You will also learn about some of the issues that a business must face when it decides to create a presence on the internet. You will see examples of the wide range of different types of organisations using it, not all of them trying to make money. In the context of this book, any organisation making use of the internet for lawful purposes can be considered a 'business'.

How can you *compare and contrast* organisations that do business on the internet? What might be the objectives of a business in setting up an internet presence and how has this affected its customers or users? What further internet opportunities are there for businesses in the future? This unit contains 'e-Business insight' sections designed to give you an insight into the practical ways that the internet is being employed to help businesses work together.

In studying this unit, your main resource is likely to be the internet itself and the websites of the many organisations doing business online. When you examine or analyse a site, you are encouraged to think of the business that lies behind it. Try to get beyond merely describing a bouncy 'home' page; dig deeper and be systematic about analysing the site, considering what you identify as its purposes.

The internet is a tool that is being used to assist business processes taking place behind the scenes out of the public eye. Technologies are increasingly being intelligently applied, so that the 'front end' (the website) connects to internal information systems working in the background. This usually relates to three sorts of information (see Figure 1.1).

Figure 1.1 The website and the e-business

A website is not magic – it needs *information* to make it alive. This information has to be in digital format so that IT applications can make sense of it and it can be used on the internet. Throughout this book you may see references to related software applications. These are software applications that can take any (or a combination) of the three categories of information shown in Figure 1.1 above and make it useful for the online business using the internet. Examples of these are **CRM (Customer Relationship Management)** software and **ERP (Enterprise Resource Planning)** software. A new industry in providing this software has evolved, known as **Application Service Providers (ASP)** and hightech companies such as the Leighton Group are starting to specialise in this field. In other words, the website itself is only a part of the e-business story.

When you analyse a site, try to judge whether the site works in terms of what the online business intends to achieve; Does it promote the organisation behind it? Does it benefit the users? Could it do more? How? **Search engines** are valuable tools for seeking out supporting information. There are many to choose from. How you use them is important; here is a selection: www.google.com; www.ask.co.uk; www.excite.co.uk; www.yahoo.com.

Before we go any further, let us at this stage clarify what is e-business is and how it is distinct from e-commerce? e-Business refers to all of the digital systems and processes that combine to make an internet presence work. An e-business might be engaged in employing a range of web facing applications e.g. stock management systems, customer relationship management system or enterprise resource planning software. All of these applications are capable of giving life to a transactional website of the business. E-commerce is a sub set of e-business and refers to the buying and selling process on the internet.

You are lucky to be doing your important e-studies in these exciting early days of the business web. Enjoy the internet, it's time to start making it work *for* you!

1.1   Range of business internet use

Range

Consider the things around you that are man-made, i.e. things that have not grown and developed naturally. The chances are you will be in some sort of building – perhaps a library or a classroom. You are reading a book, possibly making notes with a pen or in your PC notebook. These physical things – *products* – have been produced by business organisations hoping to make a profit. The school or the college you attend is an organisation offering programmes of study as a *service.* There is a huge range of business organisations of all shapes and sizes engaged in making things or offering services. Most of them today are moving online. This section will help you to understand why.

A traditional view of business structure breaks down our economy into 'sectors' of industrial activity. The **Primary sector**; agriculture, or working in producing or extracting raw materials; the **Secondary sector**; manufacturing goods from raw materials; and the **Tertiary** (third) **sector** which is providing a range of services from finance to leisure activities. The economy of any country refers to the way in which it makes use of its scarce resources. Over time, countries tend to pass through various stages of development.

Over to you   List three UK organisations and categorise them as Primary, Secondary or Tertiary. Write a paragraph explaining what they do.

In Britain we started out as an agricultural society relying mainly on resources produced from our land. Then, quite early on in a world context, Britain began using machinery and equipment to make things in factories. This 'Industrial Revolution' dramatically changed the way we worked. Nowadays Britain – in common with many other developed nations – is undergoing another sort of revolution. In this revolution, more and more business activities are being conducted via computers (digitised) across the World Wide Web.

Today, whilst many small businesses still see only a limited need for an internet presence – so called '**bricks and mortar**' enterprises – many others are beginning to see the benefits of increasing internet activity and are combining traditional selling with online selling; these are known as '**clicks and mortar**' enterprises.

More and more firms, in various parts of our economy, are recognising the opportunities the internet offers. So, the internet, which has its origins in the USA's military and defence computer network (ARPAnet) as long ago as 1966, has grown to over 1 billion indexed web pages, available on more than 20 million websites (source: Chaffey, 2002).

No wonder internet technology is helping to create a new kind of 'e-economy'!

Connect

Look at the categories below and the related web addresses – sometimes known as the Uniform Resource Indicators (URI) or **Uniform Resource Locators (URL)**. Select six sites from *contrasting* organisations and access the websites. Bookmark these sites.

Disney	www.disney.com
Mothercare	www.mothercare.com
Houses of Parliament	www.parliament.uk
The Environment Agency	www.environment-agency.gov.uk
Agencies list	www.ngfl.gov.uk
UK Local Index	www.oultwood.com/localgov/england.htm
The BBC	www.bbc.co.uk
ITV	www.itv.co.uk
Sky	www.sky.com
The Open University	www.open.ac.uk
Online Learning	www.learndirect.co.uk
The Youth Hostels Association	www.yha.org.uk
Red Cross	www.redcross.org.uk
Age Concern	www.ace.org.uk
Barnados	www.barnardos.org.uk
B & Q Hardware	www.diy.com
GUS Home Shopping	www.gus.co.uk
Manchester United	www.manutd.com
Dell	www.dell.co.uk
Courier	www.klicka.com
Food and Drink Federation	www.fdf.org.uk
Freight Transport Association	www.fta.co.uk

How do you '*contrast*' online organisations? (This is something you have to do regularly in studying internet business). It is possible to contrast organisations on the internet in several ways.

1   Who is the website intended for? Private consumers or business consumers?

2   Is the online organisation operating for profit or not for profit?

3   Is the online organisation offering physical products or non-physical services?

4   Is the organisation buying or selling?

A glance down the list of categories in the box above shows us some of the wide range of business activities now being conducted on the internet. These activities frequently involve the classical business process of buying and selling, where products or services are exchanged for money. However, the list also shows that the e-business environment includes much more than that. Not only do commercial organisations promote and sell goods and services online for profit, but government and voluntary sector organisations are present on the internet for completely different reasons.

Connect

From the list given above, take a government sector website. How is an online presence supporting the activities of the government?

Another way to categorise the e-business environment is to distinguish between the parties involved in a transaction over the internet, whether this involves exchanging a physical product, providing a service, or just providing information. Doing this shows that internet activity can be sub-divided into the following sectors.

i   Commercial sectors (for profit):

- business to consumer   (**B2C**)
- business to business   (**B2B**)
- consumer to business   (C2B)
- consumer to consumer   (C2C)

ii   Non-commercial sectors (not for profit):

- government to consumer   (G2C)
- government to business   (G2B)
- voluntary sector bodies

The online commercial sector

Business2Consumer (B2C)

A B2C business offers to sell to private consumers rather than other businesses. B2C businesses are servicing *consumer* demand. Walk down any shopping mall and you will see a range of retail outlets offering goods for sale to consumers. Before the development of the internet, shopping was restricted to particular times and places. Shops were only open at certain times and closed at others. You had to travel to the shops. A shop on the internet is unlimited in time or space and there are no limits to what an internet retailer (known as an '**e-tailer**') can *offer* to consumers (only limits as to what they can practically *do*, as some early 'dot coms' found out). Take a look at supermarket chain Asda at www.asda.com or alternatively Tesco at www.tesco.com.

One thing worth noticing is that these e-tailers are often part of an *already established* retail firm. There is a big difference between adding an online sales channel to an existing firm and trying to set up a completely new online retail service. Most of the more recent growth in e-business is due to physical businesses adopting an '**e-strategy**'. Asda, shown below, is an example of this.

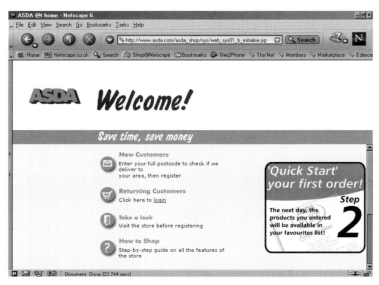

Figure 1.2 Asda.com

Connect

Have a look at the websites of some of the major retailers. Make a list of the services they offer to customers online.

The Amazon.com group is one of the most successful online businesses and a model for every online firm. Amazon.co.uk offers nearly 5 million books, together with information about them all, as well as **personalised** recommendations (see Figure 1.3 below) based on past choices from the site. The internet – a brilliant carrier of information content – not only gives e-tailers the chance to offer a wider range of choices, it also allows them to offer more backup services to consumers.

Figure 1.3 Amazon.co.uk

The problem of the abandoned shopping cart is a major issue for the e-tailer. Slow internet connections and download times, fears about intrusion, fears on security, will often drive even the most enthusiastic consumers away from internet shopping. Research has shown that sixty-seven percent of online shoppers drop out at the cart stage because of lack of speed. Despite this, online shopping is still on the increase. Greater use of faster broadband internet connection may be the solution but online suppliers still have to make a real internet offer to gain sales.

Business2Business (B2B)

In the online world, B2B is reported to be much bigger than B2C. Transactions between businesses may be less frequent over the internet, but account for more in terms of money value. The B2B business is buying from *and* selling to other businesses. It is either buying for its own internal MRO purposes (maintenance, repair and operations), or for items used as part of what is sold to another business in a supply chain. A report by *eMarketer* (www.eMarketer.com) predicted that by 2003 these kinds of transactions would amount to eighty-seven percent of total e-commerce.

Why has B2B internet trade become so significant? The reason is that there are many more opportunities for big deal transactions between businesses than there are for transactions with private customers. Figure 1.4 below illustrates this.

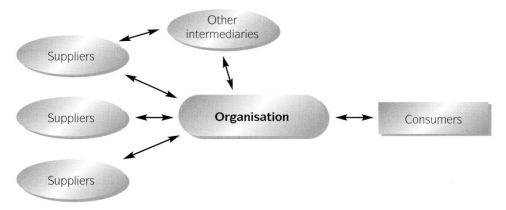

Figure 1.4 B2B and B2C interaction compared

The organisation (business) in the centre of the diagram has several suppliers (businesses); the suppliers themselves will also have suppliers (all businesses). Look at the number of (B2B) transactions that are taking place compared to those involving private consumers.

Online marketplaces for components are becoming more common. Ford and General Motors have joined forces and moved their $300 and $500 billion dollar supply chains online (see www.covisint.net).

Whilst there are millions of private consumers and more and more are using the internet to make purchases, these purchases are still relatively small scale in terms of value. The B2B online trading sector is vast, valuable and growing, because *transactions* are more frequent and are often very big value deals.

Chat room

Access the RS Components website which is available at http://rswww.com, navigate to the 'Purchasing Manager' page. Here you will find information about how the website can offer help to other business purchasers.

In pairs, discuss the main differences you can identify between a website designed for a B2C market such as www.Amazon.co.uk and one such as RS Components designed for a B2B marketplace. Prepare to present your findings using clear illustrations from the websites.

Consumer2Business (C2B)

In the C2B sector the consumer takes the lead in setting the terms of a transaction. An example of this is the pricescan.com website shown below.

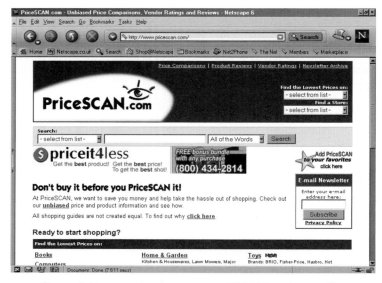

Figure 1.5 www.pricescan.com – a C2B driven transaction

Letsbuyit.com offers a website enabling collective consumer buying. By making it easy for intending purchasers to club together, better prices can be negotiated with Letsbuyit's partner suppliers (see www.letsbuyit.com).

Consumer2Consumer (C2C)

The internet enables direct transactions or interaction between consumers. Typically consumer auction sites such as eBay.com provide this facility. Other C2C interaction comes from consumer reviews e.g. Bizrate.com.

In both the C2B and the C2C online sectors, business intermediaries act as the enablers of the transactions. It is important however to be able to distinguish these sectors of internet activity.

Chat room

In pairs, select one example of a B2C website and one example of a B2B site.

What do you consider are the advantages (if any) for the <u>customer</u> in each case?

Draft a paragraph explaining why B2B transactions tend to amount to more than B2C. Explain this verbally in your own words to another student.

Non-commercial business organisations

The online non-commercial sector includes bodies that are not involved in trading goods or services for cash profit. Broadly, this falls into two sub-categories:

- government
- the voluntary sector.

Government

UK Prime Minister Tony Blair made the following announcements in 2000 with the intention of achieving these policy aims by 2005.

" *Today I am announcing a new campaign. Its goal is to get the UK online. To meet three targets: (1) Britain to be the best place in the world for e-commerce, with (2) universal access to the internet and (3) all government services on the net. In short, the UK online campaign aims to get business, people and government online...*"

"*...by 2005, people and businesses will be able to access government services 24 hours a day, seven days a week.*"

A '**portal**' is a specialist website gateway to a range of other related services and information on the internet. The government made a start on making public services accessible to us all online through its 'Citizen Portal'.

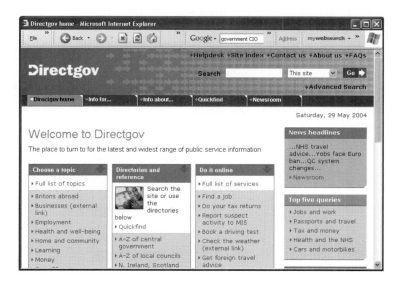

Figure 1.6 www.direct.gov.uk

The government portal at www.direct.gov.uk shown in Figure 1.6 shows how the internet can give access to a wide range of information about both local and central government services. Directgov offers links to over 1,000 related **public sector** websites. However, it is not just information that is offered. In many cases the services themselves can be provided online. Why walk to the Job Centre on a Thursday morning to sign a form if it can be done online?

The 'e-government' vision for the UK is that everyone should be able to access information from – and information about – government policies and activities. Businesses and individuals will be able to gain all the information they need about various aspects of law, policies and services. Internet technology is not just acting as a *supporting* technology here, it goes to the heart of government by helping to connect people to services and opening up the decision making process.

Connect

Access www.direct.gov.uk and follow the link to the A to Z of central government. Find the link to 'e-government'.

What is e-government?

Summarise the purpose of the e-government unit.

Just as we viewed the commercial sectors of the online world in terms of the parties involved in business transactions, we can also view the government online sector in terms of the intended users of the sites.

Government2Consumer (G2C)

Each and every citizen of the United Kingdom can be viewed as a 'consumer' of government services. There is hardly any aspect of our lives that is not in some way influenced or affected by government, both local and central. Hospitals, schools, transport, parks, employment prospects, the environment; the list can go on and on, as you will have seen from the Directgov website.

Figure 1.7 below shows how it is possible to register with the online Job Centre and gain access to all the information and documents you would need in a job search.

Figure 1.7 www.jobcentreonline.com

Government2Business (G2B)

In the UK, the British government has been recognised for one of the world's strongest and most imaginative projects in support of e-business. In September 2000, UK 'Online for Business' was launched at a cost of £67million. The services offered from ukonlineforbusiness are now available from the website of the Department for Trade and Industry (see Figure 1.8). Here, business leaders can gain detailed advice on e-business 'best practice'.

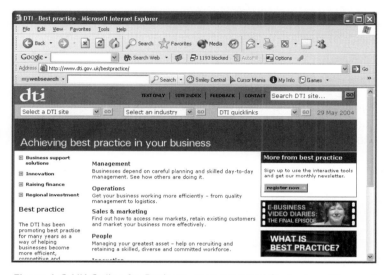

Figure 1.8 UK Online for Business, now accessed from www.dti.gov.uk

Connect

Access www.dti.gov.uk

Examine the 'best practice' part of the site, put yourself in the position of a small business manager. What services are available from this government resource?

Make a list of what benefits the site can offer someone thinking of placing his or her business online.

The voluntary sector

The voluntary sector refers to a huge range of organisations that do not operate for private profit and which depend on the voluntary support of individuals for both manpower and other resources. In 2002 there were 140,964 general charities in the UK, with a gross income of £15.6 billion (source: NCVO).

These organisations exist to offer help, or provide representation of, various groups and individuals in need. In a civilised advanced industrial society such as the United Kingdom we expect that government services will provide for the most needy groups. However, despite all the resources applied by the state, still there are many causes and interests that depend upon voluntary organisations.

See www.voluntarysectoronline.org.uk. This is another web portal promoting the activities of the voluntary sector, giving information on contact details and highlighting the importance of the internet in giving information and advice.

Connect

Visit www.voluntarysectoronline.org.uk and look at 'categories' on the left hand panel of the home page. Write a short summary outlining what you feel are the purposes of this website.

Do you think that the internet helps the voluntary sector?

Outcome activity

Internet Research
You have been asked to do some background research for the business development unit of the local authority. Senior officers want to be able to brief local members of the council about some of the latest economic developments. You have been asked to be thorough but straightforward.

1   Take three contrasting organisations from any sector and describe how they are making use of the internet for their specific purposes. You may decide to use a B2C, a B2B or a G2B organisation. Be sure that they are different in what they try to do.

2   Now take three totally web-based organisations, study what they do via the internet and make a careful critical judgement about the success of their operations. Be fully prepared to justify what you say (NB this may require some additional *background* research about a business away from the website itself).

1.2   Aims and objectives

All business organisations have aims and objectives. Before going on to look specifically at how these apply to the world of internet business, we need first of all to understand what might be the aims and objectives of *any* business organisation, whether operating in the physical or the digital world.

Purpose of business activity – the basic economic problem

Consider any group of people placed within a confined area of the world; on any piece of land, or on any remote island. What problems need to be considered straight away? First of all, is there food? Is there shelter? Have they got means of getting from one place to another? If there are none of these things, which shall be provided first? How? These basic problems – and of course many others – can be simply stated as; 'the people have *needs* and *wants*'. This is the basic *economic problem* of any country – how to exist and survive, using the scarce (limited) resources that are available.

We saw at the very beginning of this unit that in Britain we have passed through various stages in trying to solve this basic economic problem. People in the British Isles have in the distant past fought and squabbled over land, based on long forgotten kingdoms; they have settled into a peaceful agricultural way of life based on farming the fields; then they have industrialised and concentrated efforts in towns and factories using machinery – becoming 'the workshop of the world' as a result. Recently, as a nation, we have been concentrating more on services and less on manufacturing things. Now we are near the top of the world's 'e-readiness rankings', meaning we are more and more trying to make use of digital technology in doing business across the world, we seem to be getting ready for a digital future.

In the UK, our 'economic system' has been based on *private* ownership, meaning that resources have been acquired and used by private individuals and organisations for personal *profit*. People have been free to invest in businesses and offer goods and services to meet people's needs and wants. Consider an alternative situation, where a dictatorship tells you what colour clothes you can wear; where only a certain make of car shall be available; which decides whether you should eat bread or cake. In such a centrally planned system, freedom of individual choice is restricted. In our economic system and in the free enterprise (or capitalist) system that operates across most of the industrialised world today, people are free to make their own decisions about what to produce or buy and the economy is not tightly planned by any central authority.

We call this way of organising things a '*free market* economy'. By this, we mean that on the one side, consumers – wanting and needing things – generate *demand* for them. On the other side, producers (businesses) *supply* them. This interaction between demand and supply leads to a 'market price' for all kinds of goods and services.

A market economy tries to satisfy its various wants and needs by allowing and encouraging private businesses to offer goods and services wanted by consumers. Of course, our individual wants and needs are hugely varied. So in an advanced and complex economy such as ours there are many markets that can be served. Many of these markets serve private consumers (e.g. clothes, food, cars, houses, cosmetics) and many others are serving the needs of industry (e.g. machinery, raw materials).

Because we are an advanced and civilised society, for those services that are considered essential, but cannot be provided profitably by private business, the state – meaning the government – steps in, as we saw in Section 1.1. So our health services, social services, and education services are mainly organised and provided centrally by government organisations. These centrally provided services and activities are collectively known as the 'public sector' because what they do is not for profit, but for the benefit of all of us, the public. The aims and objectives of organisations must be understood against this background. Organisations exist for different reasons; some to make money, some to serve. Of course, there are many ways to make profits and many ways to serve the public.

Aims

An 'aim' for any business is a longer term goal, something that is to be achieved over a significant period of time and based upon a planned management strategy. For instance, in *private* business, aims might include:

- To survive
- To achieve profitability by a certain date
- To increase profits
- To improve the quality of our products
- To achieve technical excellence
- To be at the cutting edge of technology
- To be a leader in our market
- To improve market share
- To enter global markets.

Notice that most of these aims tend to be related to the main (but not the only) measure of private business success – *profit* and that this is achieved within the context of 'the market'. It is reasonable to assume therefore that all *private* business activity is geared –eventually – to profit *maximisation*. Among many possible definitions of profit, the most straightforward one will be used here.

Profit = the difference between TOTAL REVENUE from selling goods or services and TOTAL COSTS of selling goods and services.

Objectives

An 'objective' is a short term goal and will contribute to the strategic aims of the organisation. Whereas the strategic 'aim' tends to be expressed in general terms and provides an overall framework for activities, objectives are best described in **SMART** terms.

Specific – *'to raise profits'*

Measurable – *'by 20 percent'*

Achievable – *'by improving efficiency...'*

Realistic – *'based upon last year's figures and market trends'*

Time-related – *'in this year's trading'.*

All private business organisations hope eventually to make as much profit as possible. However, it might not be true to say that every business *at all times* is seeking profits. In the short term, many businesses are simply working to *continue* operating in a particular market. The 'objective' may well be simply to survive. This might particularly be the case where a business has undergone fairly significant changes in the way it works. A good example might be where a new technological approach has been adopted in order to open up a new channel for sales, in other words, establishing an internet presence.

Considerable investment will have been made and significant costs accepted. Managers will have planned for this expense and they will be aware that these costs cannot be recouped in a short period of time. Therefore, business 'objectives', for the short term, will have been adjusted.

Commercial reasons for going online

Break-even and profit maximisation

Private commercial online organisations generally exist to maximise profit, but they may not at *all* times be seeking profits. As we have seen; sometimes, for example at times of big investment – profits will be secondary to other things. Before considering any profit level, a business will be looking to simply *survive* by making sufficient sales in order to 'break-even'. In other words the business (at its **break-even point**) has to generate enough revenue through sales to cover its costs. See Figure 1.9.

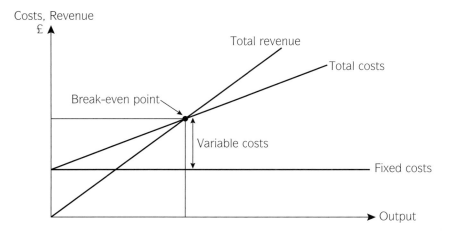

Figure 1.9 The break-even point

Costs can be 'variable' because they change according to what the business produces. For example, if a business is manufacturing football shirts, it has to pay for the material. *Each* shirt has a cost associated with it, a unit cost, so if 100 shirts are made, 100 times whatever the shirt material costs are, has to be paid. This is known as a '**variable cost**' because it varies according to the quantity of shirts manufactured. Other costs are 'fixed' because they have to be paid anyway, despite the number of shirts produced. These **fixed costs** might include rent for premises or other *overheads* such as heating. So...

Fixed costs + Variable costs = Total costs

Finally, the shirts have to be sold at a price to gain *revenue* (income). Total revenue is unit price × quantity sold.

The break-even point is the point where Total costs = Total revenue and can be calculated so long as the costs are known as well as the price that can be charged to the customer.

A business aim might – at a particular time – be to *increase sales revenue* by opening up a new internet sales channel. This will have big implications for both the costs of the firm as well as promising increased sales revenue. It is a decision that will not be taken lightly. Choosing to use the internet changes the cost base of the business as well as offering revenue benefits. These cost considerations of going online will depend on the kind of website that is planned.

Additional costs might include:

- website development and maintenance
- Internet Service Provision (**ISP**)
- hardware or software purchase
- staff training
- staff recruitment
- buying new software
- fulfilment of orders (**product fulfilment** – shipping)
- improving order response times (perhaps a call centre will be needed?).

There could be cost savings:

- on customer support as FAQs (Frequently Asked Questions) can be built into website.
- on premises as virtual malls, tours or exhibitions can be offered on the internet.
- generated from online relationships (good deals).
- on distribution where digital products can be sent via the web (e.g. printer drivers).
- as less paper documentation (e.g catalogues) is required; information can be offered electronically.

Because the internet is accessible around the world, available twenty four hours a day, seven days per week, it has enormous potential for generating sales *demand.* Remember, however, that whilst increased demand is almost a certainty from a well thought-out website offering a good, suitable product, there are considerable costs and investment decisions to be made. It is one thing to generate interest and demand for products and services, another to actually meet customer demands and satisfy his or her requirements.

The internet is all about carrying information. People choose to visit the website and place orders. This is the good news. The downside is that the order then has to be 'fulfilled'; i.e. delivered to the customer, in the right quantity, condition, to the right place, at the right time. A study in 2003 has shown that fulfilment costs in the online US retail sector were fifteen percent of total operating costs.

Kozmo.com was a **dot.com** failure in the US and a classic example of a 'pureplay' e-tailer (online only) making the seemingly irresistible offer of delivery *'within 1 hour at any time'.* The problem was that in many cases the company found it was paying as much to buy, store and deliver products as it was charging customers (see Unit 14 for more examples of poorly planned e-ventures).

Questions of storage, physical packaging and distribution, all have to be considered and costed. This will be discussed more in Unit 2.

Over to you   A small, locally successful wine business specialises in offering home brew kits and home brewed ready bottled wine. The owner is considering setting up an online presence and has asked for your expert advice.

- List the possible aims and objectives of going online
- Briefly summarise any possible problems you would anticipate.

It is worth noting that it took Amazon.com, one of the great success stories of the internet age, more than five years to achieve break-even.

The first set of objectives for an online business is therefore to do with survival and recovering initial costs, before profit maximisation.

Increase market share

A firm might go online with the different aim of increasing its market share. **Market share** is the ratio of sales of a particular product, to the total sales of that product type in a defined area, i.e. a country or a continent. A firm making a small family car in Europe will ask, out of all small family cars sold in Europe, what proportion are ours? The answer is usually expressed as a percentage and this is the market share.

Market share is an important measure of an online firm's success or otherwise. In October 2002, BarnesandNoble.com, a US-based 'clicks and mortar' bookseller working in direct online competition with Amazon.com, announced a quarterly drop in market share of book sales. BarnesandNoble.com had reported higher sales and lower costs, yet they had still lost over $30million in that trading period. Meanwhile Amazon.com were reporting a fifteen percent increase in sales over the year.

This kind of intense competition between rival online companies means that business leaders use market share analysis to measure the success or failure of their strategies. The BarnesandNoble.com decline in market share was enough to provoke a management shake-up of the business; people lost their jobs due to the fall in market share.

Connect

In pairs, research two product types in contrasting markets and summarise concisely but accurately as many details of their market share as you can find. Present the information appropriately using graphical presentation.

Growth

Many companies have taken advantage of the opportunities offered by online trading to pursue a strategy for overall **growth** of the business (see www.acmewhistles.co.uk for example). This might involve aiming to enter new global markets or extend a firm's product range. The firm will look to expand in terms of employing new staff or perhaps acquiring new capital equipment or premises. The internet has been rightly seen as an excellent new channel for sales and generating revenue.

Opening up such a new channel, as we have seen earlier, requires a great deal of investment and careful planning. Whilst a strategy for growth may offer great opportunities at first glance, it needs to be remembered that growth must be financed. An effective internet presence may well generate business and fuel growth, but it will also generate costs.

To increase and enhance the quality and variety of service delivery

A business may make a strategic decision to go online with a set of aims and objectives to do with offering a *better and more varied service* to its customers. This is best explained by examining the cases separately for B2C and B2B markets.

In *B2C markets*, every sensible business will look to improve its service to consumers in order to be competitive. Because the internet is first and foremost a content driven medium (after all, it is impossible to 'demonstrate' most products or services over the internet) an online business can seek to offer useful *information* that will benefit the consumer. Comparisons of prices, details of similar products, guarantees, product information, recommendations, can all be made available online.

In certain markets, say banking or insurance, the online firm has to ensure its *processes* are quick, secure, accurate and reasonably priced if it is to meet an objective of offering a better service. Smith and Chaffey (*e-Marketing Excellence*, 2002) list nine customer expectations from an e-retail viewpoint:

- Easy searching and browsing of a site
- Fast page downloads and no bugs

- Price, product information to be always correct

- Specification of delivery time and date to be available

- E-mail notification when despatch is made

- Personal data is secure

- Verification of high value orders

- Delivery on time, orders can be tracked

- Straightforward returns or replacement policy.

Great customer service will keep customers loyal!

Internet trading can support individual consumers on a *one to one* basis if it is properly implemented and is an excellent vehicle to improve customer service. E-mail links, FAQs, discussion forums and feedback forms can be used to enhance the offering to customers. If all else fails, consumers can make a telephone call to the online business.

In *B2B markets* the goal of offering a better service to customers becomes even more significant. B2B markets are growing rapidly and represent a huge global chunk of e-business. Within a supply chain, products must be delivered on time, they must be of the right quality and the potential purchaser must be able to find out what he/she needs to know about the product or the service. For example, a company making cars for a mass market must have components when it needs them because customers won't wait, they will simply buy an alternative model.

A business in a B2B market can achieve a great deal by going online. Indeed, in some industries (e.g. to supply Ford and Chrysler in the US) it is now becoming essential to be online or other firms will simply refuse to do business.

Chat room

In pairs, create a brief presentation clearly explaining the differences between a B2C market and a B2B. Give at least two illustrations in each case outlining how business aims and objectives might differ.

Customer relationships can be made much slicker through the use of internet connected CRM (Customer Relationship Management) software, that can link and connect all levels within a firm. External clients can access relevant company data via secure passwords. Crucial data to both a supplier and a customer can be shared. Automatic e-mail responses can be generated and digital records kept of who does what within a firm. This is important in business to business relationships when often technical issues have to be dealt with (see Unit 2). A firm requiring the replacement of a specific component of a machine for example, will not simply be 'shopping around' for the part. They will have very definite requirements and criteria and frequently specialist advice will be called for. The business able to supply not only the product, but excellent, speedy and reliable backup service will secure the business.

The concept of the '**vertical portal**' on the internet is interesting here. A vertical portal is a website which brings together all online participants within a particular industrial sector. So, for example, all firms involved in the pharmaceuticals industry will be accessible from a specific portal; all firms involved in petroleum will be accessible from another portal. The *effectively* online firm of the future may well have the competitive advantage by being present in the appropriate industrial portal. However it is not *essential* to be a participant via an industrial portal. The important thing is for the firm to be web oriented, with all of its internal systems and organisational processes geared to digital communication via the internet.

Research has shown that *retaining* existing customers is five times more profitable than acquiring new ones (Reicheld 1996). The internet is a good way of providing quick customer support services and can be a key part of a business strategy to achieve retention. The firm that achieves successful e-business implementation will increase its own standing within an industry. If properly planned and delivered, the online presence will speed up customer response times and add value to the firm's activities. Improved customer services will naturally follow. As customers experience delivery consistency and positive online relationships develop, the firm's reputation for reliability will spread.

Chat room

In groups, create a display entitled ' Business on the internet: the costs and the benefits'.

Include examples showing how three specific businesses may be achieving *different* objectives.

Non-commercial reasons for going online

Government

For the government sector there are many reasons to go online to meet their objectives. As internet usage increases the web can represent a major method of reaching citizens. Not only in terms of providing important information about government services or activities, but also as a means of *improving participation* in government. Online voting in elections has already been tried.

The government portal www.direct.gov.uk is a gateway to the whole range of services and agencies. *Improving the quality of service* to individuals and business organisations is a key aim of this citizens' portal. The term 'joined up government' was coined by Prime Minister Tony Blair. By that he was referring to the fact that the web allows the sharing of information via integrated e-services. To achieve the strategy of a 'citizen-centred e-government', three aims were set:

- Simple connectedness for all citizens
- Telephone access and e-forms widely available
- Integrated e-services.

Public disinterest towards the political process may be a dangerous thing. Political leaders and their officials must be concerned to ensure that what they do is presented factually and accurately to the people. The internet is a major tool in achieving this.

Whilst the internet represents an opportunity to improve public participation and connect people to government services, it is best not to over-exaggerate the *current* role of the internet in bringing all people closer to government services. A report published by the Department for Work and Pensions (DWP) in 2002 showed that the majority of people still prefer face to face contact when dealing with government officials. A phone call to sort out a pension problem, or a visit to the council offices to discuss a relative's home support, are still the preferred methods of contact.

Remember, many government services are geared to the elderly or those in need of social support, these are the least likely groups to; have easy access to the internet. The DWP report showed that only fourteen percent of retired people had, by November 2002, used the internet. However, the good news for e-government enthusiasts was that, of all groups questioned about the idea of dealing with the government online, a narrow majority said they would be "very, or fairly likely" to use the internet.

Chat room

Find out whether your local council has a website.

Make notes on what the site appears to offer citizens.

Discuss whether you feel the website helps the local council to deliver better services.

The voluntary sector

A 2002 'Charity channel' study in the USA showed that eighty-four percent of the general public were unsure whether charitable donations were actually put to good use; seventy-six percent said they were unsure whether to donate because they didn't know enough about the charitable organisation and fifty-eight percent claimed that they could not find a charitable body that represented the causes they felt most about. The internet has been rightly seen as an effective method of *informing the public* about the work of voluntary organisations and of seeking help. As is the case for the government sector, informing people and encouraging participation are two key aims of voluntary organisations.

Outcome activity

Visit www.VoluntarySectorOnline.org.uk and list the objectives of the site. Do you think the website is effective?

Choose three contrasting online organisations from the following categories and study their website:

- The voluntary sector
- A retailer
- A government body.

Explain in writing, with justifications, how you feel their differing objectives may be achieved using the internet.

Analyse how the aims and objectives of each organisation may in your view be more effectively achieved by being on the internet.

Use a sensible, clear layout for your work and carefully selected screen dumps where necessary to illustrate your points.

1.3 Impact

What has been the *impact* of the internet on various types of customer? How have they been affected?

In a typical business transaction money is exchanged for a product. In this exchange there are three important factors to consider. Firstly, there is the *business* that is selling; secondly the *product* that is offered for sale and thirdly the *consumer*, i.e. the business or individual wishing to purchase the product. Lawful business transactions take place within a political and legal context, a country. The government and its various agencies are at work in the background, implementing the rules and regulations and offering advice or assistance to businesses and consumers, so that they all work within the '**rule of law**'.

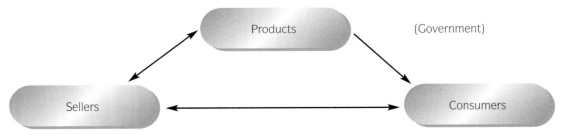

Figure 1.10 A typical business transaction

The internet is having a growing impact on this by helping to connect all of these elements. The various businesses offering products to markets can communicate with each other better, businesses can communicate with customers and *vice versa* and all parts of the community can communicate with the national government. Let's examine how this is happening.

Impact on business communication

A web page itself is the first piece of communication on the internet. The home page of any website informs anyone viewing it about the nature of the business, its contact details, its products and services. In a real sense, the website is the 'shop window' of an online business, it represents the business *brand*, giving it an identity and an 'online personality'. Placing a website up on the internet is therefore immediately an effort to communicate.

However it is *interactive* communication between the various participants that can make a real difference to performance and there are several ways in which the internet, in particular e-mail, is assisting communications between all of the component parts of a business transaction. Any business, in order to function effectively and profitably, needs to be in touch with the external environment in which it operates. This includes private customers, other businesses, government departments or agencies and voluntary bodies. No business ever operates in isolation. To receive and transmit up to the minute information is a vital part of good management.

Business to business communication – the impact of e-mail

Good *relationships* between businesses are increasingly important and all relationships depend upon good communication and understanding. E-mail combines the advantages of being immediate and in writing. Businesses can almost 'talk' to each other electronically. E-mails can attach other, sometimes complex, electronic files such as drawings, plans, reports, spreadsheets, presentations or photographs and dramatically speed up the communication process. Specialist CRM (Customer Relationship Management) software helps to integrate the whole communication process.

All businesses tend to be involved in buying and selling. Many are working exclusively with other businesses serving 'industrial markets' for example, products for use within industry, such as specific types of machinery. To be able to electronically communicate with partner firms around the world is a huge benefit. For example, an order can be placed and an e-mail can confirm receipt. An order might be delayed, an e-mail can explain and apologise quickly. An order may be despatched, and an e-mail can be sent to check all is well. Using internet technology effectively means that profiles can be built up of important clients or representatives in other firms and efficient lines of communication can be kept open. People in business expect a response to their communication and automated responses to e-mails when people are out of the office is now commonplace.

It is important to remember however that every medium of communication is dogged with problems that can prevent a message being properly received. In traditional methods of communication this can include poor handwriting, technical language not being understood, language or accent problems, inappropriate attitudes, or lack of concentration; these are all communication *barriers*.

With e-mail there is the problem of **SPAM** (**S**ending **P**ersistent **A**nnoying **M**ail, usually without permission, to *potential* customers) and there is a problem of over-mailing. This is a tendency to e-mail everything, to everybody. Whilst e-mail allows people to spread thoughts over several e-mails and 'talk' things through electronically with another firm, there are dangers in overloading people and reducing the impact of the e-mails that might be important.

Chat room

You are advising a long established small business on the question of electronic mail. What do you consider to be the main benefits? Are there any disadvantages?

E-mail is still however the most preferred method of business collaboration, (Ferris Research 2002). Even though web-based discussion forums are possible, they are regarded as too time consuming by most business managers. E-mail has the advantage of being quick, messages can cross the globe in seconds and can be sent to many recipients through mailing lists. Perhaps most importantly, e-mail saves a lot of money, being cheaper than a telephone call or postal rates.

Finally on the question of B2B communication, remember that electronic marketplaces are growing steadily in the digital world. Sometimes as we saw earlier, these are known as 'portals', 'exchanges' or hubs. In these virtual markets, (e.g. see www.bookacourse.com) businesses are able to position themselves online with other firms engaged in related products and markets. The internet in this case is allowing new relationships, increasing buyer/seller options, offering increased chances for collaboration or support and increasing the profile and status of the business.

 Connect

Access Google at www.google.co.uk. Enter a search for B2B product catalogues.

As an advisor to a catering equipment business management team considering creating an online presence, write a report advising them on the advantages of electronic catalogues for finding products or contacts.

Government to business communication

When people hear the word 'government', images of MPs shouting across the floor of the House of Commons tend to come to mind. The word 'government' does not, in fact, refer to those people in the House of Commons debating policy, but to people who actually carry out the decisions made by Parliament. The political party having the majority of seats in the House of Commons will usually get its way and is actually allowed to form a government. So, to take a specific example of putting policy into practice, Parliament decided some while ago it should be illegal to dump rubbish anywhere that is not properly supervised and steps would be taken against anybody doing so. Some people working for 'government' will actually make sure that that is implemented – in this case, the Environment Agency (not actually a government department, but working for government).

The Government is also responsible for the performance of the nation's economic policy and is working on behalf of all of us to ensure various rules and regulations controlling, as well as helping, businesses are implemented. It is therefore very important that it makes use of any medium that helps it to communicate more effectively with decision makers in firms.

The internet is allowing an increased flow of information from government departments to business and (importantly) permitting businesses to get in touch with one of the most relevant government departments to them, the **Department for Trade and Industry (DTI)**. Look for example at the following two pages from the DTI website.

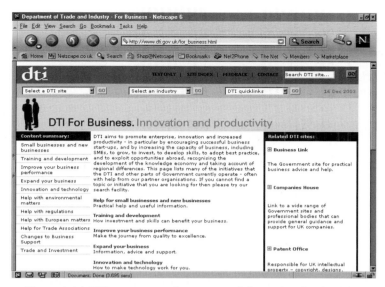

Figure 1.11 DTI page one – Government Information For Business

This is an example of how the internet carries information to the business community from government, offering structured information about all of the issues affecting every business enterprise and linking the page via links to other related services. See also Unit 6.

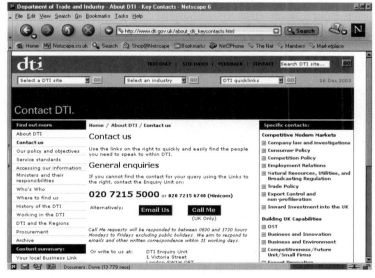

Figure 1.12 DTI Page two – web page requesting feedback from Business

This page encourages business people to contact the DTI. The *Feedback* link shown on the upper menu of the page gives an additional option for contact. These are clear illustrations of how the internet can encourage the flow and exchange of information between business and government.

Many businessmen and women, who would otherwise be unaware of the work of the DTI, now have a speedy and convenient channel of communication. Communication means that information is transmitted *and* received. Through the internet, accurate government data is posted up on the internet and made available to all businesses together with supporting information available through hyperlinks.

Connect

Visit www.dti.gov.uk and:

- Draft a description of the DTI website summarising what information it gives
- How would a small business in your opinion benefit from looking at the site?
- Write a short evaluation of how the DTI website can assist an e-business.

Business to consumer interaction

In the digital world, information flows quickly and freely across all kinds of barriers, both physical and political. It does not matter where the online business is *physically* located, products can be offered from anywhere to consumers anywhere, at any time. The most obvious impact of the internet is that it has brought *knowledge of a much wider range of products* into the homes of consumers wherever they are.

Home shopping is now made much easier and more appealing on the web, not only because there are many more retailers selling a huge range of goods online, but because a number of shopping 'portals' such as that at www.shopsafe.co.uk can offer well informed online advice and help to private consumers. A 'portal' could be thought of as a gateway site, leading to other sites dealing in a similar product.

Figure 1.13 Shopsafe – Helping the online shopper

The Shopsafe site offers a range of services aimed at making online shopping not only more convenient but a more efficient way to shop. Price *comparisons* are available to the consumer at the click of a button and products are categorised in a simple to use side bar on the home page. Static and video images can be made available so that consumers can view products in greater detail and, by using databases, experience a 'personalised' website.

Once an online store has been selected and the consumer seeks to make a purchase, all e-tailers offer a variety of options for customer contact. See the www.johnlewis.com page below. The company makes available an e-mail, telephone or fax option for customers to get in touch. This could potentially dramatically cut down the numbers of telephone queries.

Figure 1.14 John Lewis.com customer contact page

Connect

Access www.alienware.co.uk and find the link to Products. Click on Gaming Systems, then Desktop Systems and go to *Customize Case* link.

Draft a single page of A4 giving your views as to the customer's experience of this website. Do you feel that this company is making good use of internet technology?

By the end of 2002, the growth of internet shopping in the UK was running at 15 times the speed of general retail sales (IMRG group, November 2002). Retail sales over the internet in the UK, for the month of November 2002, had broken through the £1billion mark for the first time. UK consumers are clearly becoming more confident about shopping online and the increasing use of broadband will speed this up.

Chat room

Do you think private consumers are made more powerful through the internet? Justify your answer.

Equality of internet presence

On the high street or on the industrial estate – in the physical world – the size and scale of a business can obviously be seen as soon as a representative or a visitor pays a call. In the digital world, every business can, through the quality and content of its website, have an equal presence. This is an important point for many small firms. Sometimes orders are placed, or a **contract** agreed, simply on gut feelings or first impressions. These impressions can sometimes be based on preconceptions about reliability or quality. Through the medium of a well-designed website, smaller companies may communicate a message much more effectively, bypassing prejudices that might otherwise distort the message.

It is vital to remember however (as we saw in Section 1.2) that it is just as important not to *over*state your firm's capacity through a website. There are more ways than one to distort a message. The ability to meet commitments and offer reliable services or products is crucial in all markets.

Over to you   Using examples, explain why the internet is said to make firms equal irrespective of their size. Do you agree?

Impact on customer choice

By its very nature, the internet brings information about the whole world into the online consumer's home wherever they are. The only thing required is an internet connected PC or device and willingness on the part of the consumer to access the World Wide Web. The choices available on the internet are just about beyond imagination. We will examine some of the more significant areas of increased choice.

Choice of goods and services

The internet is having a growing impact on the choices available to customers in both B2C and B2B markets. Imagine walking into a physical shopping mall and instantaneously seeing all the shops available to you. A spectacular sight! Either a nightmare or a dream come true, depending on how you feel about shopping. Of course, in reality a visit to the physical shops usually means a trek around, looking for the items you want. On the internet the shops are not only arranged conveniently for you but they are classified into sectors so that the customer can access relevant online stores more easily. See www.247malls.com in Figure 1.15 for a retail shopping portal offering links to eighteen categories of store.

Figure 1.15 247 Malls.com – Increased customer choice

The Shopsafe.com and the 247malls.com sites illustrate how private online consumers have a vastly *increased variety of products* conveniently available from the internet, both physical goods as well as services such as finance and insurance. The way online providers compete with bricks and mortar firms, as we will discuss further in Unit 2, is by offering additional quality *information* for customers; as well as **customisation** opportunities such as that shown on the Alienware site earlier. Information is often about product alternatives, product and price comparisons, guarantees, offers, promotions and deals. Figure 1.16 below shows the DIY.com lawnmower price comparison chart. These things are essential if online shopping is to realistically be a serious option for consumers.

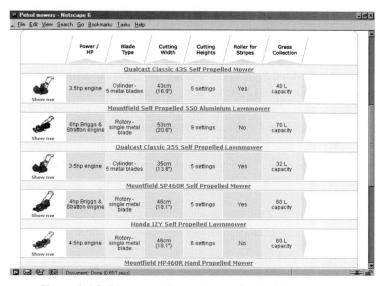

Figure 1.16 Diy.com – Comparisons of petrol lawnmowers

The B & Q Direct website at <u>www.diy.com</u> shows how customers considering buying a lawnmower can choose from seven different category menus showing a wide range of manufacturers at a range of prices. At a glance, the full range of lawnmower choices is available, together with features and prices.

A major task of any online retailer is to make the whole online shopping experience slick, enjoyable and free of stress. A big hurdle for many people is the thought that completing a transaction (payment) online will involve giving out credit card details and personal information. The task for the online business is to make the transaction quick, flexible and easy and reassure the shopper about security; yet, at the same time, the business has to acquire sufficient information about the customer to ensure that fraud does not occur. Huge losses for an online business are possible if a transaction system is not thorough and secure.

At diy.com the customer can monitor his or her 'shopping basket' at the top of the page, keep a check of the sub total showing the cost of goods selected, review and confirm their order or delete items if they wish, before 'checking out'. The transaction is a simple process of entering important personal details and even this can be speeded up by 'registering' with the website, meaning next time a shopper visits diy.com his or her details are stored.

Connect

Visit www.diy.com and select a product.

- Summarise the information that is available about that product
- Prepare to verbally describe to a student colleague the choices available
- Evaluate the quality of the shopping experience offered from the site
- Produce a brief summary of the process of making a purchase.

How do you feel customers might be affected by using this site?

Finally, in B2C markets, consumers are increasingly benefiting from the internet in making a car purchase. According to Cospirit Research, eighty-two percent of private car buyers across Europe reported in December 2002 that the internet had 'reassured' them about their purchase, fifty-eight percent had discovered new models on the internet and seventy-nine percent reported that the internet had saved them time and quickened their buying decision.

Connect

Search the UK web for car sales sites. Select a car you would like to purchase if you could afford it. Create a display showing the benefits or drawbacks of making an internet car purchase.

Services on the internet

Internet banking

Money makes the world go around, as they say. The trouble is that it does this twenty-four hours a day, so when banks were opening only at limited hours there was often a problem. Online banking is one of the most successful businesses available through the internet. A customer can access his or her accounts, view transaction histories, transfer funds and pay bills at his or her own convenience. Just about the only thing people are not presently able to do is actually make a cash deposit or withdrawal. A big effort is made to simplify the processes customers have to go through and some of the banks offer online guides and demonstrations to 'tutor' people through the steps.

Connect

Visit two internet bankers, eg. www.barclays.com and www.egg.com.

In pairs, review the main services offered. What are the features of these sites, how are they presented?. Comment on their ease of use. Why do you think 'services' seem to do well on the internet?

Internet insurance services

The internet is an ideal medium for delivering insurance information and it is possible online to get details of many types of insurance cover. Everything from pets, cars, business, life, holidays, breakdowns and home contents can be insured. Directories such as that available at www.insurance.org.uk provide a convenient source of information on the insurance companies online.

Internet auctions

A traditional auction would be held in a specific location and potential bidders would have to travel there, examine the goods and arrange to attend the event in order to bid. Online auctions enable anyone at the right time to view goods and make a live bid. Perhaps the most well known site is www.ebay.com , one of several in which online visitors can become either a bidder, an auctioneer or both.

 **Connect**

The internet carries a vast range of services.

In groups, do an internet search and create a table showing as many online services as you can. (e.g. travel, job search, CV writing).

Increased opportunities for e-learning

The internet is turning out to be a major method of delivering electronic learning to people of all ages. Recent surveys have shown that young schoolchildren know more about the internet than they know about books. Research also shows that computer-based learning can be very effective in improving results in important examinations, *if* materials are interactive and enable the user to work with and manipulate information. People can also follow many work-based courses online and complete tutorials leading to recognised qualifications.

The site at www.blackboard.com enables trainers or teachers to set up a free course site which is internet delivered, password protected and capable of holding lots of course information. Many centres are now using ***Virtual Learning Environment (VLE)*** software, in which learners become part of an internet (or **Intranet**) based group of learners. All that is needed to become part of this learning group is access to a networked PC. In this VLE, contact is maintained with tutors online, discussion threads can be set up and communication is maintained via e-mail or electronic bulletin board (see also www.fdlearning.com).

It is a central part of the government's education and skills policy that people take advantage of the opportunities offered by e-learning. We live in a so-called 'learning age' (see www.dfes.gov.uk) and the hope is that everyone, throughout life, will take advantage of electronic learning to update his or her skills and knowledge. Many work-based training courses are now delivered solely online. This gives flexibility as to the time, pace and place of learning and both the employee and employer benefit.

Connect

Divide into groups of between two and four. Access two of the following e-learning websites and prepare informative poster displays showing what they are about and assessing their benefits for both learners and teachers.

- www.bbc.co.uk/education/home
- www.campaign-for-learning.org.uk
- www.edu4kids.com
- www.ngfl.gov.uk
- www.learndirect.co.uk
- www.bookacourse.com
- www.schoolsnet.com
- www.fdlearning.com

Extended internet access

In the very earliest days of the internet the computers being used tended to be huge things that had to be transported by lorry, unloaded by crane and carefully placed within specially dedicated and air conditioned 'computer rooms'. Over the years, technological developments have allowed smaller and smaller and more portable pieces of equipment to be used. Mobile access to the internet has been possible for a number of years and the need to use a fairly bulky item of equipment was overcome by the introduction of handheld devices known as **Personal Digital Assistants (PDAs)**.

A handheld PDA

At present people all over the world tend to access the internet through a *wired* PC either at home or at work. The so-called 'next generation' of users will have the ability to make use of the internet through a much broader range of more portable devices. Currently, a minority of people have the ability to access *some* internet content through **WAP (Wireless Application Protocol)** mobile phones. Websites however, have to be specially

designed so that WAP content can be displayed on the small screens of mobiles and not all internet services are available. The latest, third generation (3G) technology allows those with the right handsets to quickly download internet video clips or MP3 files as well as make use of e-mail and messaging services. 3G technology has much quicker data transfer than previous mobile internet technologies.

Interactive digital television is offered by a number of companies and allows some internet use (Sky, ON Digital, ntl, Telewest). Using a set top decoder, messages can be received from a satellite or a cable and displayed on a TV. The set top box contains a modem that can be used to pass back selections made from the remote control across the internet. There is still a limited internet content available because suppliers have found the medium expensive.

3G (third generation)
mobile phones

Online discussions

Customers not only have an increased range of products and services available from the internet, they also have an increased ability to engage in online discussions about products or services. These discussion forums make use of the ability of the internet to enable 'synchronous' communication. This is text-based chat between different users who are logged on at the same time. Consumers can compare experiences of products and seek advice.

The power of internet consumers is increased by his or her ability to make online comment both about specific products and about particular markets. For example, see www.which.co.uk , a site containing many categories of product and offering visitors the chance not only to receive comparative reports but offering the chance to place comment about his or her own experiences.

The potential for consumers to make comment about products can be damaging for any business. To receive bad reviews about your latest product, whatever it may be, could seriously damage your image. Once an image, or 'brand' has been tarnished online, it could take quite a lot of work to repair the damage.

There seems little doubt that the internet has empowered consumers in several ways. A sub-standard product will quickly be found out and negative comment will rapidly spread. Think of it; in the physical world, if you live in a town with one cycle shop, you would be hard-pressed to decide to use another shop if it is 20 miles away. On the internet, the alternative business is only a few clicks from you.

Connect

Choose a particular product (such as Apple's iPod – see www.Apple.com) or market and seek out either an online discussion forum or a product consumer review.

Assess the value of this from the point of view of:

1 the consumer

2 the online business.

What do you think is the value of online discussion boards? Do you feel that Apple.com get any benefit from them?

Impact on product prices

The internet is having an effect on online product prices in two ways:

- **Disintermediation**
- **Dynamic pricing**.

Disintermediation

The costs associated with supplying products to the market are potentially cut through direct online trading. Traditional retail sales were serviced by products coming from the manufacturer as shown in Figure 1.17 below.

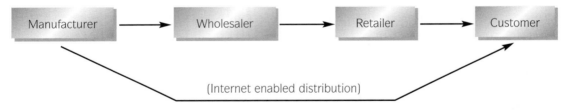

Figure 1.17 A typical distribution channel

Wholesalers and retailers, in relation to the manufacturer, are known as 'channel partners'. Because the internet allows the manufacturers in some cases to by-pass these partners and supply directly to the customer, costs are cut significantly. For example there are no selling costs (for the manufacturer) to each intermediate partner and no costs of physical distribution to them. This process, known as *disintermediation*, allows cost savings as high as sixty percent if online business eliminates all intermediaries.

The internet has a way of generating new forms of business. One of these has arisen as a direct result of disintermediation. Consumers need assistance and advice about the range of products available and comparative prices. To cater for this need, new 'intermediaries' have arisen in the form of websites offering easy price/product comparisons and reviews (e.g. Shopsafe). Now, instead of the consumer surfing from site to site and attempting to extract relevant information, possibly a slow and time consuming task, sites are available to offer this kind of consumer service. This process has become known as **reintermediation** and it is occurring in both B2C and B2B markets (the portal, exchange and hub sites mentioned earlier are examples in the B2B context). This means that a company buyer in a B2B market can access masses of data on comparative prices; the individual private consumer can look at a web directory or mall and quickly be equipped with a broad range of prices.

Connect

In groups, choose a search engine such as Google.com to access a web directory, or access a known intermediary website such as www.kelkoo.com.

Select a specific product and evaluate the service being offered. In what ways, if at all, is the consumer benefiting?

Dynamic pricing

In a traditional shop, prices of goods are determined before you ever pass through the door. Manufacturers' costs, plus retail costs for staff and overheads, plus a profit margin, give you the asking price in the shop. On the internet, where price comparisons are easy and where many specialist sites are enabling shoppers to get more and more information (see Section 1.2), fixed pricing does not work so well. Dynamic pricing means that data from the internet can be used by software tools to constantly *change* prices according to market conditions. The airline industry is a typical illustration. Today, all airlines offer ticket pricing based on dynamic pricing according to the demand for seats. High interest for a particular flight will lead to higher prices. Flights with empty seats will be cheaper particularly nearer the flight time.

In B2B markets, data about customers, competitor prices, high and low prices for the week or month is added to the firm's own knowledge about what is, or is not, an acceptable price for a product. The sales staff are obviously in touch with the pricing system and are able to quickly offer a quote. This may seem just like the old 'haggling' situation that has existed for years in B2B contexts. However, it is constantly moving with external conditions and being updated with new facts.

Outcome activity

Dynamic pricing
In your own words describe what is meant by 'dynamic pricing'.
In your view, who benefits?

Take three contrasting customers, as outlined below. Describe how the internet affects each customer and say whether you think the relevant websites improve the quality of service.

1 A young person wishes to use a YHA hostel at Kielder Forest.

2 A lady wishes to purchase a petrol lawnmower from B & Q Direct.

3 A man wishes to look for car insurance services.

1.4 Internet opportunities

In just about every business case, the internet is capable of providing new opportunities. These opportunities are particularly important for the private profit-seeking organisation because they relate to two broad areas:

- operating efficiencies
- enhanced competitiveness.

To *operate more efficiently* means that internal *processes* are smoother and they achieve something more quickly. Managers want things to be done properly (e.g. customer records kept) but they also want them done efficiently and accurately. Cash efficiencies relate to the *costs* of doing something and generating income.

To be more *competitive* means that the business improves its position to attract and serve customers so gains an advantage over its competitors. Perhaps it finds a way to know more about the competition, or sees how it can respond more quickly to changes in customers' wants and needs (see page 46).

Often, a business will make an improvement that improves operating efficiency, reduces cost and enhances competitiveness all at once. Because e-business activities are so interrelated, it is rare for an improvement to affect *only* operations, costs or competitiveness; there are usually benefits throughout.

Supply chain efficiencies

Operating efficiencies are those that relate to the way the business works, both within its own organisation and in its collaboration with outside partner firms. This relates particularly to a supply chain context, in other words buying from or selling to, other firms.

In B2B markets a business is operating as one link in the supply chain. Such a business will be *both* a buyer and a seller, buying products *from* other businesses and selling *to* others. The company that manufactures replica strips of football teams for instance, has to buy (or 'procure') the materials it uses before it can sell finished garments to the retail outlets. The Ford Motor Company uses in excess of 10,000 individual components for each car it produces. These individual car components will be manufactured by outside firms that themselves use other components. To create smoother, faster ways of dealing with firms you regularly buy from, or sell to, is a real opportunity to save on costs, be more competitive and be quicker to get products from factory to market (see Kingspan opposite).

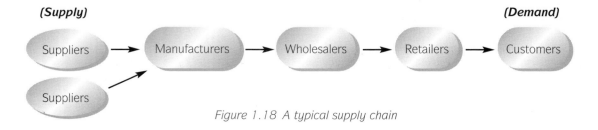

Figure 1.18 A typical supply chain

What kind of opportunities is the internet offering in this supply chain context?

The following *e-Business insight* is about an Irish firm called Kingspan. It is particularly related to how people can work together better using the web.

e-Business insight   Kingspan

Background

Kingspan Insulated Roof and Wall Systems are part of the Kingspan Group PLC. They are market leaders in the manufacture of superior quality insulated roof and wall cladding systems for the building industry and they are based in Co.Cavan, Ireland.

In 1994 Kingspan developed a paper-based design manual for architects and designers about roofing and cladding. This manual transformed the Kingspan brand and they became recognised as a leading company by architects. Soon it was decided to produce an electronic version of the manual. In 1995 the CD-ROM version of the Kingspan manual was produced.

In 1998 Kingspan appointed a company called Cadapters to develop and launch the www.kingspanpanels.com website – a static site, simply designed to offer company and product information to the industry.

Market information

The market for roof and wall insulation systems works like this:

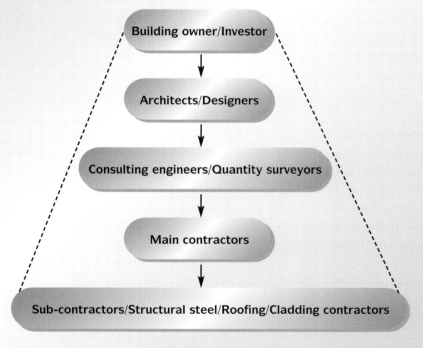

At the top of the pyramid are the building owners or investors, the most influential group of decision makers. Next the people appointed to design the building (including choosing the materials used), then the various technical specialists, down to the sub-contractors who actually buy and use the materials in the construction process.

From a sales viewpoint, Kingspan have to influence each layer of the pyramid, from the sub and main contractors up to the owner/investors. Effective communication between the layers in the hierarchy is vital. At the level of the architect, information requirements are very technical, panel specifications and precise measurements being crucial.

e-Business aims

Kingspan wanted to create an online ordering system that allowed for fast, accurate, order processing. Roofing and cladding contractors, architects or anybody else considering Kingspan products needed to be convinced that products could easily be researched, specified and prices clarified via the website. Added to this would be helpful detailed graphical images of panels and a range of complementary products.

The experience

The Kingspan online ordering system has dramatically reduced errors in order processing. The system highlights mistaken combinations in an order and automatically suggests corrections (impossible in a paper-based system).

Whilst 45 out of 47 structural steel contractors in Ireland use the Kingspan Ordering System, in the roofing and cladding sector things are slightly more slow to develop. This sector seems to be less **ICT** literate or confident. Kingspan needed to be able to identify a customer's member of staff who could deal with the information about their products and use their system. ICT literacy combined with Kingspan product understanding was important to the system.

Kingspan have been at the forefront in **innovation** using internet technologies and are influencing the roofing/cladding market. They plan to further develop an entirely online Cladding Solutions Package to meet the different needs of each level in the market.

A more detailed case study about this company is available on Enterprise Ireland's e-Business website www.openup.ie

Thanks to Tom Prendergast, Kingspan

The Kingspan insight above shows how the internet is a tremendous tool that can potentially enable all firms within a supply chain to *share and communicate relevant information*. So, in different markets, if consumer preferences change and demand is affected, retailers at the local level are usually the first to become aware, because they are closest to customers. However, using the internet, data can be picked up by retail managers, saved and made digitally available to all companies and passed back through the various supply chain partner firms.

So, if Kingspan became aware of technical changes that were required in cladding or insulation, the information could be communicated via the web to where it is needed. In this way, an integrated response by the different participating firms can be made possible. Important external factors, such as local regulatory or economic changes that might affect demand (such as unemployment) can be identified, then *shared* and acted upon. The internet offers an ideal electronic link between organisations; it has the potential to eliminate distortions in information about market conditions that is crucial to proper business operation. Later in this section, we look at the 4Projects software available from Leighton at www.4Projects.com which offers a slightly different perspective on using internet technology.

To be a participating and *connected* business within the supply chain therefore offers a real opportunity to be more *informed*, more *efficient* and more *competitive*. A November 2001 study by Stanford University and Accenture looked at 100 manufacturers and 100 retailers in the food and consumer products industry. The results showed that those companies involved in higher levels of information *sharing* had higher than average profits.

Information can easily be shared along the supply chain, but what is done with that information by business leaders is what makes the difference. One important way in which shared information can be useful is in product planning. Businesses need to make forecasts for buying (procurement) and replacing stocks, or for deciding whether stocks need replacing at all. They may need to plan for increased (or reduced) production. Should *new* products be introduced to the market? Or existing ones be developed?

Often it will be beneficial to think about these things in collaboration with others in an industry. Through the internet, electronic data is accessible not only about external trends, but also about respective companies' specialist personnel, about who should be contacted, who needs information to get decisions taken and by when. This is known as '*synchronised* planning'. Like the synchronised swimmers in the pool, who all move in planned manoeuvres at the same time, all firms are able to plan specific actions together, based on speedy and up to the minute information. Product design questions can be shared and discussed, saving time and money. The process of planning is better informed and therefore more efficient.

Over to you   Select a physical product that you are familiar with. Draw a simple diagram to illustrate the supply chain for that product. Label the diagram showing at least three ways in which online co-operation might help businesses in the chain.

Software applications are being developed to help companies make better use of the internet's improved communication abilities. Adaptec is a company with a widely dispersed supply chain and many new and changing hightech products. Using a piece of software called Alliance, the company communicates with its design centre in California, its factory in Taiwan and its manufacturing plants in Japan, Hong Kong and Singapore, exchanging detailed and complex design drawings, **prototype** plans, test results and production and delivery schedules. Orders or parts requisitions can be tracked so that managers are able to plan ahead. The internet, used like this together with well designed background software, has helped Adaptec to respond quickly to any supply chain problems and has significantly shortened product development times. This represents real cost savings and has improved Adaptec's competitiveness.

Chat room

In groups, consider yourselves as a small independent brewer. You have four real ales that you sell to local pubs very successfully. Now you wish to bottle your beers. Consider the ways in which the internet might help you develop this business. Present your findings to your whole group.

e-Business insight   attoAbrasives

Background

attoAbrasives (www.attoabrasives.com) manufacture and distribute specialised abrasives for the automotive, aerospace and medical device industries. Products range from specialist precision cutting and grinding wheels to sandpaper.

Business to business selling is the main means of distribution and attoAbrasives products are sold from a wide range of dealers, trade outlets, DIY multiples, independent retailers and builders' merchants.

Throughout the world, all manufacturers of abrasives use the American Standards System as a standard to measure and describe grades of abrasives. It is technically very important for all end-users of abrasives products to know exactly what they are ordering in relation to his or her specific requirements.

The e-business plan

In November 2000, attoAbrasives began implementation of a new e-business system designed to:

- Create a web-based customer self-service site available 24 × 7. Customers can access the full product range with immediate availability of a grade cross-referencing service

- Offer online technical support to meet the specific needs of each customer

- Offer the online ability to check technical specifications and availability of the product

- Allow online order processing and order progress tracking

- Allow online account review and invoice enquiry.

The experience

attoAbrasives have been pleased with the move to online business and feel that, although not all customers are fully ready for a complete online relationship, they as a company are extremely well placed for the future. Short term benefits have been noticed by:

- **attoAbrasives** – Improved stock control and pricing; better **targeting** of market and lots of information gathered on competitors.

- **customers** – Easier access to products and standard pricing information.

Conclusion

attoAbrasives see e-business as a growing and deepening dimension to their business strategy. Their aim is to focus on strong online technical support for customers whilst simultaneously introducing additional new products based on client requirements.

Key to achieving these objectives are strong online customer relationships and excellent internet-sourced knowledge about the markets they serve. With these things in mind, attoAbrasives aim to continue building upon the significant growth they have so far achieved.

A more detailed case study about this company is available on Enterprise Ireland's e-Business website www.openup.ie

Whilst the Kingspan example shows an admirable effort on the part of one leading firm to enhance the level of collaboration on the web, problems arise when firms take this kind of initiative in complete isolation from others. The risks involved in making a big investment in creating inhouse software, are considerable when one considers that others may not be able to (digitally) work with you.

One way to avoid this kind of risk is by employing the services of an Application Services Provider (ASP) such as Leighton (www.Leighton.com), the company who offer the 4Projects package described in the *e-Business insight* panel below.

e-Business insight · The Leighton Group – 4Projects application

The Leighton Group is a Sunderland-based company operating in the UK, Canada and Belgium. Starting out in publishing, the firm has branched out to become a leading edge provider of web-based applications, one of the most innovative products being 4Projects.

4Projects is not a project management *tool,* but a comprehensive software application designed to enable partner companies to effectively collaborate using an extranet across the web. *It particularly applies in a construction context, where a number of firms must work closely together to see a building project come to fruition.*

Leighton realised very quickly that most firms simply have neither the expertise, nor the time, to develop in-house software that will be of mutual benefit within an industry or when working on a joint project with other firms. Even if a single firm did devote resources to develop software, other partner firms may not. By offering a flexible, modularised, package that has multiple capabilities, Leighton have been able to create an application that can transform web-based collaboration.

What does the 4Projects application do?

Firstly, 4Projects is an extranet-based platform. This means that firms buying into the application enter into a secure wide area network along with other partner companies. Immediately the problems inherent in the internet, or public e-mail accounts are overcome. Extranets are robust, secure and flexible.

The software is designed to be totally flexible and capable of being configured to meet many requirements. The application consists of a number of 'component' modules. These include:

- Document management
- Task management
- Versioned forms
- Calendar management
- Search engine
- Distribution
- Work-flow management
- Discussions.

- Packaging
- Spell checker
- Contact management
- Instant messaging
- Generic forms engine
- Data interfaces
- Real time collaboration

What is it used for?

If Tesco – for example – plan to build a new store somewhere; from initial design concepts, to groundwork and roofwork, fittings and electricals, each firm that is contracted to work on the project is able to log onto 4Projects and make use of the facilities that are relevant to them. 4Projects gives potentially full access to all drawings, documents, and contacts. The software creates a 'virtual project environment', bringing all parties together (if necessary, literally whilst online).

Take a straightforward issue, common in the construction industry. An architect alters a design, a drawing is changed, a new version needs to be issued and all parties made aware. In the past, this was fraught with potential problems as one party or another failed to act upon the new design. With 4Projects new drawings can be issued, everyone gets to know, old drawings are archived and the work is fully documented. There is little or no scope for error.

If people working on a project – wherever it may physically be – need to see images of a site, a building, a room, then thumbnail images can be stored and distributed.

Contact management features within the package allow users to build up lists for document distribution, lists for e-mail or SMS and automated records of conversations and faxes.

In short, the 4Projects application is a cutting edge resource, bringing true web-based business interaction to reality. Its importance is not only what it can do *in itself*, but what it saves other businesses from having to do *for themselves*. In this way, the doubts and uncertainties mentioned earlier about the degree of internet-based awareness within certain industries is more likely to be overcome.

Further development of the 4Projects concept can have a big impact on the evolution of e-business, representing a major opportunity for many firms.

Over to you   Study the 4Projects software example described above. Draft a summary sheet in note form, for use in a meeting, describing the basics of the application and closing with your own judgement about the ways in which it offers new business opportunities.

In what ways do you feel that Kingspan may have benefited if it had made use of software such as 4Projects?

Cash efficiencies

The internet can also help a private business to improve its cash flow and working capital. Working capital refers to the amount of money needed to pay for the day to day operation of the business (wages, materials, components, electricity and gas charges). It is the 'assets', including cash, but also stocks, money owed to it (debtors) and investments that are left *after* all current debts (liabilities) have been paid. Problems with cash flow and an inability to properly control working capital are major causes of failure. Figure 1.19 shows the simplified 'cash flow cycle'.

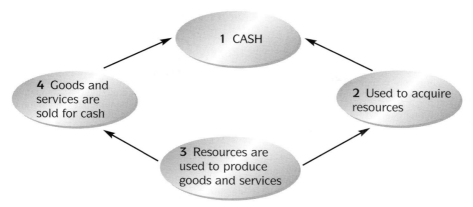

Figure 1.19 The cash flow cycle

If this flow of cash through a business is stopped or delayed, the business could be in trouble, being unable in the short term to pay its bills. However, the position might not be too bad when the working capital cycle is taken into account.

Working capital is normally calculated using a ratio known as the 'current ratio' and is...

$$\frac{\text{Current assets}}{\text{Current liabilities}}$$

If a business has a current ratio as high as 1.5:1 or 2:1, then working capital should be OK. A business must try to avoid factors that would cause it to have so called 'liquidity' problems (not enough available cash to operate comfortably). Managers need to be able to turn business activities into cash as quickly and efficiently as possible. This means efficient production, finished goods despatched quickly, with minimal storage times and bills for products that are sold settled quickly. Relating to the simplified 'cash flow cycle' shown in Figure 1.19, the internet can help the cash flow cycle in the following ways.

Goods and services are sold for cash

1   The internet has the potential to generate *increased sales revenue* (cash) for an online business with global coverage, around the clock. Acme Whistles, a UK-based manufacturing firm, sells online to customers in 119 countries, with eighty percent of their online sales going abroad (see www.acmewhistles.co.uk). Online sales are the fastest growing part of the business (Source: *Daily Telegraph*, June 2003).

2   Online secure transaction arrangements mean that *payments can be received immediately* and a build up of bad debts avoided. In B2B markets security can be gained through effective online relationships and partnerships. Payments systems and practices can be agreed. Transaction arrangements can also gain accurate data about private customers, with accurate customer histories. This can help to build up better relationships with them on a one to one basis.

3   The online firm is able to make use of the internet's sophisticated ability to *monitor customer trends* and changes in the market. By monitoring visitor statistics and accurately recording purchasing trends the firm can anticipate and prepare for strategic changes.

4 Because the internet by its nature is open and transparent, a firm can closely *monitor competing online firms* and work to stay competitive by either offering extra benefits or reducing price. By the same token, of course, competitors can see what you are offering too.

5 What is offered from a company's website can be tailored to each individual customer. From a mass broadcasted message, an online business can *customise its message* to meet specific needs or preferences.

Over to you How might *online* trading be seen as an opportunity to assist the working capital position of a firm? Prepare a verbal statement.

Cash is used to acquire resources

1 As we have seen earlier with attoAbrasives and Kingspan, by participating in supply chain partnerships and engaging in fuller online relationships with other supplying businesses, *resources can be ordered electronically* when they are needed, *orders can be tracked* and *stock availability checked* during the ordering process. This is helpful because holding too much stock can be a bad thing for any business. Space can be a problem, handling and insurance costs can be high and cash is tied up doing nothing. If market conditions change unexpectedly, the business could be left with high levels of unsold goods.

2 Prices, deals (e.g. discounts for large volume orders), promotions or design alterations affecting the resources a firm needs, can all be checked. By participating in 'exchange markets', 'portals' or 'information hubs', a firm can place itself at the heart of market trends, *discover a much broader range of potential suppliers* and possibly achieve lower costs.

3 Full technical specifications, photographs or detailed drawings are available, this can save valuable research and development time and design costs.

The opportunities to take advantage of internet technologies are significant but remember we saw earlier that there are also costs. Apart from the costs of hardware – the PCs and network facilities –there are costs associated with website design and maintenance, Internet Service Provision and the acquisition of software. Many newly online businesses are already established firms looking to create an online sales channel. The initial start up costs will be fairly straightforward to work out. Less straightforward will be staff implications. Will it be necessary to retrain existing people or will new staff be required? What organisational form will be needed?

Over to you You have been asked to prepare a presentation entitled 'How the internet can help'.

Using your understanding of business concepts 'Working capital' and 'Cash flow cycle', explain how you feel internet technologies could help a business to be more successful.

Do you think there are problems to consider too?

Staffing the e-business

Certainly staff rationalisation or training is likely to be essential in a move towards e-business. There are two sides to this:

- technical skills
- positive attitudes.

Technical skills

These are required to make an online business work. Knowing the website, being able to update the site, manipulating internal computerised processses and making use of e-mail.

Positive attitudes

It is also essential that staff in an e-business enterprise have non-technical, but positive, *attitudes*. Behind all websites and e-mail addresses there are real people requiring a service. Staff have to ensure that they carry out the processes that are needed to make an e-business work for both internal and external customers. Remember that it is staff who:

- post information into a database that will, in turn, update a web page
- are responsible for using IT applications properly
- must liaise with technical support people
- assist in keeping a business' entire bank of information, digitally relevant.

Rationalisation

Apart from training staff, sometimes it is necessary to change the structure of the organisation. There are several organisational solutions to adding an e-business channel to an existing structure:

1 Allow e-business work to be done wherever it is needed throughout the firm. No formal organisational change is implemented

2 A separate department or division is set up to look after the internet side of the business. Specialists would be transferred or appointed to that division. A separate department or division is set up to look after the internet side of the business, with specialists. An example of this is B & Q Direct which is a separate trading division of B & Q plc and which operates the www.diy.com website

3 A new operating company is set up.

Gaining staff acceptance of the changes that are needed to make e-business a success is a major management task, whatever the organisational structure. Management must decide on a staff plan, determine which staff are affected and how they are affected. The management must then sell the perceived benefits to the staff, ask them for feedback, plan implementation and monitor the implementation of the changes necessary to do to e-business.

Over to you   You are an advisor to a small to medium sized (SME) business. The business is considering the creation of a full blown website, linked to all internal business systems, i.e. purchasing, selling, stock, invoicing, customer services.

The internet technologies to be used have been agreed with managers and the new systems tested. Now you must consider the staff implications.

Create a well-written report to the management, advising them on various staff issues to consider and suggesting an outline plan to address them.

Opportunities for enhanced competitiveness

The internet offers commercial businesses real opportunities, not only to be more efficient in the way they work, but also to challenge more strongly in their markets. This means that the firm gains advantages over other firms trying to attract the same customers.

One way this happens is by being able to closely monitor (watch) what competitor firms are doing on the web. Once a web site is up on the internet it is open for everyone to see. An e-business however must accept that it's own internet proposition is also open for others to view. There is a tremendous opportunity for greater awareness of others, but greater threats from analysis by others.

Information spreads rapidly on the web. This presents an opportunity for businesses to find out much more quickly what is happening within markets at the local level. Imagine you are manufacturing sports clothing and you have a retail outlet in a particular location where economic conditions have changed dramatically. Internet connectedness (with the retailer) gives you a chance to find out about this much faster because you will be in constant touch and you can share data. When customer preferences change, you should know about this quickly.

The internet affords a range of other opportunities that are capable of putting a business way ahead of the competition. In Unit 2 we will see how personalisation can help a firm to mould its internet offer to meet individual needs. Once an order is placed it can be tracked. Partnerships can be forged and materials can be sourced from a far wider market and products can be offered to meet a far greater variety of needs.

Outcome activity

Internet opportunities
You are a consultant advising three contrasting private businesses in your local SME sector. The businesses are:

- A component manufacturer of precision parts for the aerospace industry
- A cosmetics firm selling hair and beauty products
- A fish and chip shop.

Identify and evaluate the various opportunities the internet offers these differing businesses. Illustrate your points with examples and a poster display for each business.

Unit 2   Internet marketing

After completing Unit 2 you will be able to:

- explain the *principles* of internet marketing
- explain the *benefits* of internet marketing to customers
- explain the *opportunities* offered to businesses by internet marketing
- explain the *challenges* faced by e-businesses engaged in internet marketing.

Your understanding of this unit will be tested via an externally marked Integrated Vocational Assignment (IVA).

This unit will give you an understanding about how the internet is being used to help businesses relate products or services more closely to customer needs and wants. You will learn about the traditional principles of marketing and about how these are being modified and reapplied online to help businesses in the online world. You will see how the internet is helping many businesses to create better business to customer relationships and you will gain an insight into the importance of this for businesses with an internet presence. The hugely increased opportunities offered by internet marketing will be examined for business organisations and consumers, as well as the challenges they bring to the online organisation.

2.1   Principles of internet marketing

In this section we will look at the general principles underpinning *all* marketing activities before going on to look at the ways in which internet marketing is evolving. Marketing is about communication, between a business offering products (or services) to a 'market' and the people – or organisations – within a market who may require those goods or services. It is a function within business that has become increasingly important over the years. Long before the growth of the web, it was essential for businesses – if they were to compete successfully – to think about how their products were going to meet the needs of the people who might buy them. Internet marketing is different from traditional marketing. Before looking at the distinctive and evolving features of internet marketing in the digital online world, it is necessary to have some grasp of the traditional marketing principles and processes in the physical world.

Marketing in the physical world

The traditional marketing mix

Traditional marketing always includes a **marketing mix** of tactics, revolving around the four Ps which are; Product, Price, Place and Promotion.

Product

The marketing function considers the features of a product that is offered to a market. What is it? who would it be aimed at?, what does it do? What *should* it do? The product could be a tangible item (something you could touch), e.g. a toothbrush with a manoeuvrable head, or it could be an intangible service, such as a delivery service.

Price

The marketing function also considers what price a product should be pitched at. What sort of customers will buy at a particular price? What will be the best price to attract a particular kind of customer? What price might get more people to buy? What price might create the best image? What might be the effect of a change in price?

Different 'pricing strategies' are available according to what the business is aiming to achieve:

- *penetration pricing* – setting a price at a level that will gain a foothold in a market
- *destruction pricing* – setting a price that will drive others out of the market
- *competitor pricing* – basing your price on the prices of competitors
- *skimming (or creaming) the market* – setting a high price because you have a unique product
- *discrimination pricing* – setting different prices for different customers.

Place

Marketing specialists consider how a product would find its way to consumers to a *place* where they could make a purchase. This would include physical distribution and merchandising. Physical goods must be transported from manufacturer into storage, through either distribution centres then to wholesalers, then to the high street retailer. Businesses working in between a manufacturer and a retailer are known as 'intermediaries'.

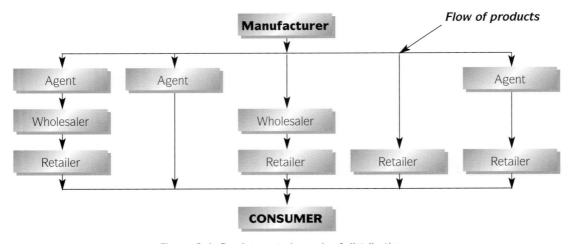

Figure 2.1 Pre-internet channels of distribution

Promotion

Marketing professionals have to consider ways of bringing products to the attention of potential customers. This includes advertising via the various media, as well as other ways of promoting products in the eyes of consumers, such as special offers. These activities, in the physical world, are designed to 'push' products and services out into the eyes and ears of potential consumers.

These four Ps are a set of tactical ingredients, to be 'mixed' according to what a firm's marketing strategy is designed to achieve; hence the term, 'marketing mix'. But what is a marketing strategy and how is one arrived at?

> **Over to you**   Take as an example your favourite chocolate bar and, using the four elements of the marketing mix outlined above, describe how marketing plays a part in the success of that product.

Marketing objectives and strategy

A business' marketing strategy, as we have seen, determines the mix of tactics to be employed by a business and it is designed to achieve long term business aims. A marketing strategy is arrived at by using careful analysis of both the external environment surrounding the business and the current state of the business itself. These two approaches can be described as:

- an industry analysis (using, for example, Porter's five forces technique)
- a situation analysis (for example, through SWOT analysis).

Devising the marketing strategy through an industry analysis

Remember that marketing, by its nature, requires a business to focus outwards in order to understand the external environment it is working in and to respond accordingly. Michael Porter's **five forces analysis** model can be used to look at a whole market or industry (e.g the motor industry or the cosmetics industry).

The 'five forces' that can determine a strategy are:

1 Existing companies in the market. This refers to companies offering the same product to the same market. These firms are clearly in direct competition to attract the *same* customers. For example, there might be two (or more) manufacturers of small cars in the £10,000 – £15,000 bracket. If one of those manufacturers mounts a promotional campaign offering big discounts, that helps other firms offering products to the same market to be aware of the first manufacturer's strategy. The marketing function needs to monitor what competitors are doing, so that an appropriate response can be made.

2 Potential new companies. There is always the chance that new firms will enter a marketplace and offer more competition by offering products in different ways. The world is increasingly a global marketplace and competition can come from anywhere.

3 Product substitutes. In a technologically complicated and changing world it is likely that new products will eventually come onto the market that can be a substitute for your own. Manufacturers of vacuum cleaners were quite complacent when James Dyson introduced a dual cyclone bagless cleaner. With hindsight, it would have been better to respond very quickly to Mr Dyson's ingenuity.

4 Suppliers to the industry. All businesses need supplies. If a business is a selling organisation, of course it must purchase supplies of whatever goods it is selling. If a business is a manufacturing organisation it cannot make anything unless it has raw materials or component parts. The day to day operation of a business calls for maintenance and repair. All of these things come from suppliers, many of whom specialise in particular markets serving particular types of business. It is beneficial for a business to keep a close eye on the various options available for supply. A business must watch for new suppliers and monitor the performance of important existing ones.

5 Customers. A marketplace exists because customers are there to be served by it. There are not just existing customers but potential customers too.

These five forces work across an entire industry and they combine to make up the business environment surrounding a particular firm. The marketing function must be completely aware of the structure of these forces and about how they interact with each other.

> **Over to you** Put yourself in the position of a marketing manager in a firm manufacturing model electric train sets. Using Porter's five forces analysis, create a set of briefing notes for the Managing Director, as a starting point for a strategy meeting.

Devising a marketing strategy using a situation analysis

This is a different kind of analysis that results in a set of information that is much more closely connected to the current situation of the *particular* business. **SWOT analysis** refers to four sub-categories of information about a business; i.e.

Strengths

Weaknesses

Opportunities

Threats.

These are then further divided into *internal* factors (strengths and weaknesses) and *external* factors (opportunities and threats). So, a business marketing team will systematically look at each factor, cataloguing the *strengths* the business has. For example, this might include things such as a well established product or brands, good customer loyalty, good staff, good equipment; the *weaknesses* might be that equipment is dated, premises are too small, the product needs updating. Both strengths and weaknesses are within a business' own control because they are internal.

The next two factors are external to the business. *Opportunities* may exist to enter new markets, to improve products and product image or to acquire new staff. *Threats* are those things that could damage a business' market position, such as economic downturn, new competition or new products.

By analysing both the wider industry as well as the business' own situation, marketing people will be far better placed to ensure that marketing objectives and long term strategic aims are soundly based. A big part of this effort involves market research.

Over to you   Visit www.saveanddrive.co.uk. Do an outline SWOT analysis of this online business, paying particular attention to the opportunities and threats you feel are created through internet marketing.

Market research

Market research is about finding out who customers are and what their requirements are. Research is designed to gather information so that business marketing decisions are based on useful, current and relevant data. New information, gathered by a particular firm for its own purposes, is called **primary research**, whereas information that is already available from elsewhere is called **secondary research**.

Chat room

1   Design and conduct a survey of students in your class to find out:

   a   What percentage of the group have internet access at home

   b   What percentage have broadband internet access at home.

2   Visit www.CyberAtlas.com and search for ANY internet trends about web use and access. Make a note of your findings.

Prepare notes consisting of a statement explaining which of the above pieces of information are based on primary data and which rely on secondary data.

A further distinction can be made between **qualitative** data, which is data that identifies opinions and feelings about something; and **quantitative** data, i.e. data that is statistical or numeric in content.

Market-led versus product-led approaches

In Britain, many businesses used to think that the things they made were the best of their type in the world (and often they were) so customers – wherever they were – would be certain to buy them. To test the wisdom of this attitude, try checking which company manufactured your TV, your HiFi, or your washing machine at home and have a look at who manufactured the cars or motor cycles in the car park. This should give you a clue as to the wisdom of holding this so called **'product led' approach**. The truth is that over the years British businesses have learned that their products will fail against overseas competition if they do not exactly meet what the customer wants. Marketing is about finding out what customer needs are and then setting out to meet them. This is why it should be interesting for all of us. We are each, after all, consumers of many products.

Over to you Think of a product you have bought. Write down a list of your main requirements from it. Can you describe how the firm that designed and made that product included the things you required?

Companies have learned that they have to look outward – towards customers in the market, in order to really be competitive. The needs of the market must lead what a business offers to it. This is the **'market led' approach**. The UK Chartered Institute of Marketing (CIM) defines marketing as:

'The management process responsible for identifying, anticipating and satisfying customer needs profitably'

Marketing principles

Marketing 'principles' are therefore aimed at satisfying customer needs profitably and they apply at all times whether a business is online, or offline. These principles underpin the tactical tools described earlier as the four Ps; they include:

- *Listening* to customers; finding out what they want from your products
- Getting as *close* to customers as possible
- *Involving* customers
- *Serving* customers well
- *Seek*ing out the best customers
- Trying to *nurture* customers into a lifelong relationship with your firm and working to repeat this every time you do business
- Constantly *testing* the market, measuring and improving
- Adding *value* in everything you do for customers.

In the traditional marketing model of the physical world a business may either choose to aim a product at the 'mass' market, with the same, undifferentiated, set of tactics for all consumers; or it may choose, as we have seen, to *target* specific groups of consumers. This involves 'segmenting' the market (think of the 'segments' of an orange), considering how to differentiate the product to meet the needs of different segments and therefore using different marketing tactics in each. This question of **segmentation**, i.e. dividing the market up, is a big issue in marketing. Traditional methods of segmentation include:

- age
- sex
- geographic location
- lifestyle
- **psychographic** profile, i.e. profiling by lifestyle characteristics, such as DINKY (Double Income No Kids).

By segmenting and **targeting** their marketing effort towards a segment of a market, businesses are able to create or modify products to meet this particular category of consumer's preferences and requirements.

Chaffey (2004) defines *customer-centric e-marketing* as:

Applying... *Digital technologies which form online channels...*
(Web, e-mail, databases, plus mobile/wireless & digital TV)

to... *Contribute to marketing activities aimed at achieving profitable acquisition and retention of customers (within a multi-channel buying process and customer lifecycle)*

through... *Improving our customer knowledge (of their profiles, behaviour, value and loyalty drivers), then delivering integrated targeted communications and online services that match their individual needs.*

---

e-Marketing in the online world

Marketing principles online

How are the marketing principles we have outlined helped or changed by using the internet?

The internet helps businesses to acquire a good *knowledge of customers* because it is a way of connecting everyone who is online. Millions of pounds, dollars, euros and many other currencies pass through wires linking computers all over the world. According to Dave Chaffey (2002) forecasts of global users of the internet show dramatic growth over the next few years and research complied by Nua Internet Surveys in September 2002 showed a worldwide total of 605.6 million people online. Of course eventually growth will slow down, but it will not stop completely, as more and more of the newly developing world (China, Russia, Eastern **trading bloc** countries and perhaps even the 'third world') come online. The number of users will continue to grow and more importantly so will the frequency of use and the time spent online. Technological improvements, increasing use of **broadband** (with much faster internet connection and download times) will almost guarantee this. Not only will more people be online, but the comfort and ease with which they use the internet will improve and fears about security issues will diminish.

Remember however, for private consumers, the internet is a '*pull* medium'; meaning that on the whole it is individual consumer's choice to visit the websites they are interested in and to 'pull' out the goods or services they want. *The audience targets the business.* It is becoming commonplace to refer to a 'remix' of the traditional marketing mix (Dave Chaffey, 2002) so that traditional marketing approaches can be reapplied in different ways in the online world. This **marketing remix** changes the traditional marketing tools and adds one or two new ingredients, described later, that are designed specifically for the online (sometimes called the digital) economy.

The specific purpose of marketing an online business is to offer something that makes visitors want to stay and look around a website. This is often referred to as the 'stickiness' of a site. To make visitors want to 'stick' around, the site has to offer something that is of value to a visitor. This is called an **Internet Value Proposition (IVP)** and it is a similar concept to the **unique selling proposition (USP)** commonly referred to in traditional marketing. In the case of the USP, marketers are trying to communicate something unique about a *physical* product that will make people want to buy it more than others. Similarly, the IVP is the special set of characteristics about a website that will make people want to stick around on the site and make a purchase. *To communicate the IVP successfully is the focus of internet marketing.* The tactical means of doing this can be described within a number of elements that are referred to as the 'e-marketing remix' (see Figure 2.2).

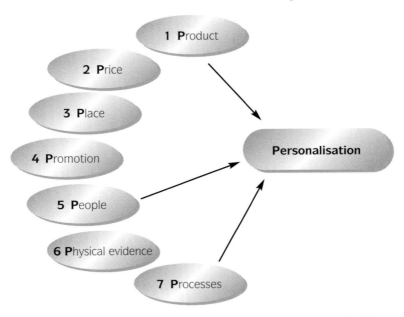

Figure 2.2 The internet e-marketing remix – the seven online Ps

The implications for the reformulated e-marketing mix of the online world differ for B2B and B2C markets, so it is convenient to look at each set of tactics separately.

Chat room

In pairs, try to identify the 'Internet Value Proposition' from the following sites:

www.saveanddrive.co.uk

www.diy.com

www.lastminute.com

www.elephant.co.uk

In writing, describe this IVP briefly in your own words and present your summary to the whole group.

How do you feel consumers might benefit from this site? Is all of your group agreed on this?

The e-marketing remix in B2C markets

Online product

Obviously it is not possible to touch, smell, or taste products on the internet, so a powerful attraction for private consumers to purchase many tangible products – the full range of human senses – is absent on the web. Furthermore, in internet shopping, a consumer wishing to buy something must wait until the product is delivered. The pleasure, or the 'buzz', of receiving *immediately* what has been paid for is missing at the point of signing over cash. So, aside from convenience, why should a private consumer consider buying online, when there are strong instinctive reasons not to bother? Internet marketers have to face up to this and find ways of making the e-shopping experience worth the wait.

The internet on the other hand is ideal for adding considerable value to *every* product made available online and marketers have to think of ways this can be done. One method of doing this is to build into the product exclusive and relevant information, often *personalised* for the customer.

At www.InternetCamerasDirect.co.uk the consumer can purchase digital cameras and supporting associated products at very competitive rates. The site offers useful technical advice and every visitor can compare and contrast the specifications of many digital cameras side by side. The customer, on registration with the website, receives 100MB of disc space in which to create his/her own online album to store photographs.

Figure 2.3 Adding product value – www.InternetCamerasDirect.co.uk

The InternetCamerasDirect site provides an illustration of how online retailers or 'e-tailers' can offer *extensions* to the basic product, thereby offering increased benefit to the customers. Examples of this can be seen in Figure 2.3 above. The services panel on the left for instance shows that several extra services are available from the site.

1   Using the idea of the 'extended product' explain, using examples from the website, how this web trader has used internet technology to add extra value to the product.

2   Make a 'screenshot' from the site, illustrating the value added to this internet product.

3   Find one other example of a B2C site offering similar added value to an online product and compare and contrast this with InternetCamerasDirect.

There are various ways of extending online products:

- Extensive product endorsements from previous customers
- Lists of customers
- Warranties
- Money back offers
- Additional customer back up services
- 'Cross-selling' of related or complementary products
- Expert advice.

Products can be extended in other ways too, improving the online experience of the private customer and encouraging a lengthier stay on the website. Take the example of Mattel's www.whatsherface.com where the user can create their own doll with personalised features, before deciding whether or not to buy. At www.orange.com it is possible to create a personalised payment package, with agreed plans for texts or calls. In these examples the consumer is actively participating in product creation and enhancement.

In a 1980 book called 'The Third Wave' (published long before the internet gained momentum!), Alvin Toffler predicted that in the future the things that we needed to possess in order to survive (i.e. our *production* needs) and our use of them, (our *consumption*) would once again be combined. In the earliest days of mankind primitive human beings had to hunt and gather food and resources for *immediate* use – or else not survive. In Toffler's view of the future, everyone would again be collaborating, involved in acquiring the things they required. Toffler predicted that consumers would become **prosumers**, not just getting what was on offer from others (businesses), but participating in producing things that they required. This would involve them being knowledgeable about products (today we can get information from the internet), being enabled to contribute to design of products (we can participate in design via the internet) and being enabled to interact with producers to assist in getting products we needed (we can contribute to surveys, research and can comment on the internet).

Take a look, just as an illustration, at some of the major motor manufacturers such as BMW or Citroen and it is possible to see how users can today actively design their own 'dream' car. The system stores this data and is able over time to monitor the most popular preferences. Has the age of 'prosumer power' arrived? One company with a policy to be at the 'cutting edge' in using internet technology is Kingfisher's B & Q Direct. The website is found at www.diy.com.

Figure 2.4 B & Q Direct – services to DIY customers

Figure 2.4 shows the services page of DIY.com. Customers can access a range of services from brochures giving product advice and information, to delivery details and terms. Customers can also become involved in interactively designing their own rooms, simultaneously placing orders for goods into the shopping cart as they proceed.

Connect

Visit www.diy.com (room designs) or any other website that allows you to be *interactive* with the content. Design a brief presentation to the whole group showing how this extends the product offering and benefits consumers.

Be prepared to present your findings to the whole group.

Online price

Traditional pricing models could work out desirable prices based on production *costs plus* a profit margin, or on set *profit targets*, or base prices on the prices of the *competition* in the market (see remarks on pricing strategies earlier). However, the overall effect of internet technology upon markets has been to exert a downward pressure on prices. One of the reasons for this is that production costs for many digital products have been reduced to almost zero. Businesses selling on the web have greater capacity to vary prices and new pricing models are tending to be based upon the old question: what is the consumer prepared to pay? The means of adding value to online products described above are therefore even more important to maintain online competitiveness. The consumer's willingness to pay a profitable price could well be determined by the value a business is able to add into its online product offer.

In the pre-internet economy, market research could usually tell business planners what price a market could accept and what the effect (*elasticity*) of an increase in price might be. Using the **price elasticity of demand (PED)** formula, marketers could make reasonably informed choices about price changes and their effect on demand for products and then make decisions. The formula is:

$$\text{Price elasticity of demand} = \frac{\text{percentage change in quantity demanded (of a product)}}{\text{percentage change in price}}$$

So, where the percentage change in quantity demanded is less than the percentage change in price, (i.e. less than 1 but greater than 0) demand is said to be *price inelastic*. This means that consumers are *not* sensitive to a change in price. A business forced to increase prices will be hoping for demand for its products to be price inelastic.

The internet can intervene in this because amongst other things it allows a great deal of price transparency for consumers. Consumers can compare prices easily between many potential suppliers. Prices can be stored digitally in databases and software (robot shoppers, shopping bots, or price search engines) can be used to search for the best prices available on the web (for example, see www.kelkoo.com). Some sites such as the BBC's internet shopping service at www.beeb.com provide instant price comparisons and at www.letsbuyit.com customers can join together in order to lower prices.

Instead of prices being set by businesses and just accepted by the market, the internet is capable of turning this situation upside down. Priceline.co.uk (www.priceline.co.uk) for instance, allows consumers to set their own prices and at several online auction sites (see www.ebay.com) consumers can place bids for consumer products having been able to view the minimum (reserve) price acceptable to the seller.

Over to you   Prepare a short display about www.ebay.co.uk summarising the bidding process and describing the benefits (if any) you feel are offered to users of the site.

The unit selling costs for each product is much less for an online product, so businesses on the internet can make cost savings that can be passed on to consumers. Those businesses that do this the quickest, will be the first to gain customer loyalty. This places a further downward pressure on prices. One way in which online traders may choose to generate revenue in this price conscious climate is by selling many products at cost price from a website and making money on selling other add-ons or services.

Businesses that have no physical network to maintain, for example finance or insurance services, may be able to lower prices even further (www.if.com, www.insdirect.co.uk).

The effect of internet technology on the ability of marketers to establish and maintain a pricing strategy has been dramatic. As we have seen, internet marketers have to acknowledge that increasingly prices are being directly *set* by consumers and not just accepted by them. Airlines can and do offer online auctions for seats. Through the internet, consumers can compare, can combine, can bid at auctions for most products and can even establish reverse auctions, whereby potential *suppliers* have to compete for their custom.

Finally, prices can nowadays be set automatically based on the level of demand and upon the stage a product is within its own life-cycle. This phenomenon is known as 'dynamic pricing' (see page 35) and it means that prices are not set in stone, only to be changed after major business strategy meetings, they are flexible and constantly moving in line with trading conditions.

Online place

The place element of traditional marketing has been significantly changed in the online economy. Consumers now have many more online options for purchasing. Distribution tactics for internet marketers have had to change. We saw in Unit 1 that **disintermediation** has tended to occur, meaning that middlemen – businesses operating as wholesalers, distribution centres, or as agents between the original manufacturers of products and retailers selling them – are often no longer required. Consumers can go directly to a supplier's site. However, new types of middle-men are appearing on the internet. These can be neutral intermediate sites that function to bring buyers and sellers together (see www.bizrate.com), or they can be **infomediaries**, i.e. sites holding information that is of benefit to both customers and suppliers. This process is known as '*reintermediation*' because it introduces another new sort of intermediary.

The significance of getting products to customers is obviously huge. One of the most successful products in the physical world for example is Coca Cola. This success is not just based on an excellent product, it is also based on excellent distribution, Coke is available almost everywhere people might want to drink it. The same approach applies in the online world. If Amazon.co.uk want to sell books then they have had to consider placing links to their site in many other places on the web where they feel people might wish to buy books. Internet marketing must therefore give consideration to which, if any, other websites might be best fitted to carrying their product information or links to it.

We have already seen that increasingly, businesses that have been traditionally based upon a purely physical presence (i.e. 'bricks and mortar'), are introducing the internet as an additional channel for their sales ('clicks and mortar'). The example of www.diy.com is such a case. Owned by the Kingfisher group, the diy.com site is the internet website of B & Q Direct. B & Q Direct management have set clear performance targets for diy.com based on a four year plan. To achieve the level of sales required to meet the strategic plan, B & Q Direct have recognised the need to have the capacity to meet customer orders from the website. This has been achieved in the short term by contracting out the whole '*product fulfilment*' function to a separate partner company, Spark Response, based at Follingsby Park, near Gateshead in Tyne and Wear. Spark Response provide warehousing and despatch services, customer service personnel and call centre staff. Apart from the website itself and associated technical ICT support, B & Q provide the whole product range and have management support permanently based at Spark Response's site, working alongside Spark Response staff.

When a customer places an internet order, it is received by Spark Response call centre staff and acknowledged. The warehouse is then given details of the customer's requirements and goods are prepared for packaging and despatch. Five separate carriage companies are used depending on the weight and nature of the goods scheduled for despatch.

Call centre

Warehouse

The parent company, the Kingfisher Group, now have within their B & Q family of companies a developing and growing 'multi-channel' approach for sales and customer service.

Online promotion

The promotion remix in internet marketing includes *presentation* and involves two aspects:

- Promoting the fact that a business website exists
- Promoting specific offerings from a website.

The first concern is usually dealt with at the creation of the site. A **domain name** is the means by which humans can make sense of where on the internet a site is. Just as most of us have an address, so that people or mail can find us among the network of roads and buildings around where we live, on the internet, every website has to have an address, so that a **browser** can locate it. While computers only understand numbers, humans understand much more. So we know, for example, that .com, .co.uk, .org, .gov, .ac., etc. etc. have meaning beyond the letters. Imagine having some kind of directory to search through containing millions of sets of twelve digit numbers! No problem for computers, but for us it is far easier to have a domain name we can make sense of. Domain names mentioned so far in this section include Diy.com, Amazon.co.uk and InternetCamerasDirect.co.uk. Every website address contains a domain name but note that the domain name is only part of the full web address which, as we saw in Unit 1, is known as the Uniform Resource Locator (URL). So, one of the first steps in internet business promotion is to choose and purchase a domain name that effectively announces the business. It is often advisable therefore for businesses to have their business name at least within the domain name. Many offline advertisements have references to domain names.

Once a website is up and a business has a presence on the internet, there are several ways of communicating a marketing message to *private* consumers.

Key activities among these include:

- **Banner advertisements**
- Web public relations
- Direct e-mails
- **Affiliate programmes**
- Pop up advertisements.

Banner advertisements

A space across the top of a web page, usually with animated content, advertising products or services from another business, is known as a 'banner' or 'banner ad'. A click on the banner by a visitor to a site leads to a referral through to the advertising business' site. This is known as a **click-through**. A major problem with banner ads is the low click-through rate, reported at only 1 percent (see www.doubleclick.net\knowledgecentral).

Figure 2.5 Banner Ad Space

The choice of which sites to place the banner will be considered by marketing specialists and there are several specialist sites offering services to help in placing, or targeting, banners. Banner ads can be exchanged between sites offering complementary products or services, or they can be specifically targeted onto sites where it is felt that the audience will be appropriate. Banner ads can be accurately targeted onto sites that are likely to have the audience a business is hoping to attract. For example, in consumer markets a business selling gardening products can target an online gardening publication and have their banner placed in a prominent page. Retired people can be targeted through sites geared towards the elderly.

Connect

Search the internet for UK-based websites that you can associate with certain hobbies, sports, or industrial sectors. See if you can identify any banner ads placed on these sites. Draw up a three-column table listing the URL (web address), summarising the banner ad and commenting on whether you can identify any targeting by the business placing it. Given the low click-through rate, would you still recommend banner ads? If so, why?

Figure 2.6 Banner advertising from 123propertynews.com

Take the illustration of www.123propertynews.com. This site offers banner advertising slots within its online magazine. This is an obvious way in which anyone involved either in travel or in the property business can target a specific audience. The 123 property news site offers various alternatives for banner placement, with differing prices for the most often viewed pages in the online magazine. Any site with a particular visitor profile can be targeted in this way.

Figure 2.7 Banner Ad alternative 1 from 123Propertynews.com

Figure 2.8 Banner Ad alternative 2 from 123Propertynews.com

Banners are of differing sizes, measured in pixels and can be placed in rotation with others from other business organisations, usually they are animated **GIF** files. The banner can be arranged to appear for a while before being rotated with others and sometimes up to four or five banners may be rotated on the one space. Other sorts of banners are static, interstitial, or **superstitial**. **Static ads**, of course, just remain in a static position on a page, interstitials usually appear between web pages and are often seen when another page is loading and superstitials are often known as 'pop ups'. Both of the latter types need to be actively closed down by the user and marketers should be careful about using them as they can be a real nuisance!

The choice for online marketers is based upon which sites attract most of the relevant target audience and where, within those sites, most visitors will view your ad. The content of the banner will be determined by what the business is trying to achieve. Some can be used to begin a transaction, others to inform about goods or services and some can be used to shape attitudes or simply remind users that a company exists. Internet technology is capable of providing information about visitor numbers, numbers clicking on the banner and the place and time of the visit, so there is a good deal of intelligence available to judge the effectiveness of a banner campaign.

The main drawback with a banner ad campaign is that it can be a relatively expensive approach.

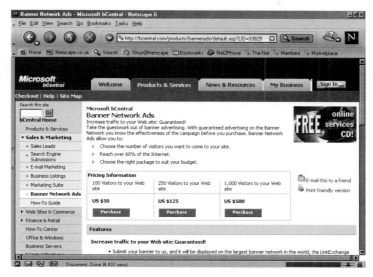

Figure 2.9 Microsoft bCentral Banner Network

The bCentral banner network shown in Figure 2.9 above also offers a service where business planners can examine statistics to do with web page views. It is possible to look at the rate of 'click-through' to see how many people actually click on your banner and are referred through to your site. As we saw earlier, the rate of click-through from banner ads has usually been low – perhaps less than half a percent – and this has led some commentators to claim that banner ads are not the most effective method of promotion.

However, banner ads can give good results if they are used as part of a wider promotional campaign and many offline advertisements now include reference to web addresses and an online promotional campaign will frequently make use of several channels other than the internet to communicate a message.

 A further technique is to incorporate, within the banner ad, something of use to a visitor to a site. A financial advisor included within a banner ad a currency converter; a life insurance company has included a quick quiz that allows users to calculate what funds they need to retire comfortably by a certain age.

 Connect

Do an internet search and collect examples of at least three different banner adverts.

In what ways, if at all, do you feel that consumers benefit from the banners you have collected?

Web public relations (PR)

A cheap and easy way of achieving publicity on the web is by releasing news stories of interest to the online public. The internet is a 'pull' medium, meaning that the whole rationale of having an online presence is that web surfers approach a website in order to extract, or 'pull' out *information.* Public relations are therefore inherent in what the internet is all about – content. Marketers must consider the perspectives of the various consumers of internet information. What angle on a news story might attract consumer interest? Distribution of news can be through e-mail pitches or through web news services. Of course, PR needs to be positive (See the award winning <u>www.Screwfix.com</u> site and go to the 'news and views' section on the Home page).

Connect

Visit <u>www.lycos.co.uk</u>. Find the Press Office link at the bottom of the home page of the site. Access this link and find the lists of press releases offered over the last two years. Select two releases on different topics. Copy and paste these into a document, or a format of your own choice.

Using the content of the press release, summarise in your own words why you consider this release to be PR. In your opinion, does it achieve its intention?

Direct e-mailing

It seems the easiest thing in the world to send out hundreds, even thousands of e-mails, to unsuspecting people. The trouble is that sending out 10,000 e-mails might get 50 people interested in whatever product a business has to offer and 9,950 people thoroughly annoyed. The practice of sending out unrequested e-mail is known as 'spamming', the term SPAM is said to mean <u>S</u>ending <u>P</u>ersistent <u>A</u>nnoying (e)<u>M</u>ail, sometimes known as 'junk'. If PR is the effort to promote an effective and positive image on the internet, spamming tends to have the opposite effect. Maturing internet users are simply learning to delete spam.

If internet marketers are going to tap into the potential benefits of e-mail, they need to consider ways of by passing any accusations of spamming. To do this they might use **opt-in mailing**. This means that, before sending anyone any mail they seek permission first, hence the sometimes used term, 'permission marketing'. Users must actively check a box giving the organisation permission to mail them in future (see <u>www.permission.com</u>).

The benefits of permission based e-mailing are considerable according to a survey quoted in eMarketer (October 2002). The survey, by Quris, found that sixty-seven percent of consumers believed that the quality of opt-in e-mails *positively* influenced their opinions about the companies sending them and fifty-three percent said that such e-mails had an influence on what they purchased. Permission mailing can initiate positive customer relationships and enable tailored offers to customers.

Marketers must be extremely careful when considering both e-mailing and PR on the internet. Because the internet is a network, the effect is that news travels very fast. Internet marketers can and do use this effect to the benefit of their businesses, but they must beware of the negative effects of bad mailing practice or bad PR. **Viral marketing** is the term used to describe the way in which marketing messages can be rapidly spread around the internet through word being passed on, either through e-mailing, (virtual word of mouth) or real world word of mouth.

Chat room

Organise a challenge among your group, entitled 'SPAM of the Week' (or a similar title of your own choice!). See if you can identify and illustrate examples of unsolicited (not asked for) e-mail. Describe in your own words why you think this kind of mail might <u>not</u> be a marketing asset.

Online people

People buy from people, not computers. Yet, private consumers are increasingly coming online to seek out both tangible (touchable) products and intangible services. Internet marketing has to overcome the major problems of gaining trust and solving an individual's personal questions about an online product offering.

The art of successful marketing of online products is to ensure that the service offered from the site is seen to be of value. But what if the user is having trouble using a site, or has a query that he or she feels should best be handled with a phone call? This is one reason why people are a crucial part of the online marketing. See <u>www.easyjet.com</u> for a simple three step process for getting in touch with the company. Easyjet's policy is obviously to try and deal with issues online. However if all else fails, the company must rely on the personal skills and knowledge of a member of staff.

Connect

Visit <u>www.easyjet.com</u> and view the three-step process described above. Summarise in your own words how you feel Easyjet have designed the getting in touch process as a 'people friendly' procedure.

Try to find a contrasting site with a different approach. As a possible user of both sites, how do you rate the people aspect of the design? Suggest improvements if you can.

The re-emergence of e-business after the dot.com crashes of the 90s is being achieved in large part through the development of many successful 'clicks and mortar' businesses. These businesses, as we have seen, combine both a physical and a developing online presence. From the marketing perspective, online customer service is the key to survival and success. At this stage in the development of the internet, many consumers still need the reassurance of knowing that people are available to assist or give friendly guidance if they are needed, either on the telephone or by e-mail. It is becoming increasingly hard for businesses to compete on the basis of price alone. While it is possible to compete through enhancing the online product with additional information or added value, excellent service from the site –offered by, or designed by, *people* with the consumer in mind – is crucial for an effective marketing effort. To be successful in internet marketing terms requires an 'outside-in' approach. Always consider the online offer from the point of view of the customer. To do this effectively requires good people at every stage.

Connect

What do you feel is meant by online customer service? Visit <u>www.diy.com</u> and write a list of examples of customer service from the website.

Find another site of your own choice and compare the two in customer service terms.

Online physical evidence

Customers often make a choice of whether or not to purchase goods or services simply based upon how the business looks or feels to them. All physical things connected with the business should therefore give out positive images. How can internet marketers create appropriate physical evidence in the online world?

The first piece of physical evidence is the website itself. In experiencing the website, consumers need to feel they are in a (virtual) professional environment. In many respects the website represents the *brand*. Because we all have certain brand loyalties or preferences and a brand is often seen as a solidly reassuring thing; the marketing intention is to help create a quality online brand using the website. Reassurances to do with awards, recommendations, professional associations or product guarantees can help and need to be prominent.

A site needs to be professionally designed, have clear and easy navigational aids and have a consistent look about it. In support of the online offer, the business needs to ensure that all offline supporting activities, such as product delivery or backup services, are communicating the right message.

Connect

In groups, carry out an internet search and create a poster display showing the main features of an e- business website. Your poster can be either critical or positive about the site, but it should refer to specific aspects of the site design and comment on whether or not you feel it represents good physical evidence for the online business.

Online processes

The ideal situation with private online consumers is to not only attract them to a website but to convert the visit to a sale. This is called the **conversion rate** and it is a key measure of a business site's effectiveness. The conversion rate links closely to one of the basic principles of internet marketing, try to convert customers into a lifetime *relationship* with the business – in other words repeat business time after time. To achieve this, as we have seen, customer experience of the site must be positive, the presentation of goods and services on the website must be clear and the content relevant and useful; the buying *process* must feel straightforward and secure and, most important of all, the business must deliver on their promises.

In ensuring that all customer orders are fulfilled, internet marketers will have to consider a subset of processes that will lead to accurate and helpful information being available, both internal to the business and external to customers. Processes must therefore be in place that update website information. Imagine you are buying toys for a children's party and you go to a website that informs you thirty are available. Satisfied, you order and relax in confidence. In reality though, none are in stock because the website information has not taken account of today's earlier orders. This is a calamity for the party and disastrous for an online business. The following set of processes is vital for online sales success:

- the process of *responding* to an enquiry
- the process of *ordering*
- the process of *updating and recording* stock available
- the process of *updating website information*
- the process of *acknowledging* an order
- the process of *tracking* the progress of an order
- the process of *notifying* the customer
- the process of *organising despatch* (shipping).

The internet marketing function needs to coordinate these processes, because ultimately they are all concerned with the relationship with the online customer. Whilst the website can be considered the front end 'shop window' (the brand!), without efficient integration of this with other systems internal to the business organisation, the internet presence becomes a sham and the reputation of the 'brand' suffers. To put this directly, the website has to be accurate – and work!

Assuming that the background processes are in place, consideration of the process that the consumer actually goes through in deciding on and making a purchase from the website is an important part of internet marketing. B & Q Direct used software to carefully analyse user interactions on their website and found that when a visitor to the site abandoned the visit, it was more often than not at the point where there personal payment details were asked for. Other reports vary in their conclusions, but the dropout rate of potential e-shoppers is a big problem. The transaction aspect of the site visit therefore had to be made very straightforward and B & Q Direct users are reassured with the words, "Placing an order is safe, simple and secure".

Amazon.com pioneered the idea of 'one click shopping', so that a very easy transaction process reinforced the feeling of convenience. Customers shopping on the web have to feel that the process is easy and that an error can be quickly put right just by simply using the 'back' button. Ideally they should receive regular reassurance on the screen that they are doing the right things to accomplish a transaction and the order screen should be clear and uncluttered. Internet marketing specialists have to consider all of these things from the point of view of a first time customer.

Although private consumers are slowly but surely getting used to making purchases through the internet, security is still a concern. Businesses hoping to make a success of online selling must use an SSL (Secure Sockets Layer) server to ensure credit card transactions remain secure. This server will use SSL technology with **encryption** processes (see unit 2) that are almost impenetrable. Many users are starting to recognise the closed padlock and key symbols at the bottom right of the screen and know that they symbolise the use of SSL. Internet marketers will consider how to reassure customers by giving full security information. People are gaining confidence and web designers and internet businesses are very concerned to reassure visitors that shopping on the web is not only convenient but is secure.

Marketing of services

A service is still a product, even though it is something that we cannot see or touch. Online services include banking, insurance, tourism, information, financial and legal advice, education and many more. Online service businesses exploit the essence of the internet as a *content driven* network. So, business activities can utilise the content to deliver services. A major difference between marketing a service product and a tangible one is that whereas a tangible product order has to be 'fulfilled' through storage and distribution to the purchaser, a service product does not so costs can be lower. Certain services of course, such as car insurance, do rely on back up support and paper documentation will be sent out from this.

In offering service products, an online business is often entering into an ongoing relationship with a client over time, rather than merely opening and closing a single transaction. This leads to additional questions for an online marketer. In the case of financial services, how is a website able to supply the same degree of confidence online, as the physical business can? With online banking, personal financial information has to be held with trust. These responsibilities, for ensuring that the people who structure website content and the processes that update it are secure and efficient, rest in large part with the internet marketing function. Great care must be taken to communicate to an online service client, concerns for care, security and *individual* attention.

The e-marketing remix in B2B markets

Internet marketing is not of course just confined to businesses selling products to private consumers. It also is very important to businesses selling to other businesses. In fact the money value of online transactions between businesses is greater than the value of transactions with private consumers. So it's sensible for businesses in these markets to get their e-marketing right.

A study by Accenture in 2001 *'Was it an Illusion? Putting more B in B2B'* showed that brand reputation, followed by service and price were by far the most important variables in buyers' decision making in B2B contexts.

How B2B e-marketing differs from B2C

The decision to make a purchase in consumer markets is usually a fairly simple and straightforward one, based upon social criteria. One individual, perhaps on occasions the whole family, choose a product for private use and enjoyment. Parents go out and choose food and drinks for family use. Sometimes the whole family might be involved in choosing a new family car. For the vast majority of household items there is no great complexity involved in the decision, or the process of making the choice, but the collective effect of these private consumer decisions in the B2C marketplace has a dramatic effect on B2B markets.

The decision of a visitor to www.next.co.uk to purchase a cotton T-shirt, for example, is likely to be a simple one. However a lot of these small-scale consumer decisions creates a 'chain of derived demand', as shown in Figure 2.10.

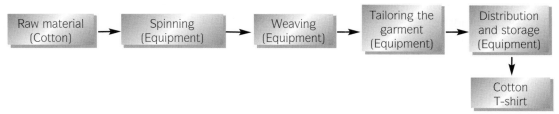

Figure 2.10 Chain of derived demand for a T-shirt

Everything from the left hand side of Figure 2.10 is pulled through the chain as a result of the demand for the end product, whether the demand comes through the online channel or otherwise. Businesses sell cotton to merchants, who sell it to spinners, who sell it to weavers, who sell it to clothing manufacturers, who finally sell the completed garments to Next Retail. This results in their distribution and storage somewhere, prior to delivery to the consumer. Value is being added (think of a **value chain**) at each stage and to add value, businesses need raw materials and equipment – things they get from other businesses.

The marketing in B2B markets is about each business meeting the needs of other businesses. The distribution company that moves clothes around on behalf of clothing e-tailers (such as Next), needs (among many other things) trucks and vans; it also needs equipment such as forklift trucks, pallets and possibly warehousing. But, do managers simply say to staff, have a look on the web and see if you can get us a couple of trucks? Of course not, because the decisions made to purchase industrial products such as forklift trucks, or significant quantities of raw materials, are much more complex than the decision to purchase the item of clothing. The decision to buy will probably be made by more than one individual and there may be important criteria used to choose a supplier.

Chat room

In pairs, create a visual display showing two products. One product should be from a consumer market and another from an industrial market. On the display, add clear bullet points showing the various criteria you feel would be used by a purchaser to decide on whether to purchase.

Whereas there are many suppliers of T-shirts, there are a limited number of forklift truck manufacturers and suppliers. Decision makers considering the purchase of such products have to consider quality, price, and delivery; just as the private consumer does. However, because of the complexity of the product and its specific purpose for a business, a degree of technical knowledge is essential.

This is the case with lots of B2B products. Plant and equipment, components, scientific instruments, pharmaceuticals, drugs, raw materials of many kinds; have to meet specific requirements. The marketing requirements for lots of industrial products are therefore quite different in character from those in B2C markets. These include:

- Lots of technical *support* must be offered from supplier to user
- Excellent technical *confidence and competence* is required from suppliers
- Confidence in *quality* is essential
- Product *image* is less important, *unless it affects someone else down the supply chain* (Brand, however, is important).

Relationship marketing in B2B markets

Because requirements differ and are often more complex in B2B markets than for private consumers, it follows that there is likely to be a bigger emphasis placed upon personal *relationships* between the firms. Technical representatives will be well known to potential buyers, they will almost certainly be on first name terms and there must be a great deal of trust and goodwill. Often products will be marketed directly from supplying business to potential purchasing business. Each business will be very well known to the other, because in many cases there will be very few customers for specialist products. However, considerable revenue will be generated from relatively few purchasing occasions. So, although a firm may only be involved in a few transactions per year, the relationship between them needs to be good.

Internet technology, through CRM software, is able to help this **relationship marketing** in several ways and has the potential to transform relationships within the supply chain. For the example of a forklift truck manufacturer, the relationships might be as shown in Figure 2.11.

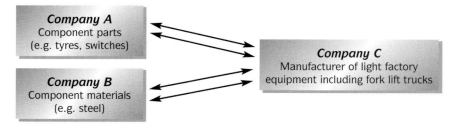

Figure 2.11 Internet B2B relationships

The three companies involved are each enabled by internet technology to *collaborate* and *communicate* very closely. If company C wishes to make design changes to the product, through the web these changes can be viewed immediately; feedback and comment can come from companies A or B. Both companies can make use of web pages that are linked to internal databases. These automatically update the web pages of the companies with the latest data available from within the firm. Web-based e-mail platforms such as OpenMail allow employees to securely access company mailboxes from anywhere. Within all three companies, design issues can be therefore be shared between specialists. The end result is that problems or complexities are avoided further down in the product development process.

Outcome activity

1   Review the e-business insight case of Kingspan from Section 1.4 of Unit 1. Produce informative notes explaining and evaluating the potential role of the internet in assisting the marketing effort of the company.

2   Explain how the marketing activities of three contrasting online businesses illustrate the principles of internet marketing.

2.2   Benefits of internet marketing

Internet marketing modifies the general principles of marketing according to the market being served on the web. The benefits derived by various online customers therefore tend to be different.

In B2B markets, businesses are trying to serve and meet the needs of other businesses and transactions are often based on long term agreements to do business with each other. The range of B2B products and services obviously varies greatly, ranging from pencils, to very sophisticated scientific or technical equipment. The more complex the product then the greater is the need to exchange detailed data and have close working relationships between expert staff. Therein lies one of the great potential benefits of internet marketing in B2B contexts. On the web, data and complex information can be stored, retrieved, communicated and manipulated. Partner businesses can use web technology to collaborate and work in a close relationship.

In B2C markets, private consumers tend to buy for social reasons to do with personal tastes and preferences. Here too there are personal benefits to be gained from the efforts of internet marketers.

Connect

Access three *contrasting* online businesses that you are familiar with; draft a statement outlining the ways in which the online marketing activities of the business:

●   offer you general benefits

●   offer greater freedom of choice

●   increase your power as a consumer.

All online businesses need to engage in marketing, whether their customers are other businesses, or private individuals. So what are the *potential* benefits of internet marketing for all of the parties involved, remembering that marketing principles are about satisfying customer needs profitably? It is essential to use the word 'potential' because in B2B markets the full benefits of the internet tend to be felt only by those firms that can enter into valuable collaborations with other firms that also have the right web-based systems. Research in America in 2001 by Accenture showed that larger companies tended to purchase online (twenty-three per cent of them doing more than a quarter of their purchases) whereas small to medium firms did less (eighteen percent). This is an important point at this stage in the evolution of internet business. Any firm considering moving to online activities needs to consider the uneven pace at which various companies are doing so. What is the point of having state of the art web based information technology if major partner firms do not? E-marketplaces (sometimes referred to as portals) are one way of ensuring higher levels of industry wide online collaboration.

Customisation

Supermarkets and hypermarkets have tended to reduce the opportunities for a personal shopping experience. Years ago people in different localities would shop at different types of outlet. Communities could be characterised by distinct sets of shops. Increasingly we have developed into a mass consumption society where every family tends to shop in similar ways, faced with similar ranges of products. One benefit of the online shopping experience is that each of us can now enjoy a personal offer from a website that is tailored to suit our individual preferences. This is 'customisation' or 'personalisation'.

Customisation is important because it gets to the heart of what marketing is about, i.e. meeting customer needs. Anything that is customised has been altered to suit a specific set of requirements. Many people customise cars by adding new panels, respraying to a fresh colour and plastering stickers all over the body. This may not be to everyone's taste, but it suits the owner. In internet marketing terms, customisation (sometimes referred to as personalisation) is when internet technology is used to tailor websites to suit the needs (or perceived needs) of individual customers.

Take the following example from a B2C transaction involving Amazon.co.uk (see www.Amazon.co.uk) and a private consumer, Mr John Goymer.

Figure 2.12 Amazon.co.uk – personalising the product

Figure 2.12 shows how Amazon.com have made use of previously gathered data to keep a log of all of the purchases a specific customer has made from their website. The example shows that John Goymer has bought before from the site and as soon as a purchase is made, Amazon's system offers other suggestions for similar books or CD's. Amazon are saying, "Hello John Goymer, if you like what you've just bought, you might like these too..." For both books and CDs. Amazon can also offer Mr Goymer – and even completely new customers – reviews of products based on other people's purchases. As with many 'e-tailers', Amazon uses the shopping cart. Shoppers can add many items to their cart and, as they do, Amazon's system maintains the full record of the shopping visit. Each time a customer visits and revisits the Amazon website, this customised and up-to-date response is automatically offered, anticipating their needs. Thanks to internet technology, each and every customer can enjoy a private and personal shopping experience.

 Connect

Do an internet search and find three websites that offer a degree of customisation of their site.

Produce a short written description of this and include screenshots to clearly illustrate the technique. What benefits, if any, are there for both the business and the customer?

John Goymer is known to Amazon as a customer because he has 'registered' with the site. His previous buying history is known to Amazon. In many cases however, site visitors are anonymous to the website. This does not necessarily mean however that they are first timers, many anonymous visitors are regular visitors to the site; they have simply chosen not to register. Marketing specialists are still able to offer the benefit of a set of customised menus for these visitors so that the site *feels* like it is personal to them. One way this can be done is by offering facilities like, 'People who bought [item X] also often bought [item Y]' and a sub-list of products is offered to the visitor. What is important is that the site user feels that the offering is personal to them.

Barnes&Noble.com offered a 'Gift Advisor' on their website. The user was asked a set of questions such as; Who are you buying a gift for? What is the person interested in? What is your price range? Next to each question was a drop-down box of alternative answers. Every time the user selected an option, the right hand side of the screen offered an updated selection of gift suggestions. No one was allowed to select a set of answers that would lead to 'no possible gifts'. Every answer would lead to the gift suggestions being dynamically updated, with items being removed or added each time. This is customisation based on user interaction, not upon asking detailed questions up front. It is a way of breaking down barriers and gently making the user feel a part of the site.

The thinking behind this kind of online marketing is to try to recreate for consumer the kind of shopping experience one would expect in a high-class shopping mall. We all expect individual attention, especially if we have a problem with something.

Customer Relationship Management (CRM) software, described in Unit 1, automates the whole response a business makes towards its regular online customers or clients. Using CRM tools enables online business to be slick, responsive and efficient. It enables an online relationship to develop that is based upon trust and goodwill.

It helps to think of every business having a personality, just as each person has a personality. Two businesses doing business with each other are better off knowing each other very well. The internet offers the chance to do this. Studies by Accenture have shown that in B2B markets service is what matters too, in most cases more than price. The firm that offers cheapness but poor backup services will not compete with those offering excellent customer support. This is known as 'customer orientation'. It means thinking always about what the customers needs are. It is a major function of internet marketing to plan an online marketing strategy with customer needs in mind. It is better to plan carefully ahead of mounting an online channel, rather than rush in with an ill conceived strategy; as they say, 'e-Right is more important than e-Speed'.

Interactive shopping

The experience of buying a product online can never be exactly the same as buying in the shop in town. However, some online businesses are attempting to use web-based technology to create a more interactive experience for the shopper and in doing so create a relationship that will keep them. It is far more productive to attract and retain customers than acquire new ones. At www.Nokey.com an effort is made to mirror the interaction of a physical shop. At any point during the shopping or browsing process, the customer can launch a live instant messaging (IM) session to seek advice or help. The latest versions of the technology allow the online store to view the items a customer has added or deleted from his or her shopping cart and initiate an IM session with shoppers at any time during their visit to site, offering help or advice at the point where it is perhaps most needed.

Over to you Prepare a brief set of notes outlining what is meant by the term 'Interactive shopping' and explaining what, if any, benefits are gained for consumers.

Ability to compare and select products

In both B2C and B2B markets the internet has offered far greater opportunities to compare the offers of online businesses. For B2C markets research quoted by Laurie Windham (2001) showed that more than a third of all internet shoppers regarded themselves as 'comparison shoppers'. Their motivation for online shopping was the ability to study and compare online products. In industrial markets the evolution of e-marketplaces (sometimes called exchanges or hubs) allows firms to enter specialist online environments in which they can develop relationships with suppliers and choose from a broad range of offerings. Several electronic marketplaces now exist, each offering a simple, single link to a wide range of suppliers (see: www.vertical.net).

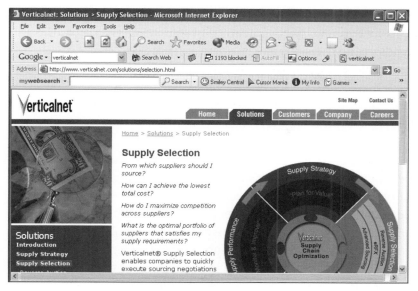

Figure 2.13 Verticalnet site offering supplier selection services

Connect

Visit www.diy.com. Prepare a presentation on the site clearly showing how it has been designed with the customers' needs in mind. Consider whether consumer choices have been improved or whether they are better informed about specific products.

Make sure that you illustrate your points with reference to specific aspects of the website (e.g. ability to try out colour schemes).

House hunting is one area where internet technology is gradually transforming the process and delivering real benefits to people. Research has shown that more than 12 million internet users accessed online estate agents in March 2003 (Nielson/NetRatings). Users can access comparative information about properties and agents, they can utilise *virtual tours* of properties, or make use of online mortgage calculators.

The travel industry is able to utilise the internet to offer consumers the full range of travel related products. Virtual tours of places of interest, photograph galleries and access to tourist office information can all be made available through a website. Online flight comparisons and reservations are now well established on the internet and consumers can benefit through the significantly lower transactional costs involved in online reservations compared to call centre reservations (the cost of an online reservation is almost ten times cheaper, source: Datamonitor, 1999).

Dynamic pricing

The benefits of dynamic pricing, were discussed in Unit 1 (page 35). The price is automatically altered to suit the particular circumstances either of the market or the buyer and everyone involved in a transaction has the chance to gain. The purchaser gets the keenest price and the seller makes something from the deal because the system is set up to ensure that they do. Using dynamic pricing means that sales people are saved the need for haggling or negotiation and decisions can be made quickly. See www.lastminute.com for example of application of dynamic pricing.

Digital complaints and chat

Online complaints services exist to make a business out of assisting consumers in any complaint about an online product or service. Consumers benefit by being able to add their complaint to those of others gathered by the specialist firm and thereby achieve added collective effect. A fee is paid to the complaints service company who are able to write to the online firm concerned and elaborate the concerns. Any complainant must have given the customer care people at the company being complained against a chance to rectify the problem before it is taken up. The matter will be passed over to legal specialists by the complaints service if it is not resolved (for example, see: www.fightback.com).

Figure 2.14 Online complaints service – www.fightback.com

The internet offers the opportunity to participate in real time online chat groups. This is especially useful to consumers as they are able to contribute opinions about products and read the opinions of many others. In this respect the power of the individual consumer is enhanced both by gaining information and the perspectives of others, as well as making collective representation.

Connect

Visit www.Apple.com and navigate your way to the 'Discussion' link about the iTunes product. Does this empower the consumer? How would you say the consumer benefits?

Payments systems

A major benefit to online consumers is the ease and speed with which transactions can be completed over the internet. A decision on the part of the private consumer to purchase tickets for an event can be quickly converted to a firm booking through a secure credit card transaction. The costs of these transactions for businesses is near zero. In B2B transactions the amount of funds involved is likely to be too high for credit cards to be used; in these cases invoicing is usually the preferred payment method and this is increasingly likely to be digitised. When both parties in a transaction are well known to each other all that is needed are passwords and login authentication. Invoicing can then be done automatically and securely, often using a third party payments service provider such as paypal or worldpay (www.worldpay.com).

Accessibility

For some people the internet is simply not accessible at all. These people have some form of disadvantage that just prevents them from taking full advantage of the benefits the internet offers. In December 2002 a survey of 159 websites conducted by Dublin University showed that ninety-four percent of the sites were inaccessible to the 'disabled'. Special 'assistive' technology is available however that can make websites useful to people with, for example, motor difficulties who may find using a mouse impossible; or for those who cannot read normal sized fonts on a screen. The benefits of the internet can and should be available to everyone and the **World Wide Web consortium (W3C)** as well as EU law makers are likely to impose regulations in future to enforce consideration of accessibility issues.

Over to you In groups, prepare a poster display illustrating as clearly as you can the alleged benefits gained from internet marketing. As the centre piece of your display, choose three contrasting websites to illustrate your points.

2.3 Opportunities for internet marketing

The internet offers several new opportunities for businesses to re-establish themselves online. A well established physical business can recreate an entirely new online personality and tap new markets on a global scale if it chooses to adopt such a strategy. There are several ways in which internet marketing generates new opportunities.

To be able to serve a market, more importantly a particular *segment* of a market, an online business needs to know all about it; it must be an intelligent business, in terms of being well informed about trends or changes. Information is the lifeblood of the internet and marketing information is readily available. Who is using a site? Where are they? What are they like? This is marketing intelligence and it is vital.

Acquiring marketing intelligence

The internet is an ideal research tool for an online business. It is possible to gather business information from all over the world, to monitor competitor activities, find out the opinions and feelings of potential customers (see www.ciao.co.uk for an example of a consumer product rating site) and study changes in the online market a business is working in. Trends and fluctuations that may affect a business' online activity can quickly be analysed It is even possible, sometimes by using the services of a specialist web analysis firm, to gain a greater insight into the impact and performance of a website. Traffic to a website can be analysed and the most popular areas of a site can be found. Marketing specialists can establish which content has been most interesting to visitors and make sure the best content is developed.

A brief word of caution, however; search engines send out little robots called '*spiders*' that are used to look at content. Also, some Internet Service Providers (ISPs) send out copies of web pages to '*proxy servers*' that store them for faster recall the next visit. *Both* of these factors can distort counts of page visits. Spiders appear as users of a site when in fact they are not. A proxy server relays requests to a site from many users, yet appears to the site as only one address. Spiders can vastly *inflate* the apparent numbers, proxy servers can *deflate* them. Marketing people therefore need to be very careful with this kind of analysis and many use specialists to do this work.

e-Business insight — Black and Decker

Business objectives
Black and Decker (USA), the leading global manufacturer and supplier of power tools and accessories, set up a consumer website at www.blackanddecker.com designed to support customers throughout the buying and home improvement process. The company wanted to build better relationships with consumers by getting them to become registered members of the site.

Challenges
1 Maximise registrations as members

2 Effectively monitor the success of the effort to build better relationships – are people registering as members of the site?

Solutions
The company appointed WebTrends (www.webtrends.com) to provide detailed analysis of the traffic on the Black and Decker website.

Question: Where was the most effective place on the site to locate a registration button?

Solution: Vary the position of the button and measure the registrations gained from each. By doing this through the *WebTrends Reporting Center*, Black and Decker discovered the best location and increased registrations by forty percent.

A vast resource of secondary data is easily available online, data that has already been researched by others can be accessed easily and new, primary data can be discovered. This primary data can be researched from the firm's own website as illustrated in the Black and Decker *e-Business insight* above. Visitor use or navigation patterns can be established by tracking, for example, pages visited, the most common entry page or the page people most often leave a site from. Obviously, visitor numbers can be checked, as well as the numbers of visitors who are converted to customers. A whole new industry supplying web analysis tools and services has developed. Businesses of all sizes now find that quite sophisticated marketing research tools are within their grasp. Check again the CIM definition of marketing given in Section 2.1; *identifying, anticipating* and (as we shall see) *satisfying* customer needs – these can all be assisted by effective and sensible use of internet marketing intelligence.

 Connect

Visit www.webtrends.com and study what this web analysis firm offers. Plan and prepare a leaflet that would inform a small business manager how this service might be of benefit to them.

Affiliate marketing

The process of carrying links from one website to the website of another business is known as *affiliate marketing* and this is an agreed arrangement between two businesses. Internet technology allows businesses to track how many visitors pass through a particular link on another site, to their own site. The affiliate business – the one carrying your link – will be paid either a flat fee or commission if a sale is generated from the referral. Commissions vary depending on sales. Some businesses pay a higher rate if more than, say, 50 sales are generated per month. Being an affiliate can be quite a lucrative thing for some online businesses depending on the value of the products concerned. If a product is worth £400 and an affiliate gets two and a half percent per sale it can add significant sums to revenue. From the point of view of internet marketing policy and strategy, the decision to add an affiliate program to a business' online presence could be a very significant addition to distribution channels.

 Connect

Visit www.affiliate.com (or alternatively find a similar equivalent site). This is a US based web service designed to help businesses join and make effective use of affiliate marketing. In your own words, note the various ways in which this kind of site can help businesses.

What specific services does this site offer?

Figure 2.15 shows how www.booksdirect.co.uk sells the advantages of an affiliate partnership scheme. This is another example of a significant marketing opportunity offered through the internet.

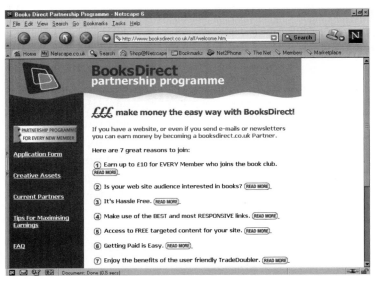

Figure 2.15 Affiliate opportunities – www.booksdirect.co.uk

Analysis of competitor activity

The internet offers the opportunity for careful and accurate analysis of what competitors are doing online. Each company that goes online immediately becomes open and transparent as they do so. By its nature, the internet is open and everyone can view its content. Marketing activities have to include keeping a close eye on the tactics, the ideas and offerings of competitor firms. The websites themselves can be looked at and are a primary source of information. The marketer will look for new ideas, for offers and tactical manoeuvres, particularly from firms competing for the same segment of the market. The idea is not to copy a website but to gain an insight into competitor strategy. There are organisations offering this kind of intelligence as a service on the web. At http://finance.yahoo.com it is possible to gather information about many companies around the world. Dunn & Bradstreet at http://dnb.com have data on more than 35 million companies.

Identifying customers

Online businesses sell to either private consumers or business clients and need to know as much about them as they can.

Private consumers in B2C markets

Only a few years ago the typical internet user was a young white male, probably of an academic background. Today there is a much more diverse pattern of internet usage and because of this the availability of many more market segments is improving for online marketers. Being a global phenomenon, there is possibly no single ethnic group that does not have access to the internet. Virtually every country on every continent has internet connection and it is essential for some companies to remember that what is offered via the web has to be tailored to meet the needs of local populations. 'Think global, act local' has become a common requirement for internet marketers. Remember, it is a fundamental principle of any marketing strategy identify and get to know customers, whether we are talking globally, nationally or regionally.

The production of statistics about internet use and trends (**webographics**) has therefore become almost an industry in itself and there are several options available for gaining such data:

- www.itu.int/ti/industryoverview/index.htm – is the website of the Telecommunications Union ITU and makes available data about internet access across countries and continents.

- www.nua.ie/surveys – offers statistical data based on European internet trends.

- www.cyberatlas.com – offers statistical data about USA internet trends.

- www.bmrb.co.uk – is the British Market Research Bureau and provides data on consumer buying behaviour.

We can categorise data about the online population in a number of ways:

- demographics – age, gender

- geographic location – continent, nationality, region

- 'psychographic' profile – characterising internet users according to major tendencies identified via research (see below)

- access device – personal computer, mobile telephone, TV

- lifestyle characteristics – interests, home ownership, car ownership

- social class – based on work status, occupation, income.

Psychographics

The 'psychographics' of online shoppers were characterised by Harris Interactive (see www.harrisinteractive.com) into six main types of online shopper:

e-Bivalent newbies (5 percent) – new to the internet and less interested in buying online. Mainly older and less often online.

Time sensitive materialists (17 percent) – interested in maximum convenience, not bothered about product reviews or comparisons.

Clicks and mortar (23 percent) – tend to shop online but buy offline. Probably female home builders who have privacy and security concerns.

Hooked, online and single (16 percent) – more likely to be young, single males with high income; been on internet longest and play games, download software, bank and invest online.

Hunter gatherers (20 percent) – Married, aged 30 – 49 with two children; often go to sites to compare prices and read analyses and product reviews.

Brand loyalists (19 percent) – people who go directly to a shopping site they know; are satisfied with online shopping and spend the most online.

Business customers (B2B)

Business users of the internet can be profiled in much the same way as private individuals:

- Do they have internet access?
- Who within the firm has internet access?
- What is their main market? (Which industrial sector? Which products?)
- Do they purchase online?
- The size of the firm
- Private or public sector?
- Country or region.

It is very important to profile potential business customers. It has already been stressed that it is essential to consider the state of 'internet readiness' of firms that may be crucial business partners, either as suppliers or purchasers of your products. So called 'vertical portals' are gateway websites to communities of firms working in specific industries and they are important means of targeting firms (see, for example, www.vertical.net).

Online and offline marketing

Marketing people may not only exploit the opportunities offered by the internet but can add to their total communication effort by integrating *offline* promotional work. This could include:

- promoting the domain name (via posters, advertising and livery, see in the photograph how Sainsbury's promote Sainsburystoyou.com on their vans)
- brand building by stressing the Internet Value Proposition (IVP) (see Section 2.1)
- promotional offers.

Sainsbury's delivery vans advertise their website

Increasingly, online businesses are building a brand identity and people are referring quite naturally to 'dot com' brands (often, adding to the physical business e.g. Diy.com). Through word of mouth, websites are able to gain a powerful reputation and this, known as 'viral' marketing, is increasingly a major concern. Similarly, web PR (public relations) can be a low cost but very effective form of promoting a site. Finally, direct mailing of website offers can be used, together with web address promotion via business cards, magazine inserts, catalogues or brochures.

Over to you　Collect and present as many examples as you can of *offline* promotional materials relating to *online* activities. Evaluate the effectiveness of this material.

Marketing through search engines

Over eighty percent of web users are reported to use search engines, so it makes sense for an online business to register with one. There are now over four billion web pages on the internet yet most of them are not registered with one of the search engines. This makes them inaccessible to all but a relatively few users. Marketers must – at a cost – submit the URL of the website to the appropriate search engine after making sure that the main web page includes important 'meta data' (i.e. data about the information on the site) at its <HEAD> (see Unit 3 for more on this). If the site is accepted then keywords from the 'meta data' on the site are added to the search engine's database and an index is created. When people do a search of this engine, the index is searched.

 Connect

Analyse three contrasting websites and, using as much evidence from the sites as you can find, specify the ways in which internet marketing has created new business opportunities.

In what ways do you feel the internet could be further used to improve business performance?

2.4　The challenges of internet marketing

Whilst the internet is offering marketing benefits and opportunities on a massive scale it also throws up many challenges. These challenges have to be faced and overcome if a business is to compete in the online world. Traditional thinking about business tends to be based on a fixed view, of a chain of value-adding activities; e.g. acquire materials, store materials, work with materials to produce something, package the product, warehouse (store) the product, market the product, sell it, move it. Often, businesses have grown to encompass several of these spheres of activity within the one organisation.

According to Chaffey (2002) one way of looking at e-business as a whole is to view it as three overlapping sets of processes:

Figure 2.16 Chaffey's view of e-business (2002)

All business involves buying and selling. This activity is at the heart of what business is about, however it is done. The internet offers a new channel through which the processes involved in adding value take place. But just as the internet represents a new channel of opportunities, so it causes potential conflict and challenges. The Chaffey approach is useful to put these challenges in perspective.

The challenge of channel conflict

All businesses have to use various channels of distribution either to acquire goods or to sell them. There are no laws or regulations forcing businesses to move online, or adopt new information technologies. The strategic decision of whether or not to introduce an additional channel of distribution is purely a management one based on whether or not business objectives will be achieved. Businesses are therefore adopting e-business at an uneven rate – some have adopted early, some are slower to introduce change. We saw in the case of Irish company Kingspan (see Unit 1) how forward thinking management can adopt new innovative processes based on the web only to find themselves way ahead of partner firms.

A variation on this sort of challenge is the generation of **channel conflict** sometimes caused when an existing business goes online. The internet, we have seen, offers the chance to use a *direct* channel to suppliers or customers. This 'disintermediation' is the tendency to directly deal with suppliers or customers over the internet and thereby eliminate the 'middle-man'. This creates efficiencies, but at the danger of destabilising many older traditional channels that are *still valuable sources of revenue* to the business. The following example scenarios show how this can occur.

Example 1: A manufacturer (e.g. Dell) sells PCs directly to customers; several long established and valued retail outlets for the product object to this and refuse to sell it any more.

Example 2: A distributor is employed to deal with physical placement of products and is made redundant for some products but not others.

Established businesses considering adding an online distribution channel, (either to their 'buy-side' or 'sell-side' channels) therefore have to consider the impact such a move may have on other dimensions of their activities. However, we have seen that, increasingly, businesses *are* making the move. Chaffey argues that today's firms have to identify what their 'core competency' is. What do they do best? Once they have identified what their core business is, they can then build key *channel partnerships* to collaborate with other firms who do other things better. Some examples will again help to clarify this.

Example 3: A manufacturer works with a retailer to offer better online customer support. Both share customer data; both work to create the brand identity.

Example 4: B & Q Direct (at www.diy.com) work in partnership with Spark Response, who provide customer service, call centre, warehousing and product fulfilment (see Section 2.1).

Example 5: Ford in the USA work in collaboration with their dealer network on an 'Internet Approved' programme, giving training and expertise to promote internet based customer relationship. In this way, Ford has developed direct customer relationships over the internet avoiding conflict with its highly valued dealership network.

Over to you Explain what is meant by 'channel conflict'. In what ways could this damage the prospects of a proposed e-business venture?

Meeting customer expectations

The internet is significantly raising customer expectations. The constant 24x7x365 (24 hours a day, 7 days a week, 365 days a year) availability and convenience of the internet has been reinforced with increased personalisation and price transparency. Even more importantly, customers are starting to expect higher levels of reliability and responsiveness, increasingly expecting not only convenience but speed; speed in terms of both delivery once an order is placed and speed whilst visiting the website. Taken together, these are heavy demands on the online business.

Through the internet, merchandise is becoming available in *mass customised* form, allowing customers to enter personal measurements for pants (for example) before ordering; or allowing a computer manufacturer to encourage customers to configure their machines online as they order. Customers will increasingly demand or expect this one to one online attention.

The process of engaging the customer is fundamental to good online marketing. Yet, it generates a fierce level of expectation that what is asked for is delivered and that every scrap of supporting information is available – and correct. A beautifully constructed website, tremendously informative content, competitive prices, smooth and easy transaction arrangements will all count for zero (or probably *less* than zero!) if a customer's product expectations or customer service expectations are not fulfilled.

A Forrester Technographics survey of 9,000 users who have made online purchases found that eighty percent of them had visited a manufacturer's site *first* before visiting the retailer selling the item. These people then revisited throughout the buying cycle and knew exactly what they wanted. Buyers on the internet are increasingly showing this willingness to bypass the retailer for product information. The internet buyer can be very well informed indeed.

The challenge for online marketers is to anticipate and understand what customer expectations will be, whatever the market context. Remember the Kozmo.com experience? The US retailer promised delivery of *any* order (*"Fancy a packet of chewing gum, Lisa? OK, I'll get those folks from Kozmo to bring it round"*). Marketing should lead to customer expectations being met *profitably* – so, the moral is not to make outrageous promises.

A business strategy for *managing customer expectations* has been suggested by Chaffey:

1 Find out what customers expect by doing some research. Include in the site a feedback form if necessary. Always work to rectify any shortcomings.

2 Make realistic promises and communicate them clearly. Do not over-promise (Kozmo!).

3 Deliver commitments with the help of staff as well as physical fulfilment.

Connect

Visit www.bizrate.com and look at customer comments. Make a note of some of the complaints made by customers.

Over to you Draft a statement for the management of a business that is proposing going online, specifying what you see as the most important things to consider in meeting customer expectations.

Information overload

Because marketing requires a business to focus beyond and outside of itself, to discover information about the market it hopes to serve, its customers and its competitors, the business will naturally be awash with data. Employees and systems can be overloaded. There is therefore a need at the outset to consider the kind of data that is crucial to the business and from that, to think of the processes and information systems that will be required to handle data.

In B2B markets especially, *customer profiles* can be usefully built up. These will characterise each customer in terms of products bought, specialist input from customer buying staff, location and size. This sort of information allows the customer to be placed in their 'market segment' and from this an appropriate marketing relationship should be formed. It is vital to capture the relevant information and to act appropriately upon it. _Information is not knowledge_ (remember that – it applies to you too!). Data has to be interpreted and made sense of. What does it mean? Managers and individual staff within the organisation should have good access to relevant data – assistance with its interpretation and the ability to act upon it. This of course generates more information and so the cycle goes on. Eventually however people can be faced with overload and this is known as 'information fatigue'.

Many organisations incorporate on their site a Frequently Asked Questions (FAQ) panel, certainly most serious online businesses include an e-mail contact and telephone number within a 'Contact us' link. This facility is likely to generate a considerable degree of feedback. The online business must be prepared to allocate resources designed to effectively deal with this, otherwise it risks damaging its reputation. If necessary, large portions of a marketing strategy may need to be revised in response to aspects of feedback. The business must process feedback and be prepared to act upon it if required.

Keeping pace with technological change

As the global world of e-business gathers pace, every business is having to face up to the challenges of what to do, when to do it and how. We saw at the start how technological change has always been with us. Our economy has changed from agriculture to manufacturing to services. Now however, we are evolving into a digital economy in which change is accelerating at a quicker pace than ever before. Businesses are having to *innovate* (find new ways of doing things) in virtually all markets, they are having to respond to new ways of working by partner firms as well as competitors. The digital economy is a *knowledge based economy*, based on providing better products, faster and more efficiently than others. In this economy, *speed* wins and for management this is pressure.

Ensuring maximum exposure through search engines and ISPs

Internet Service Providers (ISPs) are firms that offer an internet connection service to both private householders and businesses. Their primary function is to provide a link to the World Wide Web but many ISPs also host websites on their own servers.

The crucial point for business management is to ensure that the ISP is offering a satisfactory level of service for a reasonable price. ISPs have to be able to deal with fluctuating and perhaps growing traffic. Speed of access is crucial. We have just seen above that customers online demand speed. One way of helping in this respect is to have a *dedicated server*, i.e. one which is serving only content from your business. Additionally, **bandwidth** is an important factor in governing the speed of content delivery and the bandwidth between the ISP and the internet needs to be looked at. The bigger the bandwidth, the quicker data can pass (like water in a pipe). Bandwidth is measured in kilobits (1,000bits) per second and is written as kbps. A typical modem operates at 56.6kbps and will often be used by a small business; ISDN is usually twice as fast.

A further issue with ISPs is the amount of *time* that a website is made available to customers. Ideally a business needs to ensure that the site is available 24x7. Not all sites are made available one hundred percent of the time and of course this results in lost revenue.

Search engines are extremely important for the promotion of a website, as we saw earlier. Over eighty percent of web users are known to use them and if a business has not bothered to register with the search engines then they are unlikely to be found unless they have an extremely well known brand name. The registration process and the website design process are basic and fundamental to the site profile; the former for making the search engines aware of the site and the latter for elevating the site in the search engine listings. Take no care in building in *meta-tags* and *keywords* in your page's **HTML** and your site may well be listed in search results but be well down the list. Site designers have to increase the chances of a website being listed high in search results and this calls for clever use of keywords in design.

Security and payment systems

The internet has become a global phenomenon *because* it is an open network, but it is also an insecure network. Despite this, millions of internet based business transactions are taking place every minute. Confidential, sensitive and potentially damaging company data is increasingly being made available to internet-based access. Viruses, hackers and other undesirables, are constantly a danger. Malicious individuals (or firms) can attack a business' data, they can fraudulently make claims or simply attempt to thieve. Competitively vital information can be open to attack. Almost fifty percent of all credit card fraud is known to be internet related, for the e-tailer there is known to be a significant risk of fraudulent purchases. Repudiation of orders is a common problem. (people ordering goods then denying they did). Private individuals are just as open to attack and it is a real fear for online consumers. It is a task of the e-business to reassure them.

The challenge for business leaders is therefore to *plan for security*. This means, right at the outset, devising an e-business strategy that takes security issues seriously. There are several areas to cover:

- *authorisation*
- *encryption*
- *authentication.*

Authorisation

Determine who should have access rights to certain applications and information. Establish a consistent policy and ensure this is centrally controlled and monitored.

Encryption

This is a method of hiding data by jumbling it up into a hidden format. The actual meaning of text, numbers or whatever, becomes almost impossible to retrieve by anyone other than those who have access to the 'key'. Businesses in the digital world have to embrace encryption. Confidential documents such as contracts, personal data, pricing details and product research data can all be vulnerable to theft or attack. Encryption of e-mails is the equivalent of slotting a document into a sealed envelope, sensible – and private. Both **Secure Sockets Layer (SSL)** and **Secure Electronic Transactions (SET)** are standards that ensure the encryption of internet traffic. SET encompasses a whole payments system, whilst SSL encrypts only traffic between a web browser and server.

Authentication

Customers must identify themselves through a secure login and password procedure.

Linguistic and cultural issues

As use of the internet continues to grow, more and more people online are expected to be non-English speakers. According to Jupiter Research, almost sixty percent of the internet population are likely to live outside the USA by 2005. English speaking audiences are unlikely to dominate the internet for too long. Obviously it is important for any business seriously attempting to expand to consider translations of their site. Marketers must 'think global, act local', but how? It is important to remember that literal *linguistic* translations (i.e. from one language to another) are only the first step; to be a truly local service, a website needs to take account of local cultural expectations. Just take the example of payment methods. A report by NetSmartAmerica ('America.com: What makes America click': 2000 at www.netsmartamerica.com) showed that seventy percent of online shoppers in the US paid by credit card. In Japan, the most common payment method (in May 2000) was cash on delivery. This is said to reflect the Japanese preference for cash-based payment. A spin off from this was that in Japan many more websites were obliged to be based on membership, reflecting the fact that members had to pay by direct bank deposit.

Web designers of the future will increasingly need to consider cultural differences at great length. Differences in perception are significant. Oriental scripts (Japanese, Korean, Chinese) are justified and read vertically, Arabic is read from right to left, whereas English is read from left to right. These differences are *very* significant. Does a Chinese user view a left-justified web page as appealing?

Some societies can be said to be very family or group oriented (China), others much more individualistic (USA, UK, Western Europe). This difference can be reflected in marketing communications. Get the message wrong and real long-term online damage can be caused. In marketing, as we know by now, it is vital to *know your market*.

Outcome activity

Marketing challenge

Take three contrasting online businesses including at least one regional and at least one multi-national concern.

1   Identify and summarise in your own words the major internet marketing challenges you feel the business is facing.

2   Discuss in groups the ways you feel the business may deal with these challenges.

3   Evaluate ways in which the three businesses may implement an internet marketing strategy despite the challenges faced.

Unit 3 Website design and construction

After completing Unit 3 you will be able to:

- describe the range of *internet technologies* and services used to deliver content to users
- describe the *use of web authoring tools* and the impact of common *standards* on website design
- *design and plan* a functioning website to meet user requirements
- *use markup language(s)* to construct a functional website within a plan.

> **Your understanding of this unit will be assessed by an internally marked assignment.**

This Unit is designed to give you an understanding of *how* the internet works to deliver web page content and various other services to users. You will learn the basics of how computers come to be able to 'talk' to each other – through using 'protocols'. After studying the unit – in short – you will know *what* the internet is.

After learning about internet basics you will then discover the various ways in which content is created for the World Wide Web. You will learn about various web 'authoring tools', how and why these may be used and one or two potential pitfalls in using them. You will learn the basic building processes involved in creating web pages through directly applying **H**yper **T**ext **M**arkup **L**anguage (HTML). Finally you will be able to test your own skills and understanding by designing and planning a functional website, that meets an identified clients requirements.

Before going too far with your work on this unit, you are encouraged to take a moment to examine Unit 5 *e-Business project*.

3.1 Internet technologies

It's not possible to see the internet, touch it, or go and visit its headquarters. There is no grand palace, abbey, tower block or mecca that can be truthfully described as its HQ. No big corporation or big shot of any race or nationally owns it. So what is it? Is it magic? The internet is in fact a global collection of big and small computer networks that are interconnected. So there it is, the 'internet' is an *internet*-work of networks.

Questions about where the internet came from are dealt with more fully in Unit 4; let us just note now that the Russians (then part of the Soviet Union) had something to do with it. In October 1957 the then Soviet Union successfully launched a satellite (called

'Sputnik') into space to circle the globe, causing the Americans to immediately feel under threat of wholesale destruction. If the hostile Soviet Union could do that, then they could *potentially* wipe out any part of the USA. Computers were a key element of the US defence strategy. It was unthinkable that a machine holding crucial defence information could possibly be knocked out. Wouldn't it be better if computers could be linked together, so that the country was not dependant on single machines? Because of this fear, the **A**dvanced **R**esearch **P**rojects **A**gency (ARPA), an offshoot of the American Defense Department, was given a budget to *"find a way to connect all these different machines" (Bob Taylor, ARPA 1966)*.

The so called ARPA network of no more than half a dozen computers, linking east–west across the States, represents the acknowledged origins of the internet. However, it has been pointed out that to ask 'who' invented the internet is a bit like asking 'who' built Durham Cathedral. The truth is that many people have contributed in different ways and continue to do so today. The internet works day and night, twenty four hours a day, with few real disasters. Even the dreadful events of September 11th 2001, did not deluge the internet for long. The Internet Service Providers (ISPs) added more **servers** within hours to cope with the sudden huge increase in traffic.

Anyway, that's enough of the background for the moment. Let's look at the basic structures and **protocols** that make the internet work. A 'protocol', by the way, is an agreed way of doing things. You follow protocol all the time whether you are aware of it or not.

The range of basic processes of the internet

Within the network of computers that go together to make up the internet, some machines are *servers*, these machines make the internet possible because they provide services to other machines. The other machines are known as *clients* (some machines are both). The internet is therefore known as a 'client-server architecture'. When you sit at your machine at home or school/college and you access the internet, you are a 'client' and depending on what service you ask for (most commonly you will ask for a web page), you will connect to a 'server'. There are various servers offering different sorts of internet services. These include:

- **web servers**
- **FTP servers**
- application servers
- e-mail servers
- IRC servers.

Web servers

Sitting at a PC either at home or wherever, you will make use of a **browser** on the machine you are using. This is a software application – most often Internet Explorer, possibly Netscape – that is used to connect to the internet and to 'render' (display) web pages.

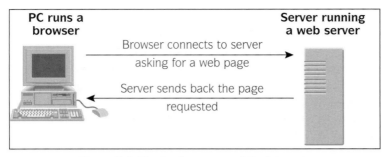

Figure 3.1 The basic process of the internet

The browser you use on your PC connects to the web server and asks – in a *particular* way – for a specific web page, the web server responds by sending back to your browser the page you have asked for. The 'particular' way, is important and takes us into just a little bit more depth about how the 'web' works.

Uniform Resource Locator (URL)

Many people refer to 'web addresses'. What they are referring to are known as 'Uniform Resource Locators' (URLs) and these are the things that users type into the browser box at the top of the screen when seeking a particular website.

Of course there are millions of URLs so let's look briefly at a single example.

Say you wanted to look at the website of B & Q Direct. You know you would need to go to http://www.diy.com so, after typing the address into the browser, certain work is done for you:

- The browser sorts out the URL into 3 parts:
  - The protocol ('http')
  - The server name ('www.diy.com')
  - The file name (separated by a / and none specified above).
- The browser connects to a *name server* and asks it to translate the server name 'www.diy.com' into an IP address which it uses to connect to the web server.
- The browser follows the **HTTP (Hyper Text Transfer Protocol)** by sending a 'GET' request to the web server.
- The server sends back to the browser the HTML text for the web page that was requested.
- The browser reads the HTML (Hypertext Markup Language – the language of the www) and formats (or 'renders') the page onto your PC screen.

IP addresses

IP addresses allow the internet to send data to the right place. Each machine on the internet is assigned a unique address called an IP address. IP stands for Internet Protocol and addresses are written as 'dotted decimal numbers', i.e. four 'octets' creating a 32-bit number. A typical IP address might look like this:

216.24.62.133

Each number, separated by a dot, is an 'octet', so called because they can each have values between $0 - 255$, which is 2^8 possibilities per octet. Each network and each host on the internet can be uniquely identified by the components of the IP address. Every IP address follows this same structure and each has to be issued by the Internet Network Information Center (InterNIC).

A final point to note on IP addresses is that they are divided into five classes – A, B, C, D & E. Class A addresses range from 1.0.0.0 to 126.0.0.0 and are reserved for very large organisations; Class B addresses range from 128.1.0.0 to 191.254.0.0 and are for medium sized organisations; Class C addresses for small; Class D for Multicast groups; Class E is experimental.

Domain names

IP addresses are obviously fabulous things and after studying the above section you will want to tell all your friends how important and crucial they are to the internet – as indeed they are. The trouble is that we mere humans could never remember all the various 'dotted decimal numbers'. So, the web servers mentioned above contain lists of human readable names (sometimes called 'symbolic names') called **domain names**. Domain names are a part of the URL described earlier. Unlike IP addresses, you will probably know many domain names by heart, for example www.yahoo.com; www.google.com and www.msn.com.

Domain names have a hierarchy. The so called *top level domain* of each of the above examples is .com. Others include .gov, .org, .co.uk, .net, .ac.uk. Of these, there are several hundred together with two letter combinations for every country. After this there is a huge list of *second level domains*. In the .com examples above you can see yahoo, google and msn. Second level domain names are usually chosen by private companies to be the same as the name of the firm There are of course millions of these. At the extreme left hand side of the domain name – very frequently www – is the *host name* of a specific machine.

Transmission Control Protocol (TCP)

IP addresses let the internet find the right route for messages, so that they get to where you want them to go (*'get me in touch with yahoo please'*). But it is Transmission Control Protocol (TCP) that takes the overall piece of data (whatever it is), breaks it down into packets, checks for errors, reassembles the packets at the other end and resends anything that gets lost.

Imagine yourself in New York and you want to send a message home. All you have is four postcards with space for only one word on each. You write 'Hello' on one, 'having' on the next, 'nice' on the next and 'time' on the last. You stick these in the post and hope. At home your folks receive, Time, hello, having and nice – eventually. Not much sense is made of this. TCP is the transport system of the internet that sorts this out. It does its best to ensure delivery of sensible data across the internetwork. TCP takes each of your 'packets' of messages and puts them in proper order at the other end and checks that each packet has been received.

Together, the **TCP/IP** protocols make the internet work.

The HTTP protocol

The Hypertext Transfer Protocol was created by Tim Berners-Lee whilst working for CERN (a research centre based in Geneva, Switzerland) in 1991. Berners-Lee is therefore correctly regarded as the creator of the World Wide Web. The function of HTTP is to specify the way in which browsers and web servers transmit data to each other. A request for a web page is sent by the client to the web server in the form of a 'GET' message containing a web address. The web server must respond with an HTML (Hypertext Markup Language) document or message. The essence of the 'protocol' is to establish which computer speaks first, how they then speak in turn and the format of the data they exchange, i.e.HTML. Clearly, without HTTP, the internet would be a vast network of variable networks all struggling to speak with each other – very limited indeed. There would be no *World Wide* Web.

Reading this sentence, you are looking at *linear* text – you can merely read from left to right – word by word. **Hypertext** refers to the text on a web page that contains *hyperlinks* embedded within it that can immediately connect a user to another document or site when the link is clicked. This 'surfing' is of course the essence of internet use, because without hypertext there would only be a very limited web. Again, hypertext is the creation of Tim Berners-Lee.

Dynamic and static content

If something is 'static' it is fixed, or standing still, something 'dynamic' is moving, energetic and consists of action. If someone calls you a 'static' person, take it as an insult. Better to be dynamic. It's not quite like that with the content of web pages but at least you know the meaning of the words.

When a user requests a particular web page, we have seen that the server on which the page is stored returns the HTML document to the browser, which then displays it. The user can interact to an extent with the document by clicking on a link, or activating a little program (such as an applet) but the information given on the page is fixed, because it is *preformatted* by the HTML. This is called a *static* web page.

On a *dynamic* web page the user can make requests for information, often through a form, for data that is contained in a database on the server. The data is then assembled according to the specific request that was made on the web page. If you wished (for example) to enquire about seats at a musical show at a theatre for certain dates, this capability can be built into the web page within the HTML. Such web pages are said to have **dynamic content** because it changes with the reality of the data behind the pages. Clearly this sort of web page is central to successful e-business.

Other internet services

The term internet refers to the infrastructure of networks that connect across the world and the World Wide Web is allowed to form because of the various established protocols that have been summarised earlier. There are several other services that are accessible on the internet, some have become less important because of the growth of the www and others have migrated to become available on the web.

- *File Transfer Protocol (FTP)* – this is a standard set of protocol for moving files around the internet. It is most commonly used for updating HTML files on web pages.

- *Internet Relay Chat (IRC)* – a tool that allows different people online at the same time to have text-based chat.

- *Internet Radio* – audio can be sent over the internet through downloads or streamed media. In downloads a compressed file (MP3 is the most popular) is stored on the user's computer. Streaming audio is not stored, only played – it is a continuous broadcast that works through an encoder, a server and the player (e.g. Real One).

e-Mail

Electronic mail or *e-mail*, was being sent in a limited form as early as 1964, during the period when computer wizards in the US were in the process of researching and developing methods of connecting computers. These messages were one-offs, capable of being sent only to another, solitary, machine. Not a lot of potential there, then. By 1971 an engineer named Ray Tomlinson had developed the ability to send messages to many machines by using the @ symbol to select the machine. In 1973, another engineer called Len Kleinrock, mistakenly left his razor in a hotel room in Brighton and e-mailed his colleague who was still in Brighton. Mr Kleinrock's razor was brought back to him. Today millions of e-mails are sent every day (a few of them probably about razors). E-mail is becoming a standard form of communication, often just standard pieces of text – but increasingly businesses are using e-mail's ability to add attachments.

To look at our e-mails we usually have to use some sort of e-mail client. Many people use a standalone client such as Microsoft Outlook Express or Microsoft Outlook but free e-mail services can be used (as you probably know!) from services such as Hotmail or Yahoo and these appear as part of a web page.

As in other internet services, the system operates through a client-server principle. Millions of machines act as e-mail servers, each server holding a list of all e-mail accounts for people who can receive e-mails on that server. In fact, most e-mail servers consist of two servers. One is an **SMTP (Simple Mail Transfer Protocol)** server; this server handles *outgoing* mail. The other is a POP3 or IMAP server, both handling *incoming* mail. **POP** stands for Post Office Protocol and IMAP for Internet Mail Access Protocol. Servers 'listen' for requests through 'ports' that are numbered in a standard way and always used for the same services.

An SMTP server listens on port number 25. When an e-mail client sends an e-mail, a connection is made to the SMTP server holding the senders account (through port 25). The e-mail client (e.g. Outlook) tells the SMTP server the address of the sender, the address of the recipient and the message body. The SMTP server takes what it has received and breaks into the three parts. The SMTP server contacts the Domain Name Server – assuming the message is intended for another domain – and effectively says, '*please give me the IP address of the SMTP server at so-and-so'.* The Domain Name Server replies with the IP address. The SMTP server with the sender's message then connects to the SMTP server to receive the message (through port 25) and has a brief conversation handing over the message. The receiving SMTP server recognises the address it has received and hands over the message to the POP3 server (listening on port 110) waiting to handle incoming mail. The POP3 server puts the mail into the inbox of the recipient.

Outcome activity

Internet technologies

Task 1

To achieve a Pass…

Describe what is meant by client–server protocols. How do they help provide web and e-mail services?

Task 2

To achieve a Merit…

Several services – other than the web – are available on the internet. Explain what these are, how they interact and what their main functions might be.

Extension task 3

To achieve a Distinction…

Explain the impact and the role of the various services available on the internet. Investigate how they may be applied in business.

3.2 Use of web authoring tools and standards

The creation of web pages tends to be done either:

- by direct coding in HTML or
- using a 'web authoring' tool.

HTML, as we know, is at the foundation of all websites. It is the basic markup language that is read by browsers and used by them to display the web page. However, although HTML has to be learned, it is reasonably straightforward to use (by the way, don't trust anybody in computing that says *anything* is easy!). However, it can be quite time consuming for some. Many people, not just professionals, want to create web-based materials for all sorts of reasons. Web **authoring tools** help in this by placing the HTML code automatically for you. Using a WYSIWYG (what you see is what you get) interface, it is possible to create pages and entire sites knowing nothing about the structure of HTML.

Here we will look at the range of authoring tools that are available for creating web pages, have a brief survey of what they do – with a little more detailed look at one product, Macromedia Dreamweaver. We will then deal with the issues of 'web standards' before going on to investigate various 'markup' languages also used to create web content.

Web authoring tools

Several companies specialise in developing highly sophisticated authoring tools for website creation. These make it possible for an amateur developer to work within a WYSIWYG (what you see is what you get) environment, to create useful and usable web pages. There are several advantages in using web authoring tools, especially:

- speed of creation
- ease of use by non-HTML experts
- ability to create large numbers of consistent pages.

Macromedia Dreamweaver

Dreamweaver has been available for several years in quite a number of versions. It is both an HTML editor *and* a site management tool. Each version has encompassed new features and improvements; Dreamweaver MX is the current version.

Figure 3.2 shows the latest (2004) Dreamweaver MX authoring environment. Notice the menu bar running along the top of the screen, allowing a web designer to (among other things), create a new file (page), modify a page's properties or set background colours or images. In the central area, the designer can see directly the results of his/her design work A site management tool is shown at lower left of the working area, showing all the related files and above that is the option to add 'behaviours' to certain elements in a website.(e.g. make text change colour on mouseover).

Dreamweaver, among other visual web development tools, offers a powerful means to create web pages within an environment that could be said to be 'developer friendly'. The effects you are looking for can be seen immediately, libraries of content can be created, cascading style sheets (CSS) used as well as Dynamic HTML.

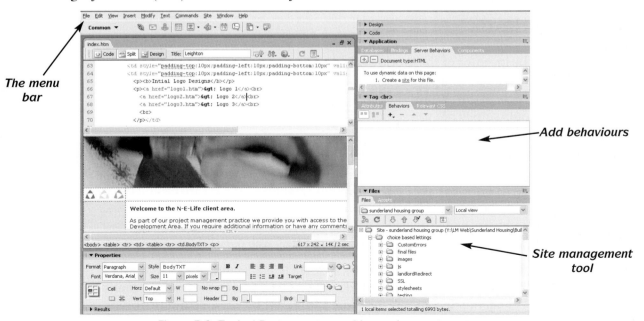

Figure 3.2 Typical Dreamweaver working environment

Macromedia Flash

Flash is usually used to create *animated* content within a web page, or to incorporate multimedia (sound and video) content. Most web pages of these days have some content that moves on the screen. Often these are GIF (Graphical Interchange File) images such as the Union Jack flag that appears to blow in the wind, or a fisherman shaking his fishing rod.

Flash users can create animated images using a timeline feature that makes use of 'keyframes'. A static image can be made to appear animated by making slight adjustments frame by frame. A developer can place an image in a Flash 'keyframe' in the timeline, another slightly changed one in another and Flash will, on command, insert 'tweened' motion. The software works out the images needed in between the two keyframes. When the 'motion' picture is played, the image appears to move.

Flash has all sorts of other features such as video import that can be used to enliven and enrich a web page. It is commonplace these days to have interaction on websites. Flash even allows for interactive quizzes.

Web standards

Tim Berners-Lee, the inventor of the World Wide Web, had in mind a fully open, interoperable and accessible web of information. HTTP and HTML were the techniques he created that would enable this. Whilst the HTTP protocol, by its very nature, would persist – otherwise data could simply not be exchanged – HTML could be modified or extended during its use. A major problem arose very early in the development of the web when two competing corporations Netscape and Microsoft, created two browser versions. This separate development (still persisting today) of the two leading browsers, meant that people developing web pages had to consider different versions of the HTML coding to take account of browser preferences. As later browser versions emerged, the problems became more severe. Web designers had to consider different browser versions as well as different browsers. Could developers afford multiple versions of every web page?

Although nobody actually owns the World Wide Web, there are leading bodies that work to try and ensure that it develops in an open and accessible way that will benefit as many people as possible. A major contributor is the **World Wide Web Consortium (known as W3C)** and they among others attempt to define web standards.

A web standard is made up of elements and structures. The purpose of developing a core of web standards is to ensure as far as possible that:

- web-based content is designed and structured in such a way that the greatest benefit will be gained by the greatest number of web users

- as many applications as possible can understand the source code of a page

- any document published on the web will have long term viability.

The intention is to try and secure the basics of the web, by creating uniform standards accepted by as many web creators – and browser manufacturers – as possible. In this way, it is hoped that sites will continue to function correctly as browsers change, that they will be 'backwardly compatible' too and they will become more accessible to more and more people, using a greater variety of internet connecting devices (the Web Standards Project is accessible at www.webstandards.org).

Authoring tools and web standards

There is obviously a major temptation to use authoring tools. They allow for easy site management and these days increasingly allow for powerful design features. However, by definition they generate HTML code *automatically* and frequently they have been shown to break out of W3C standards guidelines. A study completed in 2000 by the Special Needs Opportunity Window (SNOW) at the University of Toronto, showed that authoring tools that were being used for creating web-based learning courseware all tended to breach W3C standards. This meant that materials might not be usable on particular browsers or operating systems; it meant that for some users of web-based courseware, the materials were not accessible (authoring tools did not generate HTML code that would help users with special requirements, e.g. extra large fonts). Authoring tools also tend to introduce scripting languages (such as Javascript) embedded in a page, that are sometimes unnecessary and yet significantly increase file sizes. This has the negative effect of slowing web page download times to the detriment of users.

In using authoring tools, it is necessary to make sure that any that are used are capable of promoting accessibility, for one thing. For the remaining issues, developers should be able to adjust the HTML or other code manually. Alternatively, there are some tools available on the web that can be used to refine and rationalise the HTML produced by an authoring tool. (e.g. HTML Tidy or the W3C HTML Validation Tool).

Markup and scripting languages

HTML

This is the standard language that is used to define the text and layout of web pages. HTML can be written in a text editor – typically Notepad – and saved with the file extension .HTM or .HTML. HTML uses '**tags**' that are enclosed within angled brackets, like this <HTML>, to identify the different elements in a web page. HTML is described in more detail in Section 3.4.

XML (extensible markup language)

HTML has been a straightforward and powerful method for arranging the presentation of components of a web page, but it has no ability to describe the kind of data that is on a page. XML, a direct product of the work of the W3C, is an attempt to provide a common structured format for web design.

Because HTML is a generalised set of tags, a person creating a web page purely in HTML does not have the capacity to define tags for specific *sorts* of data. If you are running a fish business you need a markup language that allows you to build web pages containing well defined (fish related!) data. So appropriate tags, set within new document types, can be developed, say <cod> <plaice>. This means that businesses can define the language to suit their own particular requirements for the data they are working with on the web – whereas HTML *predefines* the way to describe web page information for you – inflexibly.

For e-business, the development of XML is very important indeed. It releases e-businesses from the constraints of HTML tags and elements and permits the kind of business interaction online that is needed. XML allows two parties to agree on a **document type definition (DTD)** that can then be used to exchange data of importance to both.

Cascading Style Sheets (CSS)

In 1998, the W3C discussed the future of HTML and decided that it should be reformulated *within* XML. Under the name of XHTML (*extensible* hypertext markup language), this new language was to include a general set of core tags that would create headings, lists, paragraphs, images or other basic features of a web page. Other important tags such as for forms, graphics, multimedia or tables could be written as XML and combined as required. Work could be done at different speeds on each.

The introduction of XHTML meant that as this markup language had no control over layout, **cascading style sheets (CSS)** would take on the role of displaying documents on a device.

Why 'cascading'? The term comes from the fact that several style sheets could be created to specify aspects of page style – say paragraphs, fonts, heading sizes, etc. – and they all 'cascade' to apply to the same page. Style sheets are of two types:

1 Separately created and placed on each page

2 Created singly, with all pages referenced to it.

A style sheet is employed by placing it within the <HEAD> and </HEAD> tags on a page. For example...

```
<HEAD>
<STYLE="text/css">
<!--
BODY {background: #FFFFFF}
A:link  {color: #4169E1}
A: visited {color: #000080}
H1 {font-size: 24pt; font-family: arial}
H2 {font-size: 18pt; font-family: arial}
H3 {font-size: 14pt; font-family: arial}
-->
</STYLE>
</HEAD>
```

The above example is actually technically called a 'style block' but is it is simpler to think of these as sheets. The result of the above is to tell a web browser exactly how to display a page. In the above example, the background will be white, links will be Royal Blue, visited links Navy Blue and headings will be of three sizes, all in Arial font.

There are many more tags available in style sheets, of course. The use of a standardised format for XHTML, dealing with the presentation and format of particular data *types*, creates a good level of stability in the way that data is understood by web browsers. The use of cascading style sheets offers the same benefits relating to presentational style. By standardising these things it has been possible to specify 'conformance profiles' for different devices that may be designed to access the web in the future (as we know, internet access in future will be commonly enjoyed from more than just the PC). Conformance profiles will specify the HTML tags a device *must* support.

Client side/server side processing

The processing of data derived from XML documents can be done either at a server or at a client browser or application. Sometimes data must be transferred without any user interaction (e.g between businesses operating online in the same sector in partnership) because it is done automatically. Sometimes data must be processed because it is a part of a customisation process for delivering content to a website. In both of these cases XML is used to deal with data content.

A problem may arise however if data is processed on a server and is presented to a client in a form that is not readable to the browser or application. The problem may be overcome if a 'raw' XML document is transferred to the client and the client is left to decide how to display it. This is 'client-side' processing and various languages have been developed to deal with it, for example Javascript, VBScript, Java and Perl.

Javascript

Javascript – no relation to Java – is a 'scripting language' that can be used to extend the capabilities of internet applications in ways which are crucial for e-business. By embedding Javascript within HTML, a degree of user interaction can be developed, such as checking entered text and alerting users with a message dialogue if the input is invalid. Javascript can also be used to perform actions on the page, such as play an audio file. Javascript is a means of creating dynamic content because page displays can be made to change, depending on user input on the page. A piece of information stored in a browser for later retrieval (by the server that placed it there) called a **cookie** can be generated by Javascript; this means that user identity can be checked together with previous order history. The advantage of Javascript over other programming languages is that it integrates well within a web browser and is able to access all objects on a web page without connecting back to the server. This saves both time and network load.

Outcome activity

Web authoring tools and standards

1 Describe the main features of web authoring tools and outline the major web standards. Do authoring tools conform to these in your view? Illustrate your responses.

2 Explain how web authoring tools can be integrated into the production and maintenance of a website and in what ways could a programming language such as Javascript be used to enhance a website?

3 Evaluate the contribution of web authoring tools to website development, using:
   a Your own impressions of a tool
   b Other developer views
   c Product marketing information.

3.3 Design and plan a website

User requirements

You have been asked to design the production of a website for a particular, *identified,* group of users. The first thing you need to consider is, why? What is the purpose of the site? Say you were asked to design a website for elderly people, over 65 years of age. You should ask yourself (and others) if the site is (among possibly other things):

- intended to save them money?
- give them advice?
- help them buy things?
- help them get information?
- entertain them?
- give them a joyful online experience?

These things are considering the website from the perspective of the user, but what about the originator of the site (the e-business)? What does *he or she* require the site to do?

- maximise sales revenue?
- to offer great services?
- retain clients?
- save lives?
- entertain?
- educate?

As a web designer, it is your job to find these things out and the answers to some of the above questions should be your *starting point* in planning your design. To illustrate the approach, let's look at an imaginary scenario of a different kind.

Sample project – The Copt Hill Preservation Society
Copt Hill is a well known local landmark thought to be a pre-historic burial site. It is topped by seven large trees known in the region as The 'Seven Sisters' and these can be seen for miles around. Archaeological digs completed in the nineteenth century found evidence of several burials and quite a number of artefacts.

The Copt Hill Preservation Society (CHPS) aims to maintain and improve the Copt Hill site. The society wishes to encourage visitors by informing people about its importance as a site of national historic interest. Educational materials are felt to be a good idea and a new membership scheme, the 'Friends of Copt Hill' is envisaged. This would entail the collection of personal data, so registration under the Data Protection Act would be needed.

It has been decided that a website would be a good way of promoting the activities of the Society and reaching a broader audience. Perhaps such a website would encourage many more visitors from abroad.

Over to you   You are planning the design of the Copt Hill website.

1   List in your own words the requirements of the CHPS

2   List all desirable design features that would be needed by visitors to the site.

Designing the Copt Hill website

You have a clear idea of what the site should do. It is to be promotional and raise the status of the Copt Hill landmark, it has to be informational, it has to be educational and it has to encourage membership. You need a site that is easy to use and navigate, people must know who to contact to get more information, people should enjoy looking at the site and the site should be accessible through a range of browsers.

Plan the site

Using just paper and pencil (you have the technology!), draw up a rough sketch of the structure of the website. It might look like this...

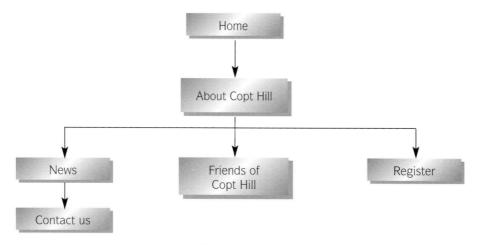

Figure 3.3 Planning the website

Looking at each of the planned pages in turn, now summarise what they will offer the user.

HOME page

Needs to be attractive, atmospheric and interesting. Must have photograph of the 'Seven Sisters' on the Copt Hill. Will have a navigation bar linking to the other pages of the site. Page includes a hit counter.

ABOUT page

Will show largely text about the Copt Hill, its history and the story of the 19th Century excavation. A Javascript slide show will show photographs of the various artefacts that were found on the site. Dynamic text effects will emphasise the landmark's importance.

NEWS page

Mainly text about current activities or future events.

FRIENDS page

This will be a text-based page describing the hopes and plans for this group.

REGISTRATION page

This will contain a form to be filled in online and submitted to an online database. Data entered by a site visitor will automatically be saved into the database.

CONTACT page

Text-based details of how to contact the society, meeting times/dates of the Friends group, how to make a contribution and a feedback form which can be mailed to an officer of the society.

Other aspects of the site plan

Having considered the basics of the site structure, it is vital to think about other crucial matters:

- ease of *navigation* between the pages on the site. Which pages should link with each other? Should all pages refer back to the home page?
- consider the requirements of all *kinds of user*; those with special requirements, novice users, expert users
- graphics; what sort of *images* will improve the site?; photographs, animations, multimedia content (e.g. audio?)
- *sources for content*; where will the content come from? How will it be verified? Who will update or maintain the site content? Will training be required?

Test plan

All pages and all links must be tested as the site is developed. If a site is to include advanced features such as Javascript or other scripts, these will be tested as the site is uploaded onto the web.

It is always advisable to test a site on both major browsers – Internet Explorer (latest version) and Netscape – and sometimes on earlier versions of the browsers too.

A test plan can be created in the following structure.

Test number	Test	Method	Expected outcome
1	Access to site	Open browser and type in web address	CHPS Home page is displayed
2	Enter the site	Click on Home page link	User should be taken to 'about' page
3	Javascript	Click on hyperlink to 'slide show' marked 'Artefacts'	User should be able to view series of pictures of urns, pottery etc with ability to move to and fro
4	Hit counter	Check Home page to see that hit counter is working	Number of hits increases by *at least* 1 each time site is accessed
5	etc.	etc.	etc.

Figure 3.4 Test plan structure

This is the structure of a test plan and of course in the above illustration this is far from complete. In reality, every link, every script, every button or form, each e-mail link, *must* be tested and the outcomes *thoroughly* documented. Remember, you are expected to adopt a professional approach. Test the feedback form, test the registration process and make sure that the site works in as many browsers as possible. If your site is to gather data from users, make sure that it does so.

Communication is vital during this testing and site evaluation process. You must strive to keep the site sponsors well informed and comfortable about your plans. Consult at every stage, in this way you are more likely to have a happy client, a successful site and a happy user!

Outcome activity

Design and plan a website

Task 1
Design the *production* of a website for an identified group of users (N.B. Don't design the site itself! – just design the process of preparation and planning).

Task 2
Plan the inclusion of all media elements, show awareness of resource and timing implications (e.g images, audio, video?).

Task 3
Evaluate the (planned) site with reference to the needs of the user group and with reference to standards of good practice.

3.4 Use markup languages

As we already know, HTML is the markup language that is used to create web pages. The standards (see Section 3.3) for HTML are managed by the World Wide Web Consortium (W3C) www.w3c.org. In this section you will be given the basics to start creating useful web documents. However, an even better way might be to access www.w3schools.com and teach yourself!

Languages

The basic HTML document structure

All HTML documents have the following structure.

```
<HTML>  ←————————————————————————————————  Opening tag
        <HEAD>
                <TITLE>Document Title</TITLE>
        </HEAD>
        <BODY>  ←
                Main contents of the page  ————  Element
        </BODY>  ←
</HTML>  ←————————————————————————————————  Closing tag
```

All HTML tags are enclosed within angled brackets (<>). Tags tell the browser what to do. Most tags are created by enclosing a piece of text within an opening tag (<TAG_X>) and a closing tag (</TAG_X>). Together, the opening tag and the closing tag and the content between them, are called an *element*.

All HTML documents must be enclosed within an opening <HTML> tag and a closing </HTML> tag. Within the document there are two main sections:

- The Document Head
  - The header is enclosed within <HEAD> and </HEAD> tags and it contains information about the document. It also serves as a container for other tags.
  - The document *title* element should be placed within the header.
- The Document Body. The body element, enclosed within the <BODY> tags, contains the main content of the page that will be displayed within a browser window.

Attributes

These give the browser additional information about a tag.
For example, a piece of text is presented using a font. A font can have attributes such as size, colour and alignment.

HTML uses a <FONT> tag and its size attribute can be set like this:

<FONT SIZE = "2"> Some text.</FONT>

Its colour attribute is set like this:

<FONT COLOR = "red"> Some red text</FONT>

Alignment is set like this:

<CENTER> Some centred text </CENTER>

Meta data

Meta data refers to data about the document itself – when was it created, its author, copyright details and content description (NB: 'keywords' that should be included in here, are vital for search engines to pick up in their listings). Data in meta tags is not *displayed* by browsers but is utilised by servers, browsers and search engines. Meta tags are always located in the HEAD of an HTML document.

```
<!DOCTYPE HTML PUBLIC  " - // W3C//DTD HTML 4.0 // EN ">

<HTML>
<HEAD>
        <TITLE> Document Title </TITLE>
        <META NAME = "author"   CONTENT = "Me Student">
        <META NAME> = "Last revised"
                <CONTENT = "16th September 2003">
</HEAD>
<BODY> Main contents of the document. </BODY>
</HTML>
```

The <!DOCTYPE> tag is the only tag that can be shown outside of the HTML containing tags. It specifies the version of HTML that a document is written in.

HTML validation

HTML is read by the browser when a web page is opened. The correct way to write HTML is recommended by W3C and all web developers are expected to follow the guidelines. If guidelines are followed, the chances are that your HTML will be correctly displayed by the greatest number of browsers.

HTML validation services are available online. www.w3c.org/QA/Tools?#validators is able to check your HTML and report back to you with any problems.

Coding standards:

○ Tags should be capitalised. They are not case sensitive but they should stand out from the rest of the document.

○ Each new level of tag should be indented one step from the previous one. The <HTML> tag is the exception.

- All HTML elements containing further elements should begin a new line.
- In a list of attributes, separate the attributes with a single white space.
- Attribute values should be lower case and enclosed in double quotes.
- Do not use unnecessary tags as this increases file size.
- Keep line length to less than 80 characters.
- Always use the .html suffix when naming files, (.htm will work but should not now be used).
- Always use lower case when naming files.
- Do not use special characters or spaces when naming files.

Page elements

Remembering the basic HTML document structure given above, here are some of the more important elements making up a web page.

Paragraphs

```
<BODY>
      <P>
```

The <P> is the paragraph tag. Browsers ignore indentations and blank lines. A new paragraph should be specified using another <P> tag. When this is done the closing </P> tag can be omitted.

```
      </P>
</BODY>
```

Headings

```
<BODY>
      <P>
              <H1 ALIGN = "center">Big Heading </H1>
              <H2 ALIGN = "right"> Smaller Heading </H2>
              <H3 ALIGN = "left">Next Smaller Heading </H3>
              <H4 ALIGN = "center"> Even Smaller Heading </H4>
              <H5 ALIGN = "right"> Very Small Heading </H5>
              <H6 ALIGN = "center"> Tiny Heading </H6>
      </P>
</BODY>
```

Headings help to bring a sense of order to a document. Headings range in size from H1 down to H6 and can be given alignments attributes as shown. Remember the attribute conventions for inverted commas and American spelling of 'center'.

Text

HTML offers a large number of ways to format your text on a web page including these common ones:

<B> **Bold text** </B>

<I> *Italic text* </I>

<U> <u>Underlined</u> </U>

Font

The <FONT> tag allows the characteristics of text enclosed within it to be specified with a number of attributes and is described on pages 107–8.

Horizontal rule

The <HR> tag inserts a horizontal line in the text. It does not need a closing tag as it does not act upon any block of text. Attributes can be specified as follows:

<HR ALIGN = "left", "center">   *alignment of the line.*

<HR NOSHADE = "0 ">   *displays as a solid non shaded line.*

<HR SIZE = "3 ">   *thickness of the line* (1 to 6).

<HR WIDTH = "20% ">   *width of the rule across the page.*

Lists

An ordered list is enclosed within the tags <OL> and </OL> and each item in the list is enclosed by <LI> and </LI>. For example...

<OL>

<LI> The first item</LI>

<LI> The second item </LI>

</OL>

An unordered list is enclosed within tags <UL> and </UL> with each item enclosed by <LI> and </LI>

Creating links

No website of any real use can work without employing links to other documents. This is at the heart of what the web is about. Links can usefully be made to documents within your site, or outside your site (offsite links). Links are created using the <A HREF> tag. (Anchor – Hypertext Reference)

Offsite links

For example, an offsite link (to www.amazon.co.uk) is set like this.

Within your HTML structure...

<A HREF = "http://www.amazon.co.uk"> Amazon is here!</A>

By clicking on the words Amazon is here! (which will display on your page) a user is taken offsite to the Amazon site. (N.B. always use the FULL web address when including links to external sites)

Insite links

When creating a website, all files that are created are suffixed by .html. All of these files must be included within the same folder. If you were creating the Copt Hill Preservation Society website (see earlier example), and you were linking from the Home page to the About page, this would be your HTML.

Within your HTML structure,

> **<A HREF = "About.html"> About us </A>**

You have anchored a reference to a hyperlink that takes the user to the About us page *within* your site. Because the file is within your own site, you do not need the full address (URL) telling the server exactly where the file is. The server looks within the home directory first. When a website is uploaded to an ISP's server, all files needed to make the site function have to be uploaded into the same folder.

Page jumps

Have you ever noticed that sometimes you can click on a link in a page and you are taken to just another section (a fragment) of a page? If you are especially interested in archaeological finds at Copt Hill, you simply see the hypertext link and click. As the site designer, you know that people might be interested, so you allow them to quickly go to the section that interests them. This is how it's done.

At the top of the browser screen, place an anchor tag <A> referring to a NAME attribute called a 'codeword' (call the 'codeword' whatever you want to refer to the section). For example...

At top of browser window, place the command....

> **<A NAME = "Digs">**   (or anything, inside " ")

Then when you want to point to another section of the document, you include a basic hypertext link.

> **<A HREF = "#Digs"> Archaeological digs </A>**

The <A NAME> command has created a target where the page must scroll to. The <A HREF> tag then references to the codeword, in this case 'Digs'. Notice the # must be included before the codeword to show the browser it is an internal link. The user clicks on 'Archaeological digs' and is taken to a relevant section of the document.

Background

The background of a web page is one of the first things anyone notices about the page. Often, an image is used as background, here we will try to keep things fairly simple and just use a plain colour.

Two things are needed to change the background colour, a command to tell the browser that the colour is going to be changed and a code for the colour required. In the <BODY> command, immediately after the </HEAD> command, place the following.

<BODY BGCOLOR = "##">   (where ## is a hexadecimal code number)

Sample hexadecimal code = 4682B4   creates Steelblue.

So, **<BODY BGCOLOR = "4682B4">** creates a steelblue page background.

Images

The first type of image to be used on the web was GIF (Graphical Interchange Format), launched by Compuserve. It is still supported by all browsers and uses a relatively small number of colours (256). GIF images tend to be best used in solid colours as 'vectors' because it is a lossless format that loses none of its quality when images are compressed or scaled. There are two types of GIF image files, GIF87a and GIF89a, only the latter supports animation or transparency.

The alternative web image format is **JPEG (Joint Photographics Experts Group)**. These contain millions of colours and are most suited to handling photographs that may have very subtle changes in shades of colour. However, they can be large files so can take a while to download onto a page. Additionally, JPEG files tend to lose quality in compression or scaling.

Another format, PNG (Portable Network Graphics) was recommended by W3C in 1995 but has not really taken off. PNG has a number of desirable features but due to its relatively poor level of support to date it is not advisable to use it.

Adding an image

An image can be added within the flow of a document by inserting the following...

<IMG SRC = "image.gif">

The source of the image to be inserted is the file 'image.gif'. Note that, by default, an image is added to the base of the text (remember that the image file in this case has to be in the same directory).

Tables

Tables are useful not only for bringing order to data but they are also useful for creating a layout for your page.

A table is enclosed within the <TABLE> ...</TABLE> tags. Table content is defined by row <TR> ..</TR> and columns are defined by the number of cells within a row. Cells are defined using <TD> ..</TD> tags. For example, this is a basic table...

```
<TABLE>
        <CAPTION>Member Addresses</CAPTION>
                <TR>
                        <TH>Member</TH>
                        <TH>Address</TH>
                        <TH>Tel. No.</TH>
                </TR>
                <TR>
                        <TD>Mr Smith</TD>
                        <TD>1 Smith Street</TD>
                        <TD>123456</TD>
                </TR>
</TABLE>
```

Style elements

Style sheets

Style sheets have already been mentioned in Section 3.1 but as they are important to web design they will be briefly covered again here. There are three ways that style instructions can be incorporated within a document:

- embedded style details at the top of the HTML document.
- linking an external style document to the HTML document.
- inline style directions.

Embedded style sheets

The style rules are simply placed within the <HEAD>...</HEAD> tags.

External style sheets

This method allows you to use the same style sheet for different documents and is a powerful technique allowing for consistency and economy of effort. A style sheet is created in a text editor such as Notepad and the file is saved with the suffix .css. The <LINK> tag is placed in the <HEAD> element of a page to link to the external .css file. For example...

```
<HEAD>
        <TITLE> External Style Sheet</TITLE>
                <LINK  REL = "STYLESHEET"  HREF = "new_style.css"
                        TYPE = "text/css">
</HEAD>
```

The above example shows that the link relates to a 'stylesheet' (always this) and that the sheet (in this case) is named new_style.css. The TYPE command must be set to "text/css".

Inline style

It is possible to set individual styles for each tag within the HTML document. This is no longer the recommended method as it mixes content with style and as far as possible these should be kept separate in the design process. For example:

```
<H1 STYLE = "color : blue"> BLUE HEADING </H1>
<P STYLE = "font-size: 12; font-family: arial">
        Much to his Mam and Dad's dismay... <BR>
        Charlie ate himself one day...<BR>
```

Conclusions on HTML

HTML manuals can run to well over a thousand pages so this Unit can hardly be said to be comprehensive in its approach. It was not meant to be. However there should be enough in here to help you get to the stage where you can produce a website that functions with links and is well formatted with the user and the client in mind. Before starting on your assignment work, you are encouraged to experiment with the various techniques, always bearing in mind the W3C coding standards. Concentrate on developing your HTML coding ability as far as you can. Good luck and have fun!

Outcome activity

Build a website

Following on from the *Outcome activity* at the end of section 3.3...
You have identified a group of users for a planned website. Choose an area that interests you:

- night club members
- sports club members
- your school/college.

Task 1

To achieve a Pass grade:
Build several pages of the site you have planned, using HTML. (Do NOT build solely using an authoring tool, you are being assessed on your skill in doing some HTML).

Task 2

To achieve a Merit you must also:
Verify that the site as you have built conforms to current standards for use of markup languages (HTML). Explain how you have done this.

Task 3

To achieve a Distinction you must in addition:
Verify that the site implementation conforms to current standards for separation of style and content. Explain how this has been achieved.

Unit 5   e-Business project

After completing Unit 5 you will be able to:

- identify an appropriate e-business *project*, using all relevant information
- identify the appropriate *resources* required to develop the project
- monitor and control progress of the project, using appropriate *processes* to ensure completion
- draw *conclusions* and make *recommendations*.

> ***Your understanding of this unit will be assessed by an internally marked assignment.***

This means that you must *plan, specify* and *monitor* the delivery of an e-business project for a real 'client' and subsequently *write a detailed report* on the process. The project will give you a chance to integrate and use the skills and knowledge gained in other units. It is designed to be a practical exercise that will reinforce understanding. In working on the project you should try as far as practical to liaise with a real organisation, preferably one at least *considering* some form of e-business. The sections within Unit 5 will take you through the stages of specification, resourcing, planning and monitoring and finally reporting on your project.

Some general advice: you need to be careful as to the timing of your work. Much of what you are able to offer a real business client will depend upon what you have properly covered in other units. As you will see, Unit 3 *Website design and construction* and Unit 7 *Database systems* are ideal foundations for delivering productive e-business ideas to a client. At least one of these units should have been completed before you embark on the e-business project.

For assessment, you will submit a written report of *no more* than 5,000 words and this will consist of a minimum of four sections (look at the structure shown in Section 5.4 on page 129). Each of the sections within this part of the text is designed to cover the needs of each component section of your report. The structure of your report should therefore logically follow the sections given here in Unit 5.

The *Outcome activities* in this unit are offered as three or four separate tasks. Yet, if you read them as one, you will see that they all refer to the *same* product of your work.

For example, the first activity asks for a choice of project and a Project plan and specification. Task 1 tells you this and offers you a Pass grade for doing it (good). Task 2 says 'by the way, if you also add some more details about methods, the business situation and **contingency planning**, you will get a Merit' (very good). Task 3 says 'add something in as well about how the project could be extended to other issues and you have a Distinction' (excellent).

5.1 Project

When deciding on a project, you don't have to be over-ambitious. Remember you are learning e-business. This project is a chance to develop your awareness not just about the nature and impact of e-business, but about how real projects are planned and delivered by professionals in the IT industry.

It is important when you are doing the preliminary planning that you work systematically to get information, before writing down the basic framework of your approach, this section will tell you how to do this.

Identifying and selecting a project

On what basis do you select a project? Remember that the term e-*business* refers to more than just selling on the internet. If we were to confine our scrutiny of the internet to just the selling process, we might more accurately call the subject e-*commerce*. In reality, e-commerce is a part of e-business.

When you think about e-business, you should consider a broader range of business activities that are influenced – and in many ways these days controlled – by internet technology. It is difficult to deal with a company website, unless some consideration is given to 'behind the scenes' processes that place content on the site. This point was made very early in Unit 1. A business cannot successfully develop an internet presence, if it does not have background processes in place to support the site. This entails making use of sophisticated applications that will support the online presence. These processes, storing, arranging, presenting and digitising data – together with the website and the vast range of connections together making up the www, go together to make what we call e-*business.*

Take an example of how this can apply. In motor retailing, a motor retailer might wish to develop an online brand (i.e. an identified and strong internet presence) in order to draw customers to his showrooms. A new website is designed, but also in support of it must be a connected inventory (stock) management system and customer relationship management system. Customers can then view vehicles in stock online, make enquiries, check histories and be dealt with efficiently.

Over to you In your own words write a brief statement distinguishing e-commerce from e-business.

Verbally explain the difference to a class colleague, or your tutor.

What has this got to do with your e-business project? Well, in choosing a project, you need to remember that there are several e-*business* avenues you could pursue, each of them contributing to developing e-business. A project you choose to do could be quite small scale, yet make a big difference. It is feasible that you could consider a project to set up a *database* for a real small business; alternatively, you could agree to design a small *website*. The point is that whatever project you decide to follow, you should be able to *justify* it in terms of its significance or potential significance for the client concerned.

It should be fairly apparent by now that you would be well advised to choose your project with reference either to Unit 3 *Website design and construction*, or Unit 7 *Database systems*.

Two things should govern your selection:

- Your own abilities and skills in delivering the project aims
- The identified needs of a business client.

Whichever kind of 'system' you choose to offer, you should be able to state clearly how the proposed implementation will impact on the business. Look at it in the following ways:

- What is the main business of the client? (i.e. the business you are creating a new 'system' for.) Is it for profit? Not for profit? Does it sell tangible products? Offer intangible service?
- What 'systems' does it currently have?
- What problems exist with the current systems?
- How does it hope to benefit from changing the system?
- What constraints or restrictions are there on hardware, software or timescale?

Over to you   Prepare an effective data capture document designed to secure the above information from a potential client.

By conducting initial research thoroughly, you will gain an idea of the significance of a new 'e-system' to the client. This will then form the basis of planning. Communication is the key. Find out what clients want. Consider carefully their business needs and at the outset, decide what is feasible for them. Do not suggest, for example, a new system involving a high degree of ongoing maintenance, when the business does not have the resources to do it.

Project specification

Once you have decided upon a particular project *with a client* and it has been agreed by your tutor, it is a good idea to write a clear statement of the *aims and objectives* you intend to achieve. You have already carried out initial research from a business scenario and you are clear about business needs.

Now you have to start specifying, in a structured way, what your project aims to achieve – always referring back to the client.

Writing your specification

The following is a *possible framework* for writing your detailed specification.

1.   Introduction

1.1   Background

The business you are to work for. What type of business, main products or services, history of the business.

1.2   Statement of the current situation

An overview of the particular aspects of the businesses work that you hope to improve through your project.

2.   Investigation

2.1   Current systems

Based on your interviews and research within the business, specific descriptions of tasks and data flows. (include a data flow diagram if necessary)

2.2   Problems

Problems that have been identified in current methods.

3.   Requirements of the new system

3.1   General objectives

3.2   Specific **quantitative** objectives

Objectives written in numbers, in terms of precisely what is intended, e.g. 'customer records will be retrievable within 20 seconds'

3.3   Specific **qualitative** objectives

Objectives written in more non-specific, general terms, e.g. ' it is hoped that this will promote the business more effectively'

4.   Constraints

4.1   Hardware requirements

A description of the hardware that is available both for the development of the system and at the client businesses location.

4.2   Software available

Name the software you have available to make use of (including the version number) and briefly outline what it does.

4.3   Client ICT skills and knowledge

Briefly describe the level of skills that available to the client business and say what effect if any this will have on the design.

Remember that this is a *possible* framework. Feel free to modify the structure according to what you are planning to do. Your specification should show good links with an organisation that could benefit from an 'e-system'

Project plan

Once you have established your project you need to carefully plan its progress and delivery. There is no point at all in setting out on a project unless you have a firm idea of how long it will take to deliver. There must be a timescale, a deadline by which time the 'system' you have proposed, is delivered and implemented. This is of course mirrored in the real world. In the IT industry, a potential client will approach the specialist firm inviting them to quote for some work. The IT firm will examine the request, will liaise and consult before offering a quotation based upon the time it will take to deliver. The hours spent (by various staff) on a project determines cost – in your case (sadly) cost is not the issue, but sensible planning of time is essential.

There will be *key project milestones* within the following general series of activities:

Liaise with client:
- problem identification
- establish aims of the project
- specification of the project.

Check project progress:
- Draft 'system' solution:
  - Website? – site map, screen drafts, establish mood.
  - Database? – data descriptions, flow diagrams, entity relationships.
- Consult with client
- Design new system:
  - Website – draft designs for pages in 'flat' screens. (no working links)
  - Database – tables, forms, dataflow diagram.
- Consult with client
- Incorporate changes at client request
- Consult and test
- Monitor and review.

It is likely that however diligent you are in your planning, something will happen that will cause your project to diverge from your plan. Always be careful to build in some contingency time, time that will be available to cover for unforeseen factors. Be realistic in your time allocation.

Finally, in planning your project remember that you are working to meet the needs of a client. As far as possible you must be prepared to be flexible and willing to revise or amend your system in order to meet the client wishes. If you submit a web page that simply clashes with the tastes of the client then you must be prepared to change it. This is why communication and consultation is so vital. Never go off into a darkened workshop and simply plough on, without reference to the needs of your client. The early stages of your project are crucial for this. At regular stages throughout your work, you *must* consult. If possible, document these discussions, if you make changes, record them against your well documented plan and indicate who requested them and when.

Outcome activity

Report section 1: Project plan

Task 1

To achieve a Pass grade:

Identify an appropriate e-business project and produce a well structured project plan and specification.

Task 2

To achieve a Merit you must also:

Include fully detailed plan and specification, giving due attention to the current business situation, the methodology of the project and contingency plans for unforeseen problems.

Task 3

To achieve a Distinction, you must in addition:

Indicate how the project could be extended to address other significant issues facing e-business professionals (in the client business and in specialist IT firms).

5.2 Resources

We know by now that e-business is revolutionising the way much business is being done. Many businesses of all shapes and sizes are starting to adapt to this e-revolution and, in one way or another, are changing the way they work. This is happening in virtually all industries. Some are leading the way, others are holding back. We have discussed the fact that in some cases early adopters (of internet based business) are having to deal with the problems associated with having partner firms that are not ready to do business online. This is happening because in some businesses the *resources* are simply not there to maintain a totally new way.

One of the most important things to consider therefore, in planning a project, is what resources are available both to you – as the *deliverer* of a new way, and to the client business– as the *user* of the new system? Resources are almost always scarce and fall into several categories:

1 Human resources

2 Information

3 Time

4 Software

5 Hardware and financial.

Human resources

The point has been made elsewhere that no matter what computerised system is in place, behind it there has to be staff who are capable of making use of it and who are willing and competent in using it. A website, for instance, can transform a businesses image and have all the bells and whistles in the world. A website can elevate even the smallest business and place it online alongside the biggest there is and no one will be aware of the difference in resources behind the public online face. Until, that is, things begin to go wrong.

e-Business insight   Joe's Brew

Joe has a small business selling bottled home brew from a modest shop in a small town. He decides he will go online to sell more, but he knows nothing about the internet or computers. However, his nephew – Richard, a bright lad, does.

Richard is doing a project so he designs a website for Uncle Joe. Joe buys a domain name for £1.99 and chooses a low cost web hosting firm to put his site live on the internet. The cost for Joe is £250 plus £40 per year after that.

Joe thinks this is lovely and after talking to Richard they spend another few days submitting the site and its keywords to different search engines.

In the first two weeks Joe gets two enquiries. One from round the corner, the other from Dublin. This is not as good as he is hoping for. He gets in touch with the local paper, telling them how he's now online and business has taken off. They carry a story on him saying that 'brew business is booming'.

The following day, Joe is interviewed by every newspaper and radio station in the region. A few more enquiries come in, but still not as much as Joe hopes for. Two weeks later the Mail On Sunday does a feature on Joe headed 'The Online Brewer Makes It!'.

On the Monday after the Mail On Sunday article Joe gets 3,500 e-mails, most of them trying to place orders for home brew.

The website however was not designed to take money online, so Joe asks some people to send cheques or credit card details with their orders. From doing nothing online Joe is now getting between £4,000 and £5,000 worth of orders a day. But because he can't keep up with orders anyway, he knows nothing about most of them. Other sites have started putting links to Joe's site and traffic increases even more. Joe has his head in his hands after checking his e-mails.

Complaints have started, Joe pulls the plug out of his computer and decides to pretend his website does not exist.

Talk about the internet now to Joe and he changes the subject, fast!

Chat room

What resources do you feel were lacking in the case of Joe's Brew? Discuss this in pairs and agree an action plan for Joe.

The story of Joe's Brew tells us that resources are vital. Joe didn't have the staff to take orders, to fulfil the orders or to respond to complaints. Joe didn't even have the staff to update his website. In fact, Joe didn't have *any* staff – just him. Far from being a boom to business, the website became a millstone around Joe's neck, an embarrassment.

A functioning e-business must adopt processes that ensure customers get what they want. Expectations on the internet are high. Human resources are fundamental to e-business success; attitudes as well as skills need to be right. When thinking about human resource needs, a business must either be prepared to invest in training, or it must appoint new staff. Either way, there are costs to be considered. Highly skilled staff can be costly to employ.

Over to you   Acting as an e-business consultant, draft a skills analysis for your client business. Clearly set out the skills you feel staff should possess in order to make your proposed system work well. Do you feel training will be required?

If there are any skills gaps, what would you propose to remedy them?

Information

The information requirements for your project are specific to that particular work so it is not possible to be specific about what you will need. However, broadly there are two approaches to gathering information, primary sources and secondary sources.

Primary data

Primary data is information that you gather directly yourself from the client business. Information about products or services, weekly sales, aims and strategies of the management; where do they want the business to go? What problems do they have that can be addressed by an e-business approach? To do this successfully requires knowing the right person or people to talk to, you need to access the right documentation and ask the right questions. Primary data is crucial for a successful project.

Secondary data

Secondary data is second hand information; company files and records, manuals, reports, books, articles, statistics compiled by someone else. In many situations secondary data will be the only source of data available. In such cases you must trust the accuracy and the integrity of the source. Always check your sources and record where you got data.

Time

Time is the one resource you often seem to have absolutely no control over. All you can do is set a target date for completion, allocate a number of weeks, days, hours until that date and work hard to stick to that plan. Within the plan, as discussed earlier, you would be advised to build in contingency (what if?) plans. Several tools and techniques are available to help you plan your time (see Section 5.3 on processes). One of the simplest and most straightforward methods is to detail your timescale on a spreadsheet.

Software

Don't disappear into a computer workshop to design either a website or a new database system only to discover that the business does not possess the software that you are basing your system on. When identifying resource needs one of the first considerations must be software. If a business is lacking it, will they buy it?

Hardware and financial resources

Hardware refers to the actual machines (PCs, printers, cables, modem, scanners) that will be essential to run your system. Ideally you want the client to already possess the hardware they will need and in most cases this will be the case. However, if not you must cost the equipment carefully and communicate this to the client as well as the possible ongoing costs of the new system.

It is desirable at the outset that you consider a *budget* for the project. A budget is an *agreed* plan, established at the start. You have discussed the project aims, the existing problems faced by the business, now time to establish what is it worth to them to try and address these problems. The basis of the budgeting process will be costings covering:

- hardware
- software
- licences
- internet service provision
- labour (hours worked on project)
- maintenance.

Over to you Using the above, or any other cost headings relevant to your particular project, create a spreadsheet showing a weekly breakdown of project costs.

Prepare to present and justify these costs to your class group.

Roles and responsibilities

Throughout the whole project planning process it is essential to be clear about who is responsible for what. At every stage you are strongly urged to keep in close touch with your client business. Some mechanism for ensuring that you are mutually clear about the project direction and intentions is helpful. To achieve this, always be certain that following any liaison meeting, both you and your client are in no doubt *who* is to act on something. Note and record discussions and give copies to the client. If you use a spreadsheet technique, a heading 'Action by' is important. There should be no room for dispute later. You need to know the roles of everyone you are dealing with and how they relate to your work.

Report Section 2 : Project resources

Task 1

To achieve a Pass grade:

Identify and specify suitable project resources.

Task 2

To achieve a Merit you must also:

Present a detailed costing of the project resource requirements.

Task 3

To achieve a Distinction you must in addition:

Evaluate the conditions under which the project resource requirements might be justified.

5.3 Processes

In the IT industry the process of project management often refers to projects in which a number of separate individuals – sometimes separate teams – work apart from each other on different 'modules', or component parts, of a project before combining at certain key points to achieve their collective goal. In this exercise you are likely to be working individually, yet nevertheless you are encouraged and expected to use a professional approach to delivering your project aims. The processes you employ in managing your work are therefore important. You will have quite a number of tasks to complete, deadlines to meet and a number of people to consult with. This calls for organisation and planning. The more thorough you are the better.

Figure 5.1 below shows how your project can be broken down into a number of separate processes, each in its own way contributing to the achievement of the overall aim – the resolution of a problem.

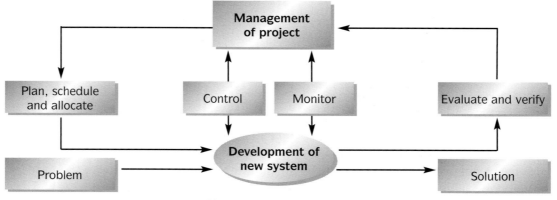

Figure 5.1 Project structure

With the above overall structure in mind, it will help to examine each of the general processes to be followed.

Review project aims

The initial planning is done in consultation with the client business. You will have been in discussions and discovered several new facts about the business, in terms of its resources and expectations, as well as its hopes for a new system. After fully investigating the existing situation and reporting on it, in *consultation with the client*, you will need to actively review the aims of your project. This means going back over them and evaluating them. Were your *initial* aims likely to be the solution to the problems the business is seeking to solve? A project is useless if it addresses the wrong issues. Be certain the project has the right aims. Once you are comfortable with this, then you can move on.

Progress and pace against key milestones

Once your project is based on a firm and solid purpose, you can begin to properly plan its delivery. At the heart of project planning is a process of scheduling. You must define the tasks or jobs you have to do and set these against *key milestones* within the time you have available. You may, for instance, have ten weeks in which to deliver your project. Within this period you must set milestones that act as target dates for completion of key tasks. Some of these tasks must be completed *before* you can begin others (i.e. dependent tasks). Some tasks can be started whilst another is still going on.

One well-established method for visualising the planning out and tracking of a schedule of project activities is the **Gantt Chart**. This is a horizontal bar chart that was developed by engineer Henry L. Gantt in 1917. These can range in complexity and detail. Figure 5.2 shows a simple example.

Project date	Week 1	Week 2	Week 3	Week 4	Week 5	Week 6	Week 7	Week 8
Preliminary research	▓	▓						
Interviews/consultation		▓						▓
Write specification			▓					
Design new system			▓	▓		▓		
Test new system						▓		
Consultation/review		▓		▓		▓		
Tutor review of project		▓			▓			▓
Write up report						▓		▓

Figure 5.2 The Gantt Chart

In the simple Gantt chart above it is easy to see the point in the timescale during which the different phases occur and to identify the key milestones. The Gantt chart gives an *at a glance* view. In the example, by the end of week 2, all preliminary research and initial interviews and reviews should have been done. By the end of week 6 all design work should be complete. These are key milestones and should be used to track progress.

The Gantt chart does have limitations for large scale projects involving lots of people. It is difficult to see how tasks relate to each other, or the effect of a particular delay upon the whole project. Of course Gantt charts can be made more sophisticated or detailed and software tools can produce them automatically if required.

Network (or activity) charts, use a system of notation that helps to overcome the limitations of the Gantt (bar) chart. There are variations of them. The best known is the **PERT** (programme evaluation and review technique).

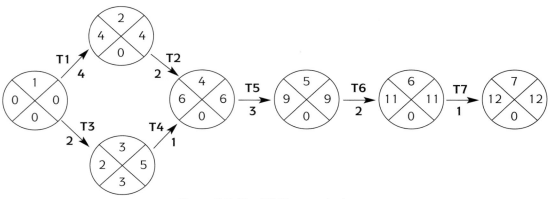

Figure 5.3 The PERT network chart

On a network chart, the tasks are represented by lines, with the estimated duration of the task written below each line (in this case in weeks). Circular symbols represent events or project milestones and can be divided into four segments. The top segment shows the milestone number, the second (anti-clockwise) shows the earliest completion time, the third (opposite) shows the latest completion time and the bottom segment is known as a contingency factor and is the difference between the earliest and the latest completion times. Using the tasks and milestones on the PERT chart, it is possible to see the longest path on the network of things to be done. This is known as *the critical path*. Tasks that are *not* on the critical path can safely be delayed if necessary, tasks *on* the critical path must be performed on schedule otherwise they will delay the entire project.

Over to you   Compare the Gantt Chart approach to the PERT network diagram. What do you feel are the pros ands cons of each method?

Which planning technique do you feel will best suit you and why?

Project planning software

There are several project planning and management tools available and one of the most well established is Microsoft Project software, of which there has been seven versions at the time of writing. There are claimed to be over 3 million users of this product worldwide so it is worth examining briefly what the software can do.

Summary of Microsoft Project (2000 version) features

Collaborative planning: Team members, project members and senior managers can utilise a companion website called Microsoft Central to keep up to date with project progress. Personal Gantt charts are available from this site, members can enter new tasks and non-working time (such as a holiday). The project manager can view timesheets for each team member.

Status reports: A manager can request text based status reports and set these up to be generated at key moments in the timescale.

Graphical indicators: The Project software allows managers to set up alerts within the various data fields in the project schedule. For example, budget figures can be set up for aspects of project expenditure. If any of these predefined ranges are exceeded a 'stoplight' report is generated to flag up possible problem areas of a project.

Chart generation: It is possible to generate both Gantt and PERT charts, as well as calendars and budget and resource schedules.

Connect

Do an 'additive' search by entering **Microsoft+Project+Software** in a search engine such as www.Google.com.

Gather as much information as you can about this software tool and prepare a presentation concisely describing its use.

---

e-Business insight **Leighton Media: The Noel Wright Project**

Innovation as standard

Leighton Media is a part of the Leighton Group based at Doxford International Business Park near the city of Sunderland, in the north east of England. The company originated in 1979 in academic publishing. As the World Wide Web expanded, Leighton was at the forefront of evolving internet technology. Today, Leighton Media has firmly established itself as a cutting edge company, offering the whole suite of internet related applications for many types of organisations; Premiership football clubs, national governments, private firms, schools, colleges and universities.

Leighton Media have a systematic, yet straightforward method of planning client projects. Using a simple spreadsheet, a project is configured into distinct phases and key milestone dates, with tasks and responsibilities for each listed.

The example shown below is for the Noel Wright (recruitment consultancy) website.

Phase	Planned delivery date	Task	Responsibility	Actual completion date
Pre-production	26th March 2003	Configure Project area	Leighton	26th March 2003
Weeks 1–4	28/3/03	Preliminary Plan	Leighton	3/4/03
	2/4/03	Delivery of virtual mood boards	Leighton	2/4/03
	7/4/03	Sign off mood/ direction	Noel Wright	8/4/03
	7/4/03	Delivery Structure/ site map	Leighton	14/4/03
	7/4/03	Tech. spec. of site and content man. system	Leighton	2/4/03
	11/4/03	Homepage design	Leighton	14/4/03
	11/4/03 amended	1st/2nd level navigation design	Leighton	24/4/03
	24/4/03	Sign off Homepage design	Noel Wright	24/4/03
	24/4/03	Sign off site map with titles and order of nagivation	Noel Wright	17/4/03
	18/4/03	Design of e-mail templates	Leighton	23/4/03
	29/4/03	Sign off e-mail templates	Noel Wright	
		Content Management Database	Leighton	
Broad Prototype	9/4/03	Delivery of all static content for prototype	Noel Wright	
	9/4/03	Develop prototype content recovery and display	Leighton	
Deep Prototype	6/6/03	Delivery of full content management system.	Leighton	
Integration of existing systems	13/6/03	Accept candidate registration. Upload job postings	Leighton/ENV	
Beta testing & training		Testing and acceptance	Noel Wright/ Leighton/ENV	

Investing time in proper project planning can save you time in the long run and more importantly can vastly increase your chances of success. Notice that the Leighton approach does not make use of project management software. They like to keep things simple. Using straightforward spreadsheets ensures that many more varieties of clients can engage in the planning process and true collaboration can develop within a commonly understood framework. Perhaps the more sophisticated software tools have their place when specialist teams come together for very large scale projects. For the purposes of smaller projects, involving the single specialist/client relationship, a simpler approach works better.

Outcome activity

Report section 3 – Project planning processes

Task 1

To achieve a Pass grade:

Monitor project progress against agreed milestones showing evidence of appropriate action taken to ensure punctual completion.

Task 2

To achieve a Merit you must also:

Monitor project milestones with reference to the use of project planning software, giving a full explanation of its use.

Task 3

To achieve a Distinction you must in addition:

Evaluate the effectiveness of a major project management software package in facilitating the effective monitoring of the project.

5.4 Conclusions and recommendations

The conclusions and recommendations from the project allow you to sum up your major findings, to evaluate what has been achieved and to make clear recommendations where possible. *If* the project was successfully planned, the plan was followed and all deliverables were achieved, you should already at this stage have the information you need; importantly, this information will already be *structured* too. What you need to do now is to present your considered conclusions by analysing the facts you have drawn from completing each assignment in the unit.

Report structure

For assessment purposes, you have a substantial report (maximum 5,000 words) to submit. Structure the report as follows:

- **Introduction and project summary**
  - The initial project purpose
  - What the report is about.

- **Procedure and method** (from your answers to the first activity)
  - Detail steps taken to choose the project
  - Project specification and plan
  - Detail interviews and data capture methods
  - Background research
  - Technical matters (e.g. choice of software).
- **Resources employed** (from your answers to the second activity)
  - Human
  - Information
  - Financial
  - Hardware.
- **Processes** (from your answers to the third activity)
  - Review of aims
  - Milestone planning
  - Alternative methods of planning.
  - Diagrams (possibly appendices)
  - Microsoft Project software.
- **Conclusions and recommendations**
  - Summary of each section *in own words*
  - Brief recommendations
  - Costings
  - Comment on need for further related development
  - Evaluation of project.

Evaluating the project

In any assessment, the process of evaluation attracts a small but very significant number of marks. Evaluation is a tough thing to do well and calls for 'higher level' thinking. However it is not beyond anyone. Think of it like this. You have done your project, no one else. Therefore who else is better positioned to judge its successes or failures? No one has said at any stage that your e-business system has to function *perfectly* – there will be shortcomings and things that do not quite match your own hopes. This is natural and one of the joys of evaluation – you can turn your failures into successes!

At the beginning of the project you should have stated your aims and objectives. Do you feel you have achieved them? What does the client feel? What does your tutor feel? What areas of the project work have you enjoyed? What areas have you found a pain? Say something about how you feel about yourself after having made this attempt.

Impact on stakeholders

Stakeholders are people or groups that have an interest in a business, a 'stake' in it. The most obvious people will be the proprietors (owners) who have invested their time and capital into the venture. Then there are other shareholders and managers, together with all staff. Every person employed within a business has an interest and a concern that it survives and prospers. Beyond the business there are suppliers, neighbours and customers. Each of these, in different ways, has a stake in the business.

What will be the impact on the various stakeholders of a decision to embark on e-business? Obviously this will depend on the nature of the organisation and the type of business, but some generalisation is possible.

Owners – investment will be required. Costs of hardware and software, training, staff time, own time. Discussions, strategic planning, assessment of risk.

Managers – handling change, communicating to staff, managing resources, dealing with customers and suppliers. Monitoring business performance. Dealing with own changing role.

Shareholders – keeping informed of effects on business performance, monitoring key indicators.

Staff – handling job changes, keeping informed of business plans, seeking security, reassurance about job roles.

All stakeholders should be kept informed of what is happening. As an outsider preparing changes and procedures that will impact directly and indirectly upon a number of people, the I.T. consultant should be prepared to answer questions and where possible give reassurance.

Ethical and social considerations

The nature of *employment* has been changing over a number of years. Modern employers tend to look for flexible, committed and often multi-skilled people. A business often has a small number of core workers of this type, the remainder of staff being temporary or part-time. People are expected to be lifelong learners, always ready to take on new skills and tasks.

When you are considering the introduction of a new business e-system, you are directly affecting the work, possibly the livelihood, of members of staff. In some cases you may be causing worry and stress, as workers feels threatened by possible changes or are worried about whether they can cope. Be prepared to consult or advise your client about this.

Many people have legitimate *fears about the internet* itself. They fear that their business will be plagued by computer viruses, they fear security breaches and that staff will access unsuitable websites. Of course there are many methods of securing a business network so that data is 'firewalled' and access to any sensitive information is controlled and restricted. You should be comfortable about security issues and aware of potential fears.

The implementation of an e-business strategy can cause many ripples of discontent and unease within a business. Having investigated the business' situation fully it is essential that all sources of possible conflict are anticipated and dealt with. As consultant on the matter you have responsibilities to help in this. The e-strategy should contribute to the business aims and objectives. It should clearly add value to the business and as consultant it is also your responsibility to outline precisely and honestly how. If, having looked at all the facts, the e-strategy is not worth it – say so and why.

Outcome activity

Bringing it all together

Task 1

To achieve a Pass grade:

Draw up appropriate conclusions from your project and present these to a professional standard.

Task 2

To achieve a Merit you must also:

Draw analytical conclusions, present them professionally and illustrate by detailed and costed implementation plans, with due reference to ethical and social implications.

Task 3

To achieve a Distinction you must in addition:

Evaluate your project conclusions and use these as a basis for an extended project proposal that is resourced, costed, scheduled and presented to a high standard.

Unit 6   Government, e-business and society

After completing Unit 6 you will be able to:

1   identify national and European *government support* for e-business
2   identify the major *legal implications* of e-business operations
3   identify the relevant *legislation and codes of practice* relating to e-business operations
4   identify the *social implications* of e-business development.

> *Your understanding of this unit will be assessed by an internally marked assignment*.

This is a wide-ranging unit, dealing with some of the background issues associated with the internet and e-business. To fully understand and make sense of e-business requires some consideration and thought about these important topics. You will be much better informed for making the effort.

At the start of the twentieth century the world had evolved into many separate, self governing nations, each one trying to look after or protect its own interests. This, of course – as we know – led to two horrific world wars and millions of innocent lives lost. The start of the twenty first century now sees us in a dual world; the physical world, still with its boundaries mapping out nations, states, continents and trading blocs; and the virtual (digital) world in which there are no boundaries at all. This unit will help you to understand some of the problems faced by online businesses trying to comply with regulations globally and by national governments trying to protect their citizens in the virtual world.

You will also learn about some of the ways in which the UK government is helping **Small to Medium sized Enterprises (SMEs)** move their businesses online so that they can take advantages of the opportunities available from e-business (An SME is defined as any business that employs between 50 and 250 staff.) You will consider some of the unique legal problems and issues that can arise in a world wide digital economy and look at the developing set of codes, rules and regulations that are being formulated for the global digital world of e-trade.

Finally, you will examine some of the social implications of a significant growth in the volume of e-business activity. How will people be affected and in what ways? Is the digital world a force for good, or bad?

A brief word of caution: government actions and policies are changing all the time. What is given here as policy may not be policy in the future. Always check using the websites referred to. Similarly, rules and regulations change constantly, especially in the field of the *evolving* internet. Never take descriptions of current law as permanent. What can be said is that government regulators are likely to have similar *intentions* for the foreseeable future (for example, to protect children). You are always advised to look first hand at what the regulations are.

6.1 Government support

Research carried out by the **Confederation of British Industry (CBI)** a few years ago found that if UK business could achieve even the *average* level of performance of their main global competitors, an estimated £300 bn could be added to this country's economy, meaning we would be a lot better off as a country. Furthermore, if companies, large or small, could learn from each other, picking each other's brains, finding better ways of doing things, then *everyone* would benefit; staff, managers, owners and customers (Source: *The Sunday Telegraph* April 6th 2003).

This knowledge underpins much of what the government has been trying to do through the Department for Trade and Industry (the DTI), the government department largely responsible for promoting the UK development of e-business. Everything that follows in this section describes the British government's three-dimensional effort (see Figure 6.1) to encourage:

- businesses
- individual citizens
- Government departments and agencies (i.e. services)

to go online.

Government therefore has a crucial role to play in promoting the effective use of the internet by a variety of citizens and organisations; after all, it was US *government* money in the 1950s that led to the original development of the internet.

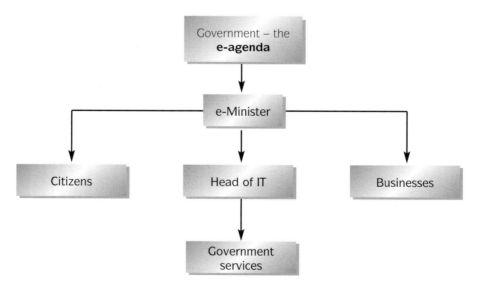

Figure 6.1 The outline framework of the UK government's e-agenda

Why is the government making such a big effort to help everyone to use the internet? We know that the world is undergoing a revolution in the way that goods and services are produced and traded; we also know that this is not restricted within national boundaries.

The only boundaries to be overcome are those related to understanding, expertise, skills or attitudes. The UK government, largely through the DTI, is investing a lot of effort in helping with these things.

One of the problems faced by individual nations is the uneven pace with which firms are taking up the opportunities offered during this time of change. Larger firms are better placed in terms of resources – finance, staff, hardware and software – but the small to medium firms are less willing, or able, to take up the challenge of moving a business online, even when they have real opportunities to benefit by doing so. Managers therefore need to be given help in making difficult decisions about changing the way they do business. While the big firm probably already has the right sort of staff skills and attitudes, the SME may not. Government help directed towards the SMEs is therefore important.

In a situation in which firms are working increasingly in global market places, those firms that stand still will almost certainly lose out to overseas firms that decide to innovate (do things differently) and go online. As the population increasingly adopts internet purchasing patterns and wakes up to internet opportunities, online business will grow. Businesses that have been slow to react will fall behind the competition; do badly and as a result will have to shed jobs. As this happens, government economic performance begins to suffer, unemployment rises and the country becomes poorer. This is another important reason why the UK government has been very keen to help SMEs move online. It has done this in a number of ways.

The UK Online for Business strategy

In September 1999 Prime Minister Tony Blair said:

> "There is a revolution going on. A fundamental change, not a dot.com fad, but a real transformation towards a knowledge economy. So, today, I am announcing a new campaign. Its goal is to get the UK online. To meet the three stretching targets we have set: for Britain to be the best place in the world for e-commerce, with universal access to the internet and all government services on the net. In short, the UK online campaign aims to get business, people and government online".

The UK government policy is very clear. *The aim has been to make the UK the best place in the world for e-commerce, with targets aimed at getting people, businesses and government services online by 2005.*

The business focus of this came from the **UK Online for Business** program. This was a Department for Trade and Industry led programme that worked in a number of ways to support small to medium sized enterprises. Now, the DTI website at www.dti.gov.uk (see Figure 6.2), offers many forms of help, with the overall aim to give impartial advice and fully brief business managers, so that their firms can exploit Information and Communications Technology (ICT) more effectively.

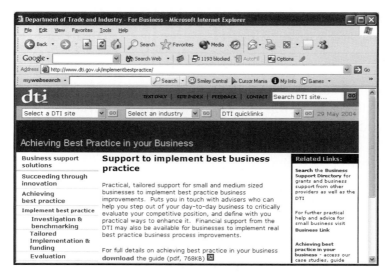

Figure 6.2 www.dti.gov.uk – 'Best Practice Support'

The major features of the UK government support for business are:

- *Advice* about ICT from experts, both online and offline; including step-by-step guides and written publications.

- An online *business planning* tool to assess the current situation of a business

- A *benchmarking* tool to compare a businesses use of IT with those of similar businesses in a sector or region

- A bank of *case studies* to see how others have achieved success in e-business

- Details about e-commerce within various *industrial sectors*

- A network of more than 70 *local centres* where advisors can offer impartial help and advice.

> **Connect**
>
> In pairs, access the www.dti.gov.uk website. Research the site and prepare a presentation aimed for the management of an SME in your area, showing the main features of the support offered through the site.
>
> What is 'Best Practice'?

The e-Minister

The office of the **e-Minister** is a recognition of the high priority that the British government places on e-business in the UK. It is the job of the e-Minister to 'champion the e-business agenda' within the cabinet. To be a cabinet member of the government means that the issues you are responsible for can be heard at the very top level of government decision making. It is at Cabinet meetings that government policy tends to be agreed. At the time of writing, Patricia Hewitt M.P. is the Secretary of State for Trade and Industry and leads the DTI; she has overall responsibility for the 'e-business agenda' and provides monthly reports to cabinet. Answerable to her is (currently) Stephen Timms M.P. who holds the office of Minister of State for e-Commerce and Competitiveness. Together, the Secretary of State at the DTI and the Minister for e-Commerce formulate the government's e-strategy.

Head of e-government

On 25th May 2004, the government appointed its first formal Head of Information Technology, Ian Watmore. This is a top level Cabinet Office post with responsibility for leading the national government's drive to achieve its promise of delivering excellent e-government services to ordinary people.

Prior to 2004 the government recognised the importance of offering online services through the office of the so-called 'e-Envoy'. This office was designed to promote the use by citizens of e-government services, largely through the ukonline website discussed earlier. However, the decision to replace the e-Envoy post was taken because it was felt there was a need to focus more closely on the needs of ordinary citizens. The Head of e-government will be responsible not only for delivering better online services to ordinary citizens, but will also deal with the whole **IT (Information Technology)** infrastructure surrounding the UK government.

As we saw earlier, a new government website, available at <u>www.direct.gov.uk</u>, aims to pool together information from a number of government departments and make it easier for people to navigate around online government services.

> **Over to you** Research the roles of the e-Minister and the Head of e-government. In what ways do you think that e-government can help ordinary citizens?

Helping the private citizen

Lifelong learning

The promotion of lifelong learning (see <u>www.lifelonglearning.co.uk</u>) is important to the government's stated aim of developing the UK as the best place for doing e-business. Lifelong learning is a government initiative delivered through the Department for Education and Skills. It is designed to help both private citizens and the business community to identify and deliver a range of learning opportunities for people of any age. By encouraging people *of all age groups* to re-enter training and education; better still, to encourage everyone to view learning as a lifelong process, industry can be better assured that they will have a ready supply of people with the aptitudes and abilities they need.

e-Business, like all business, needs people with skills and positive attitudes. More and more businesses rely on a multi-skilled and flexible group of core workers at the heart of their operations (see Section 6.4 on social implications). Schooling may well formally end at sixteen, but learning – throughout life – certainly does not. During an era when technology changes quickly, people have to accept they may need to learn new things. A willingness to accept change and respond positively to it is vital for the e-business sector to develop and prosper. It is crucial for those in the sector, to know that people will be constantly willing to update their skills and to feel too that the general population is taking up the e-culture with a positive approach.

Connect

Visit www.lifelonglearning.co.uk. Write a well-organised set of briefing notes for a small business manager outlining the ways in which this programme might be of help to a developing e-business.

The ukonline website

The UKonline campaign has an overall aim to help all sectors of UK society take advantage of the internet. Everyone is being encouraged to experience the World Wide Web and the 'getting.ukonline' site (http://getconnected.ngfl.gov.uk) encourages people to become involved in helping others to use the web. After all, the more people there are online, the better for online business and the better for our 'knowledge-based' economy.

Connect

Visit http://getconnected.ngfl.gov.uk and prepare a brief verbal report to your tutor about the methods and purposes of the campaign.

What does an 'Internet angel' do?

Promoting business innovation

To' innovate' means to introduce changes or new ways of doing things. It is a particularly important word in relation to e-business, as to place a business online is (of course) to do things in a new way.

British business – in the past – was often accused of being far too conservative in its approach to change. As a nation, we tended to be stuck in old fashioned ways of doing things, always believing that we were the best anyway. Partly for this reason, the government has been keen to promote innovation at this time of worldwide change towards a virtual business world. If it did not, Britain might again fall behind other countries.

A lot of the features of the UK Online for Business programme described earlier are designed to offer practical help for businesses preparing and adapting to change. The DTI, responsible for the programme, have also started another service called *The Innovators Club* (see http.//innovation.gov.uk). This service aims to help and inspire businesses by sharing good ideas and better ways of doing things.

Connect

In pairs or groups, visit www.theinnovatorsclub.org.uk and www.businesslink.org.uk. What do you think are the differences between these two sites in terms of what they are aiming to do?

Prepare a poster display about each site, clearly explaining the main features and saying how a small business might benefit.

European Union grants

The UK government works to help purely UK-based businesses and citizens, but it is important to bear in mind that we are part of a much larger economic bloc, the European Union (the EU). The EU is a powerful and growing influence representing the combined efforts of more than twenty European nations working together. An important aspect of EU policy is to develop within the EU an 'information society'.

The EU currently offers assistance to SMEs through its Information Society Programs. One of these is Framework Program 6, the priority of which is, *"enabling anywhere, anytime, natural and enjoyable access to IST (information society technologies) services for ALL"*. In 2003, the level of funding available from this programme was 3.6 billion Euros, aimed at helping research in the relevant industries and encouraging academic and industrial cooperation.

The importance of government support

In the real world, very few business leaders wake up one day and have a *Eureka!* 'flash' of genius – just one single moment of inspiration that encourages him or her to take a bold decision that makes the business a world leader. Serious research shows that real genius comes from quiet thought, humility and constantly looking for new ideas and approaches. To expect an owner or manager to simply pick up the e-business opportunity, just because he or she is *told* it has benefits, is in many cases asking too much. This is why much of the government's effort is towards *sharing* experiences. To hear first hand from other SMEs what their experience of e-business has been is a real boost to confidence. Government efforts are often trying to create an atmosphere of collaboration, of togetherness and willingness, to share and support.

The smaller businesses do not have the same resources as the larger firms. Government advisors can cover for the absence of in-house skills and give added confidence to a firm that is thinking about embarking on the e-business route. Advice can be about technical issues, legal issues, the pitfalls to avoid, or the availability of financial grant aid. By assisting the SMEs, government can help to develop a more productive and rewarding e-business sector. Government cannot afford to just leave the sector to look after itself, it is too important for everyone's jobs and prosperity for that.

Outcome activity

Government support for the SME
You have been asked to visit the Directors of a small cosmetics company to give them advice about developing an internet sales channel for their products.

Task 1
For Pass grade award…

Identify the principle features of government support for organisations developing an e-business strategy.

Task 2

For Merit grade, work must also...

Explain in detail how government support for organisations developing an e-business strategy is likely to lead to growth in the e-business sector.

Task 3

For Distinction grade, work must also...

Evaluate the potential contribution of government support for organisations developing an e-business strategy. Make recommendations for key ways in which such support might be improved.

6.2 Legal implications

Discussing the legal implications of doing internet business is complicated because as the law changes to meet technological change, then technology changes again and overtakes the law! It's hard to keep up. Nevertheless, in this section we must try to isolate the main principles and areas of the law that need to be considered by an e-business.

It is the mark of a civilised country that everyone is expected to abide by the law. This is what gives us all a sense of security. When we feel comfortable that people – and businesses around us – are acting lawfully, we feel safe. At times when we are unsure about this, we feel anxious. Have you ever walked through an area, say an estate, where you think there might be people who will attack or mug you? Or, have you ever had the feeling that you were being 'ripped off'? Of course, most of us have experienced these uncomfortable sensations. People who violently attack others or thieve from them are behaving unlawfully and we can all seek protection. Laws exist to create order and stability and if we feel wronged we can refer to the law. This idea, known as the '*rule of law*', is basic to our country and to most advanced nations. It means that everyone – no matter who they are – is subject to the same legal rules.

This brings us immediately to the heart of a problem in the digital world – laws are created by *individual* nation states to operate within their own boundaries. Yet, the internet is a global thing – there are no national boundaries – so *which* laws apply? If you set up an online store from your bedroom here in the UK, selling little hand-made dolls, the entire world could see what you are offering to sell. This is great as long as all goes well, but what happens if it does not? This is when people look to turn to laws and regulations.

There are many potential *disputes* when you sell on the internet, for example:

- A customer might pay you for a doll but you can't deliver.
- You deliver the dolls, but the customer does not pay.
- The customer pays, but you deliver the wrong doll, a broken doll, or the wrong quantity.
- You deliver, but the customer says he has not ordered any dolls.

The process of legally examining a dispute and making a decision based on the law is called **jurisdiction**. The law exists to regulate in these matters and to protect both buyers and sellers, but the internet means that the buyer and the seller might be in two different countries and the web server could be in another. Whose 'jurisdiction' counts? Which set of regulations should apply? Those where the buyer is located? Or, those where the seller is located? Or, those where the web server is located?

The law courts therefore have to decide *where* a transaction has taken place. In most cases, the location of the web server is disregarded. It is not always clear where a server is located anyway. In addition, top level domain names can be bought by anyone willing to invest in them, so a .com domain need not belong to a company in the USA, or a .de domain in Germany, the originating business can be anywhere.

Before going on to look at some of the further legal issues specifically in e-commerce, it will help to very briefly outline some of the most basic aspects of contract law as it applies in the UK.

Contracts

What is a contract? A contract is an agreement between two parties that binds them both in law. This agreement has to have certain characteristics so that it can be enforced in a court. There has to be *mutual (both parties)* intent between the parties and usually there must be proof that an agreement existed.

How is a contract formed? A contract is formed by an *offer* being made and an *acceptance* of it being received. This is the agreement. A contract does not exist until an offer is communicated, with the terms known in advance, and acceptance is in return communicated.

Consideration: A contract exists when both parties have agreed to exchange one thing in return for something else (Latin: *quid pro quo*). This is the *consideration*.

Intention to create legal relations – it is presumed in the UK that, in business at least, there is an intention to create legally enforceable relations in the sale of goods or the provision of services.

Contracts in the digital age

When the law of contract was first established in Britain, most people were dealing with each other on a face to face basis. Communication was usually immediate and the form of the 'deal' was easily agreed. People exchanged 'binding' agreements that were under (wax) seal. In the internet age contracts are capable of many forms.

When a transaction is done on the internet with a foreign business, it is important to know if the deal that has been made is covered by the law of that other country. In the real world there are many sets of regulations that exist to protect the rights of customers by making the laws of their own countries take first priority. On the internet, as we know, customers from all over the world can deal with a particular business; therefore it seems the electronic business needs to create online terms and conditions that will comply with the laws of *every* country. This is a global solution and achieved by some companies by establishing separate websites for each set of local laws; by others through setting up one megasite meeting the needs of every conceivable national and local legal requirement. This, however, can be both costly – an option available to only the biggest businesses, and possibly inefficient.

Digital signatures

A contract has to consist of an offer and an acceptance. How is it possible to know for sure who you are dealing with on the internet? Paper and pen signatures are hardly suitable. To overcome this it is possible to substitute a digital (electronic) signature. A **digital signature** is not a scanned image of someone's handwritten name. It is an electronic identifier made up of a certain sequence of bits created through a hash function. This is then **encrypted** (made unreadable) using a sender's private 'key'. Anyone authorised to open a document digitally signed, can do so if they have the private 'key'. A digital signature added to a digital document means it can be fully checked for who sent it, when and whether the document has been altered in any way, during transit.

Digital certificates are hard to forge and form the basis for legally binding contracts on the internet. Remember, the contents of an agreement must be clearly stated and communicated. Terms can be *expressly* stated and incorporated into a contract document itself, for this reason it is vital that a document's content can be proved to be original. The only question remaining is the extent to which each country accepts their use and it seems that a legal framework is starting to emerge.

> **Over to you** Summarise the main features of a lawful contract. In your own words, explain why doing business over the internet complicates the formation of a contract.

Problems of website content

The web is about delivering content to users. There are several matters relating to content regulation and control that every online business should be aware of.

Privacy

Internet technology (through for example, *data-mining*) gives businesses, or any online organisation, the opportunity to collect information about consumers and other businesses purchasing trends. In the case of private consumers, what they liked or disliked, how they shopped, when they shopped. In the case of a business corporation, major competitors can get an insight into sensitive strategic marketing plans.

Messages can be targeted to a large number of consumers, whilst tailoring the content for specific groups. This information gathering potential of the internet has led to a good deal of sensitivity about online *privacy*. In fact, studies have shown that privacy is the number one concern of internet users and remains an obstacle to internet take up (Centre for Democracy and Technology, 1999).

The Information Commissioner

The Data Protection Act 1998 (see page 151) established the office of Information Commissioner.

The Information Commissioner has the following mission.

'We shall develop respect for the private lives of individuals and encourage the openess and accountability of public authorities by:

- promoting good information handling practice and enforcing data protection and freedom of information legislation;

- seeking to influence national and international thinking on privacy and information access issues.'

Figure 6.3 The website for the office of the Information Commissioner

Connect

In groups of two or three, access the Information Commissioner's website at www.informationcommissioner.gov.uk. Click on the link to 'Electronic communications'. Produce a joint presentation summarising the guidelines for 'Privacy and electronic communications'.

Defamation and libel

Can you legally set up a website and put harmful comment on it, say about David Beckham, because you happen to dislike him? Can you carry articles on a website about other people, that will do harm to them, or their business, just because they are competing against you? The answer in the UK is no, because you can be accused of 'defaming' them.

Defamation is the *publication of a statement which reflects on a person's reputation and tends to lower him (or her) in the eyes of wider society*. It has two forms, *slander* – not relevant to the web because it refers to the spoken word or gesture – and *libel*, which tends to be viewed as more serious, because it is a more permanent form. Anything which is written, say in a newspaper, or (importantly) broadcast via media such as TV or radio, can be regarded by the courts as libel, if it is viewed as being not true and the person's reputation suffers. The internet has now been established as being *in the same category* as the broadcasting media.

Internet content is potentially dangerous because it can be regarded as 'published' information, once it is up on the web. The only question is, how is *publication* defined on the internet? If a website carries anything which is 'defamatory' as defined earlier, then the publisher of the site can be sued. The question arises as to *who* is responsible for publishing the site? Is it the Internet Service Provider? Or the person or firm that uploads the site? Does 'publication' occur at the point of uploading, or at the point where it is read by users? This issue affects all matters connected with website content.

A CompuServe executive, Felix Somm, was convicted in Germany in 1998 for allegedly trafficking pornography and Nazi propaganda, yet his company was not the originator of the sites concerned. This was a major scare in the industry until it was overturned later. Now it is clear in Germany that the content provider, not the ISP, is responsible. In an earlier case in Britain however, Demon Internet, one of Britain's oldest ISPs, failed to convince a court that they were not the publishers when they were sued by a physicist, Laurence Godfrey. The judge ruled that Demon had the chance to remove offending material but had refused to do so, therefore they were the publisher.

The question of internet libel has been a growing concern. In 2002, the Law Commission found that businesses had been increasingly using legal threats against ISPs to close down websites set up by angry customers or protest groups. The Commission argued that the situation was in danger of stifling free speech, because many of the allegations on the sites were true! In the United States, where freedom of speech is much more strongly protected than in Europe, ISPs are exempt from legal liability for materials they publish on the web.

Chat room

In pairs, discuss the question of internet libel. Prepare a brief summary in your own words of the dangers anyone publishing on the web should be aware of.

Negative campaigning

Internet marketing shows us the power of the internet in getting positive messages over about a business and its products. A good website that works well, backed up by good products that are delivered and supplied efficiently, should be a real benefit to a business. The effect we know as viral marketing means that people will refer favourably to your web-based presence if they experience something good. However, just as this can be used positively, it can also be used negatively. Bad news about a site spreads rapidly.

Negative campaigning refers to web-based content that deliberately attempts to undermine your business by finding anything wrong or problematic about it that it can. For example, in 1995, the Ford Motor Company suffered because a group of disgruntled Ford buyers put up a website about the 'Flaming Ford' (which *used* to be at www.flamingfords.com) causing the company to spend millions recalling cars they felt had an electrical fault. A counter website, properly constructed and giving good information can eventually turn this bad situation for Ford into a positive piece of public relations.

Unhappy customers of a particular website have been known to purchase domain names that put a joke angle on a business. The Chase Manhattan Bank got in first by buying the domains, Chasesucks.com, IhateChase.com and ChaseStinks.com, and the chief executive of Priceline.com, bought Priceline-sucks.com to prevent dissatisfied customers from using that name (perhaps UK-based customers are more imaginative in this respect?).

In the European Union, negative campaigning or comparison advertising (e.g. ours is better than yours) is not permitted. As we know, on the internet, national laws are not always applicable. Putting up information on a web server in another country is fairly simple and there are still countries where internet regulation is very weak. A vicious competitor could maliciously place a negative website about you online from a base with weak regulation. It is always advisable for a business of any standing to closely monitor the internet for such a thing.

Daniel Amor, in his book *The e-business (r)evolution* recommends that online businesses to develop a 'Dark Site', a website that is kept on standby with full details of products just in case there is a problem. As Amor says, in the physical world, if a person buys a product that fails, possibly fifty people will get to know. In the online world, a single mouse click can send the message out to thousands of people.

Intellectual property

If you are in college or school as you work through this text, have a look around the place and the chances are you will be looking at someone who has come close to infringing someone's copyright.

As we all know, it is possible to cut and paste another's work into your own and this can be done very quickly and easily. Today it is worth knowing that almost every piece of information is copyrighted, whether a copyright statement is visible or not. Anyone who reuses material from another person's site can be in breach of copyright – especially if this is done for commercial purposes.

A while ago, people were setting up fan pages for fun, so long as there was no commercial gain involved this was fine; however, eventually, banner ads appeared on them and money began to be made. Copyright issues suddenly emerged. Star Trek fan pages are a good illustration. Logos and images of the Star Trek 'brand' (www.startrek.com) were widely used on the fan pages until the owners of their copyright asked for them to be removed.

The biggest problem on the web does not concern text-based information but music, images and programs. The MP3 format compresses music files in such a way that whole CDs can be copied in little time. The JPEG format similarly allows images to be downloaded and copied easily and software piracy is a worry for many software corporations. However, there are of course issues of copyright for the owners of the material.

The domain name

Domain names, as we know, are vital unique business identifiers on the web. The IP address being a twelve digit number is almost incomprehensible to most of us, so we need something that is easily readable by humans. If I wanted to set up an online business, the domain name John.com is probably already registered but maybe worth a try. If I wanted to be really 'clever' however, perhaps I'd be better off registering a domain name such as WeetabixJohn.com. Why? Because I'm incorporating someone else's trademark and this may be a benefit to me. Problem is that if I did this I would probably be violating the Weetabix owners trademark rights (if doing similar business) and it has now been established that trademark owners *do* have first rights to these in the domain name question.

Anyone can buy any domain name so long as it is not already registered and many did so in the past just to make money. A new online business needs to be careful to check existing trademarks, (as in my fictitious case above) register a new domain name as a trademark and carefully check foreign countries and domain name register wherever business might be done.

Data protection

The question of data has already been mentioned when discussing the problem of privacy. However, any business handling any data must comply with the principles of data protection, meaning that data must:

be fairly and lawfully processed

- be processed for limited purposes only
- be adequate, relevant and not excessive
- not be kept longer than necessary
- be processed in accordance with the data subjects rights
- be secure
- not be transferred to countries without adequate protection.

Disclaimers

A disclaimer can be placed on a website that, if properly and clearly worded, can warn customers that a business can accept no liability in the event of any difficulty with products or services. Depending on the nature of the business, a disclaimer can be very simple in content, or as watertight as possible. The disclaimer should be placed in a visible place, with clear links from other pages. If, for example, your business provides a delivery service and someone claims a late delivery has cost them a fortune, an appropriate disclaimer may save considerable financial losses.

Connect

Research a variety of websites. Collect at least three examples of online disclaimers and try to collect one from a service product.

Framing and 'deep linking'

The use of frames in a web page allows the page to be divided into separate parts that can then be loaded onto the page individually. A navigation bar can be created with logos contained in it that will load another site into a 'frame' on your own, without reloading the entire page. This is not a problem in itself but becomes an issue if your page also contains revenue raising banner advertising. You are in effect using other people's content to raise money from your site.

Creating hypertext is the essence of the web, in fact it is at the core of its whole purpose. Any page can be linked to any other web page without restrictions. Web creators – by using links – are adding resources to their sites and adding value, it is part of web culture. However if a website incorporates links to other pages on a large scale, by passes the home pages and then deliberately promotes this as part of their own service, then this process, known as **deep linking** is regarded as pirating. It is perfectly safe and acceptable to link to other specific external documents, but dubious practice to link to other people's *services*. Microsoft found this in 1997 when they where sued by Ticketmaster (www.ticketmaster.com) for directly linking to their ticket sales page without reference to the home page of the site.

Non-content issues

Not all problem areas to do with the web relate to content. These are best considered too, before a business considers implementing an e-strategy. Taxation issues are particularly important.

Taxation

National governments are understandably concerned about possible loss of tax revenues due to the borderless internet. By 2001, internet shopping was expected to cost Britain up to £10billion a year in *lost* taxes (source: Reuters *'Britain Adds Up Net Tax Losses'* Wired News, 1999). Needless to say, governments are looking into the question of taxing e-commerce. In the meantime, the issue again is one of location. You sell something as a web-based retailer, over the internet to a person in Ireland, whose tax applies? The general view is that national governments must maintain rights to tax, that there should be a fair share of the tax base between countries and no double taxation. For a new online business, taxation questions need to be monitored.

Outcome activity

Legal implications of doing e-business

A local medium sized firm specialises in acquiring spares for a range of classic 1970s cars and the management are considering moving the business online, so that the rewarding US market can be opened to them. You have been informally approached and asked to give them some advice before they go any further with their plans.

Task 1
To achieve a Pass grade:

Identify the major legal implications for this business in implementing an online strategy.

Task 2
To achieve a Merit you must also:
Analyse the major legal issues that any SME would need to consider before going to an online sales strategy.

Task 3
To achieve a Distinction you must in addition:
Evaluate the extent to which the legal implications of doing e-business are serious obstacles to successfully implementing an online strategy.

6.3 Legislation and codes of practice

The word 'legislation' (in the UK context) means an *Act of Parliament*. In this country, before something can be called 'law', it has to go through a fairly lengthy process (the 'legislative process') of being introduced to Parliament as a 'Bill', discussed and possibly amended in parliamentary committee, debated and discussed in both Houses of Parliament (i.e House of Commons and House of Lords) before it is signed on behalf of the Monarch and becomes the law of the land. Some Acts of Parliament go back hundreds of years and (in theory at least!) represent the collective wishes of us all. Many Acts of Parliament are amended time and again, so that they keep up with modern trends. Some – dealing with similar issues – are consolidated (combined) so that they make more sense. Lawyers, in the form of barristers, solicitors and judges, have to interpret and implement the law in the way that Parliament intended.

The huge changes that have been at the heart of e-business are yet to be *fully* embraced by the law. Many of the Acts that we will describe here were of course conceived and implemented long before the web had spread successfully around the world. Nevertheless, they remain law. Many of the intentions and protections that they established for consumers remain in place whether we are dealing in electronic commerce, or buying from a stallholder in the street.

What follows in this section is not intended, therefore, as a definitive listing of every piece of e-business related legislation that has been enacted by the UK Parliament. It is however, a general guide. Taken all together, this should be seen as a starting point guide as to the important matters that any online business needs to consider. Some of these matters require action by the business, some of them will call for expert advice.

Before summarising the legal framework, it is essential to remember too that the UK is only one nation state within a wider economic/political union, the European Union (EU). European legislation is discussed and agreed in the European Parliament that meets mainly in Brussels and to a lesser extent, Strasbourg. The law of the EU over-rules our own national law and *when the European Commission introduces a 'directive' to member states it is an instruction to introduce legislation on an issue.* The member state is free to choose *how* to implement a directive.

There are also 'codes of practice' that not have the force of law behind them. They tend to be voluntary regulations that represent the collective opinions of an industry. People working in advertising for instance, or marketing, recognise that they need acceptance and credibility to succeed. The ASA code of practice described later attempts to create a framework for this.

Acts of Parliament

Acts of Parliament can be seen at www.hmso.gov.uk under Legislation, Acts of the UK Parliament.

Consumer Credit Act 1974

People who enter into credit agreements (i.e. agree to buy goods on credit terms) valued under £25,000 are entitled to cancel as long as they signed the agreement in their own home and did not make the deal over the phone, or sign in the seller's shop.

The seller must give written notice about how to cancel and how long is available to cancel. The person giving the credit, (the creditor) cannot demand payment, or try to get goods back, without giving 7 days written notice of their intention to take such action. This notice has to be written in a particular way:

- How much needs to be paid to bring the agreement up to date.
- When payments should be made.
- How the agreement can be ended.

If a customer has paid more than a third of the total price of the goods, a creditor cannot get the goods back without a court order.

If a credit agreement is unfair, the courts can be asked to examine it and change it.

In a credit agreement, the creditor must provide written details about the agreement, including:

- The total charge for credit.
- The Annual Percentage Rate (APR)
- The cash price for the goods.

Consumer Protection Act 1987

This Act deals with the safety of products sold onto the market. The Act (as many Acts of Parliament do) 'consolidates' (i.e. brings together) things that have been implemented in earlier Acts. The Act deals with:

- Product liability
- Consumer safety.

Product liability

People injured by defective products may have the right to sue for damages and the Act removes the need to prove negligence on the part of a supplier. The product *does not* have to have been sold to the injured person. An injured person can sue Producers, Importers or other suppliers. All *food* is covered under the Act, *building materials* (not a whole building), *component parts* (of other products) and *raw materials*.

Information is not covered, nor is printed matter, unless it is part of inadequate instructions or warnings for a product that is defective. Design consultants are not liable for a mistake in design that causes a product to fail, a producer is. Software designers are not liable for software faults causing a product to fail, it is the company producing the product that carries the liability.

The Act also defines the meaning of 'defective'. It refers to a situation where *safety* is not as one would expect. Poor quality is not in itself considered defective. It is important to be conscious of 'what might reasonably be expected to be done with' a product. In other words, someone using a product for a purpose it was not manufactured for, cannot expect to successfully sue.

Consumer safety

The 1987 Act set out safety regulations that had to be complied with in the case of both new and second hand products. This includes methods of construction, safety warnings (and fire warnings) and instructions for use. A fine can be imposed for failure to meet safety standards. *Trading Standards Officers* in local authorities had the responsibility for enforcing the Act; these officers can seize goods, make test purchases, or enter warehouses or premises. The 1994 Safety Regulations effectively consolidate the 1987 section on consumer safety by introducing the General Product Safety (GPS) regulations. These fit in with EU directives and mean there is now an EU wide set of safety regulations.

Copyright, Designs and Patents Act 1988

Copyright arises when an individual (or an organisation) creates an original work that has involved a degree of labour, skill or judgement. Normally, an individual or group that has authored the work will own the copyright; however, if the work has been produced as part of employment then the employer owns the copyright. Copyright has limited duration, varying from 70 years for literary, musical, film or artistic work, to 25 years for magazine articles.

The Act gives protection for literary, dramatic, musical or artistic works and the creators of these have the right to control the ways in which they are used. The rights cover performance, copying, adapting, issuing, renting or lending to the public.

The Act also covers software copyright. It is an offence to make unauthorised copies of a software package, whether this is for personal use or for sale (duration is for 70 years).

Computer Misuse Act 1990

This Act created three new offences;

1   unauthorised access to computer material;

2   unauthorised access with intent to commit further offences and

3   unauthorised modification of computer material.

Cause a computer to access any program, or any data held in any computer – intentionally, without permission – knowing it is happening, is an offence liable to result in a 6 month prison sentence or a maximum £2000 fine. Persistent hacking is a more serious Crown Court offence and can get an offender 5 years in prison.

Altering data without permission can get an offender 6 months in prison, as can unauthorised copying of data.

Data Protection Act 1998

The power of computers to find and store data is awesome to many people. Data about everyone can be processed rapidly; allowing mail shots, instant credit references and detailed personal profiles to be built up, based on previous online buying. Added to this capability is the possibility of hacking and data misuse.

These concerns led to an early EU directive that personal data could only be exchanged between member states that had data protection rules. Hence the UK government passed the original 1984 Data Protection Act that began to regulate the automatic processing of data. The 1998 legislation strengthens that Act and adds further controls about how personal data about people can be used.

The 1998 Data Protection Act established the office of Information Commissioner (see page 143) and set out eight basic but important principles relating to processing personal data.

1   Data must be processed fairly and lawfully. When data is collected, the data subject should be told it is being collected and what it is for and its intended destination. Written consent is needed for any sensitive data to be processed; e.g. about a person's sexual orientation or criminal record.

2   Data must be collected for specified purposes and cannot be used in ways that are incompatible with those purposes.

3   Data must be adequate, relevant and not excessive for those purposes.

4   Data must be accurate and kept up to date.

5   Data must not be kept longer than necessary.

6   Data must be processed in accordance with the data subjects rights under the Act. (see below).

7   The data must be protected against unauthorised access and against accidental loss or damage.

8   Data must not be transferred to a country which does not have appropriate data protection.

The data subject (the person about whom data is held) has certain rights in relation to a data controller (the person or business processing data):

1   The subject has rights to a copy from the data controller of personal data held about him/her, although a fee may be charged.

2   The subject can make a written request to the data controller, that data processing about them is stopped.

3   The subject can give the data controller notice to halt, or prevent, the sending of advertising or marketing material to them.

4   The data subject can give written notice to prevent decisions affecting them being made on the basis of automated data processing.

5   The data subject can claim compensation where they have suffered damage or distress when the Act has been contravened.

6   The data subject can obtain a court order to have inaccurate data corrected or erased.

7   Anyone can ask the Commissioner to assess whether or not personal data is being processed according to the Act.

Electronic Communications Act 2000

This Act has also become known as 'The e-Commerce Act' because its aim was to help the UK *really* to become the 'best environment for electronic commerce' as the government intended. The Act aimed to modernise the law and ensure there was a climate of confidence (in relation to security issues) for the conduct of e-business. The purpose of the Act was to implement most of the EU Electronic Signatures Directive. In effect, the Act does the following:

●   Makes authentic electronic signatures acceptable

●   Sets up a register of cryptographer service providers (CSPs) (these are private sector organisations offering services designed to secure electronic data).

●   Allows the use of electronic forms of data in areas previously restricted to paper documents.

Sale of Goods Act 1979

This Act lays down that goods sold must 'conform to contract', that is they must be:

●   of satisfactory quality

●   as described

●   fit for purpose.

'Satisfactory quality' covers minor and cosmetic defects as well as substantial problems. It means that products must last a reasonable time, but does not extend to goods a consumer knew to be faulted at the time of purchase.

'As described' refers to any advertisement or verbal description made by a trader.

'Fit for Purpose' means not only the obvious uses, but also purposes asked about given assurances about, by a trader.

The Act covers second hand items and sales.

A consumer can ask to have the goods repaired or replaced; he or she can then ask for a price reduction; or, he or she can return the goods and get a refund.

Within the first six months, the retailer has to prove that goods 'conformed to contract', after six months until the end of six years, it is for the consumer to prove there has been a lack of conformity.

Trade Description Act 1968

This Act makes it an offence to:

- apply a false trade description to any goods
- supply, or offer to supply, goods to which a false trade description is applied.
- make certain kinds of false statement about the provision of any services, accommodation or facilities.

A false description

A *false* trade description could be related to size, quantity, how they were made, (e.g. products were 'handmade') fitness for purpose, strength, performance, (e.g. it is 'unbreakable') or physical characteristics (e.g. car is 'fitted with disc brakes'). A false statement within a description could be that goods have been 'tested', or 'approved', or 'this is an 18th century item'.

There are a number of ways in which false statements can be made about:

- *services*; such as the time, place of provision of the service
- *accommodation and facilities*; e.g. place, facilities available or approved by someone else.

Spoken, as well as written statements, including statements in advertisements, are covered by the Act.

Unfair Contract Terms Act 1977

As we know, a contract is an agreement between two parties containing terms and conditions. This Act makes it unlawful to create clauses in a contract that attempt to limit liability for: personal injury, death, loss or damage, breach of contract, unless they can be proved to be 'reasonable' (the Act defines certain conditions about 'reasonableness').

Regulation of Investigatory Powers Act 2000

This Act regulates the sensitive issues of interception, surveillance and investigation of electronic data by government security services and law enforcement authorities. These bodies are allowed to intercept and monitor electronic exchanges in specific situations when they are preventing or detecting crime. The powers the authorities are given includes being able to demand the disclosure of encryption keys, i.e. to open up encrypted (hidden) documents or data.

The Act also gives the Secretary of State powers to make regulations that allow businesses to intercept communications, in the lawful conduct of their business, in special circumstances, without the consent of the sender or receiver of the data.

Chat room

In groups, take *one* of the Acts of Parliament listed above and prepare a jointly agreed paragraph summarising its relevance to a new e-business.

Agree and plan, in your groups, a brief presentation about the legislation to the whole group.

European Union influence

EU law takes precedence over national law. This means that if there was ever to be a conflict between EU and UK law (or the law of any other EU member state), EU law has to be applied. *Directives* are the most common form of EU legislation and these are *instructions* to member states to introduce legislation. Directives indicate the goals to be achieved within the EU. It is left to member states to decide *how* to achieve them. Usually, member states have two years from the date of publication of an EU directive to transform it into national law.

The electronic commerce directive

By 2003, it was expected that Europe's online population would have exceeded that of America and also that 80 percent of the value of European business (as measured by the Gross Domestic Product) would be conducted by companies that were connected to the web. Just as the UK government has set out its policy to make the UK the best place to do e-business, the European Union has in place a framework for an *e-Europe.* The aim is to get everyone in Europe, every citizen, every school, every company, online as quickly as possible. Overall, EU policy is geared towards harmonising the differences between the laws of different member states and in this way, paving the way for complete freedom of e-trade across Europe.

The electronic commerce directive attempts to ensure that e-business can benefit from both freedom of establishment and freedom of movement. In general, e-business can be provided throughout the EU so long as it can comply with the laws of its *home* member state. A number of principles are established by the directive, including:

- Contracts should be capable of being concluded by electronic means (with some exceptions, such as real estate).
- As already said, the law of the country of establishment of the e-business has to be complied with.

B2B contracts

Generally, a contract is governed by the laws chosen by the parties involved in the contract. Usually (understandably) suppliers favour the laws of their own national government. They must make this clear however, and therefore should inform customers of the organisations identity, place of establishment and trading status.

The e-commerce directive requires that an e-business should communicate 'comprehensively and unambiguously' the steps to follow to conclude an e-contract, the language available to do it, the technical means for identifying and correcting errors and whether the contract will be stored and accessible later.

B2C contracts

The parties to a contract can choose the applicable law. However, this choice cannot deprive a consumer of the mandatory consumer protection rules of his/her own country. When contracts are drawn up, the supplier must state which is the governing law.

According to *The Distance Selling Directive* the supplier must provide the consumer with clear and understandable information about; his identity and address, characteristics of the goods and their price, delivery times and costs, details of terms for return of goods, details of deadlines for returns, general terms and conditions of business, arrangements for payment and delivery, existence of the right of withdrawal, the period during which an offer remains valid, cost of using distance communication and finally, the minimum duration of the contract in cases where something is to be done over a longer period of time.

Under the e-commerce directive, the consumer must get written confirmation (or other durable medium) of a contract, telling him or her how to withdraw, the place where he or she can complain, details of after sales service, and conditions under which the contract can be rescinded. Apart from contracts concluded exclusively via e-mail messages, the e-business should communicate 'comprehensibly and unambiguously', the technical steps to conclude the contract, the language available to conclude the contract and technical means to correct errors.

e-Business insight

A medium sized business opened a new sales channel via the internet, mainly trading within the European Union. The Managing Director is delighted with the increased sales and the legal support she feels the business enjoys within the EU.

In planning the website, designers have made it clear where the business is based; that the law of the UK will apply and they have included all of the information detailed above. Consumers know they have rights and the business can work within a developing legal framework.

The Advertising Standards Authority code of practice

The ASA was set up in 1962 to provide independent scrutiny of the advertising industry's *self regulatory* system. It administers the *British Code of Advertising, Sales Promotion and Direct Marketing* and this contains explicit rules dealing with distance selling. See www.asa.org.uk.

Summary of the ASA rules

1 Delivery date should be no more than 30 days. Some goods may take longer but this should be clearly indicated in the advert. If there is a delay in fulfilment of an order, and the customer wishes to have a refund, the advertiser must provide this.

2 The full name and address of the advertiser should be given so that a consumer may keep a record.

3 The product received by the customer should be accurately described in the advertisement and the advertiser is obliged to repay any money received if the goods do not conform to their description.

4 If unwanted goods are returned – unused – within seven working days, the advertiser must send a full refund to the customer. Exemptions from this are perishable, personalised or made to measure products.

The essence of the system is *self* regulation. It is believed that everyone in the advertising and marketing industry has an interest in ensuring that marketing communications are welcomed and trusted by their audience; if they are not accepted or trusted they cannot be effective. If they offend in any way, the whole industry is discredited.

Outcome activity

The legal framework

A medium sized firm, local to you, manufactures and supplies a range of personalized coffee mugs. The firm has opened an online service and is attracting a good deal of business from across the European Union. The website offers the firm's products and services in six European languages and they are receiving a lot of online orders from Spain. The MD has asked for your advice on legal codes and you have been asked to respond in a formal report.

Task 1

To achieve a Pass grade:

Produce a management report summarising the key features of major pieces of legislation and codes of practice relating to internet business in the UK.

Task 2

To achieve a Merit grade you must also:

In the report, analyse the key features of the major legislation and codes and make recommendations to management on the appropriate actions to be taken.

Task 3

To achieve a Distinction you must in addition:

In the conclusions to the report, evaluate the extent to which you feel doing e-business subjects the firm to significantly increased regulation.

6.4   Social implications

What is the effect of e-business upon people? This is important because the way in which a country produces the things it needs has a tremendous impact upon the way its people live. In the 17th century, the change in Britain from open field farming to enclosed compact farms had an effect on the people. The development of machines for use in manufacturing at the end of the 18th century, started a chain of change that brought people across Europe into towns to find work in the factories.

The *implications* (effects) of this for *people* were huge. Work changed, living conditions changed, wealthy factory owners emerged and a labouring 'working' class was created. Patterns of building changed too, as accommodation for these workers had to be created near where they worked. Often, these hastily erected cramped houses led to poor standards of public sanitation (sewage systems) and the eventual side effect was disease and ill-health (if you could be transported back in time to those days now, the first thing you would notice would be the *stench*). The 'social implications' of this 'industrial revolution' were enormous. The effect was to change people's entire pattern of life and eventually force the government of the time to take a much more active role in 'social' matters.

The current digital 'revolution' is not causing these kinds of dramatic shifts in life experiences – yet. Most people's *way of life* is untouched by the internet. A minority however have made a living out of it, have created wealth out of it and become themselves wealthy out of it (legally and illegally). Others have had to develop new skills as their job roles have changed, some – hopefully not many – have lost their jobs, some – hopefully many – have acquired jobs, directly because of the internet, as businesses have grown and taken advantage of new opportunities. There *are* then, social implications and these can be serious for us all. This section looks at some of the social implications of the digital revolution, each one having in its own way a potentially significant impact on every one of us.

Potential for falling tax revenues

Tax is a dirty word for many people. None of us likes to examine our pay packet and see that thanks to PAYE (pay as you earn), we have had a big chunk of our hard-earned cash taken away by the government in Income Tax. For businesses, the pain is sometimes worse as they have to pay taxes based on the trade they have done and the tax due has to be paid all at once. Taxes are either based directly on what is earned, or they are based on sales (Value Added Tax). It is the question of taxation on sales that poses a problem for the digital age.

Whilst taxes are not popular, they are important, because tax revenue is what the government uses to provide services that are essential in a civilised country. Whilst we hate paying tax, we want our children to have the best education; if we are poorly we want to be able to have health care; if we want to travel, we want decent roads and transport systems. Whilst a private firm spends money on the things it needs for *itself*, the government spends money on things it needs to provide for all of us, the general public. Some people would say that taxation is the mark of a civilised society. What it does is to help *redistribute* money around (the rich pay more tax so that the poor can get decent health services).

It is a concern then, to consider that the creation of a digital economy has had the effect of reducing tax revenues for government. Instead of a straightforward pattern of trade between businesses and customers *within* national boundaries, a new pattern is emerging in which there are no national boundaries at all. The problem, again, is one of location. If a person buys on the internet, where are the taxes due? At the point of sale, or purchase?

The American news service ABC reported in 2000 that between $300 million and $3.8 billion of potential tax revenue was lost by the authorities due to online shopping in the USA (source: Dave Chaffey, p.138). This happened because retailers only needed to impose taxes on sales when goods were being sent to consumers who lived where the retailer had a 'bricks and mortar' store. Buyers were supposed to pay taxes voluntarily when buying online, but this rarely happened. The internet therefore became a tax free area within the USA. US government policy seems to have been that taxation of internet trade would only stifle its development.

In Europe, tax free betting became available because betting companies offered internet-based betting from offshore locations such as Gibraltar. These countries had lower tax levels and the betting companies could make betting significantly cheaper for punters. This trend was dubbed 'Location Optimized Commerce on the Internet' (LOCI) by Mougayer in 1998. The UK government responded to this loss of tax revenue by lowering its own tax on betting, so as to reduce the differential and deter betting companies from relocating.

e-Business insight — Betting

In 1998, NetBet launched an internet duty-free betting site licensed by the States of Alderney in the Channel Islands. Customers were not therefore subject to UK tax. The Alderney authorities charged a £50,000 licensing fee and 20 percent tax on company profits; making this relocation an extremely beneficial one for the firm.

This gave the UK Customs and Excise people a bout of real anxiety. In effect, this sort of development was a leakage from tax revenue raising ability. When you consider the UK has a total offcourse betting market valued at £6.2 billion – and growing, the issue was understandably regarded as a serious one.

(source: *Global e-Commerce* A.Farhoomand and P.Lovelock, Prentice Hall, 2001)

EU (VAT) Directive on Electronically Supplied Services

In July 2003, new EU VAT rules came into effect requiring all non-EU businesses to collect VAT-based upon the rate of VAT in the country of residence *of the consumer*. The rules mean that non-EU businesses, selling to an EU-based consumer, have to register within an EU member state, file a single VAT return, and pay the tax to that country.

Chat room

Do you feel that there should be some form of international body looking at the question of taxation of e-commerce? Discuss this question in pairs, then write down a justified response.

e-Learning

Learning any place, anywhere, anytime?

e-Learning refers to *internet enabled learning* and this means far more than just computer *assisted* learning, or computer-based learning. In the latter cases, individual PCs are employed by a user to interact with learning materials often delivered from CDs or other disc media. e-Learning uses the technology of the internet. In e-learning, the internet and the content power of the web are both used to deliver educational courses, training and other structured information as and when required, either at home, in public libraries, internet cafés, learning centres or in workplaces. Additionally, e-learning today offers not just learning materials, it offers online administration, grading and communication; offering learner support, tracking and individual performance development. Online, a virtual learning environment (VLE) can be created.

e-Learning broadly falls into four categories:

- Knowledge database – accessed via *search facilities*; a key word or phrase is typed and matched to a database. This is a very basic form of e-learning and commonly used in all forms of formal education.
- Online support – where forums, chat rooms, bulletin boards, e-mail, or live instant messaging support are used. These are slightly more interactive that mere searches.
- Asynchronous training – this is training that is self paced, based often on CD-ROM, network-based, or internet-based. These courses are often accessed through tutor bulletins, online discussion groups or e-mail.
- Synchronous training – this is training done in real time, in which everyone logs on at the same time and can communicate directly with the tutor and with each other. It is possible to view the cyber-whiteboard over an internet website, audio, or video-conferencing facility.

e-Learning is now becoming a huge business. Businesses have found that e-learning can be a tremendous asset in delivering their own *in-house training* requirements. Research done in the US in 2001 by Unisys Corporation showed that by using e-learning, training costs can be cut by 25-45 percent; training time reduced by 35–35 percent and learning effectiveness by 15–25 percent. Paul Harris of Mentor-UK.com has said that it is only a matter of time before 90 percent of professional training is web-based and e-learning centred. Computer firm Dell, for example, now has 90 percent of its own employee training done online.

The People's Network

The People's Network is a project to connect all public libraries to the internet. In July 2003 there were over 30,000 terminals, in 4,000 public libraries, offering 60 million hours of free internet access to people of all ages, interests and backgrounds. The project, which is funded largely from the New Opportunities Fund, aims to get more people online so that they can access a range of government services as well as take up e-learning opportunities (see www.peoplesnetwork.gov.uk).

The knowledge-based society

Your parents, maybe – your grandparents, almost certainly – will have started their working lives by immediately getting a job after leaving school. They will have expected to keep that job for most, if not all, of their working life. In the north east of England for example, huge coal reserves were discovered underground in the 19th century, bringing many thousands of people to the region for jobs in the developing coal industry. Coal also needed to be shipped away from the region to wherever else it was required. This meant that ships had to be built and so the two staple north east industries, coal and shipbuilding, came to dominate the region and gave it its economic base.

Today, physical and capital resources such as coal and ships no longer drive the economy. Instead, knowledge (information) and human intellect are taking over. This has massive effect on people's lives and jobs. Instead of leaving formal education and getting a job for life, people are expected to go on learning all their lives. In the north east, in the traditional economy, a man may have become a miner or a shipbuilder for all of his working life; today, people are expected to move around. Firms expect flexibility, responsiveness, willingness to acquire multi-skills, to adapt to new methods. Firms are much leaner, employing fewer people on permanent contracts.

In this knowledge-based economy, the needs of individual learners have to govern what is offered in training. E-learning is ideal because it can offer personalised training, can offer flexibility, new models and access as and when required. Learning today is a lifelong process, not a distinct event that comes to an end at 16 years of age. New regulations come from government or from Europe and have to be taken on board and learned; new products, new technologies arrive and need to be learned; new techniques for offering customer service – e.g. call centres, are employed and they have to have trained and skilled operators. This is the significance of e-learning and one of the reasons why it is set to grow at such a phenomenal rate. There are new things to learn all the time; and the pace is getting faster!

Internet cafés

Public access to the internet is an important aspect of government policy. Public access to the internet is, as we have seen, offered in public libraries and now throughout the formal education system. The private sector is also offering access through internet cafés and salons.

Connect

Access the following two websites and do a survey to discover the nearest internet café facility to where you live.

- www.Cafeindex.co.uk
- www.eats.co.uk

Produce a brief informal report on these businesses describing the service they offer.

Potential for e-business to cause structural unemployment

In a free market economy, firms can be created and dissolved depending upon market conditions. For example, if people want pink plastic elephants, industrial leaders are at liberty to produce and sell them if they feel they can make profits out of it. When markets are buoyant, people are spending money and firms become very active and take on workers. In general, free markets are said to operate for the benefit of both workers and business owners. However, at times workers are not required by firms and they become unemployed. There are several reasons why unemployment happens. Sometimes it can be part of the so-called natural business cycle (cyclical unemployment) or, at other times, industrial change causes some jobs to permanently disappear and *'structural unemployment'* is caused. It is this kind of unemployment that concerns us about the growth in e-business.

Earlier, we saw how the north east of England underwent big economic changes due to the closure of coal mines and shipbuilding firms. Many people lost their jobs. This 'structural unemployment' becomes such a social problem that governments have to deal with it. Some people may argue that people should move to where the new jobs are located. However, the reality is that this factor, called 'labour mobility,' is still a problem for many people, who prefer to stay near their families and home community are.

Today, the emerging digital economy is causing further structural changes in our national economy. For many firms, it has been essential that they change the way they work in order to stay competitive. If they stood still, then competitors would move into the market space they occupy and take their place. For several years there has been a trend for businesses to trim their workforce. Labour is a major cost for any firm and technological change has meant some workers could be replaced. The trend has been for firms to employ a central core workforce, consisting of relatively few full time, permanent staff. These workers have had to be highly skilled in a variety of areas; and be flexible.

Today's e-business must find people with the relevant skills in order to stay competitive. Traditional office skills still have a place, but on their own they are likely to be inadequate. Staff will be expected to be familiar with concepts like 'intranet', **'extranet'**, 'network', or 'webmaster'. As the trend shifts towards electronic sales, all job roles can possibly change and some jobs go altogether. Take B & Q Direct for instance. We saw earlier how B & Q offer the whole range of products from their DIY.com website. Yet, unlike their physical stores, where customer service jobs are located within the stores, where warehousing and distribution is dealt with on site, in B & Q Direct, these matters are contracted out to a separate business that takes responsibility for product fulfilment and call centre customer response.

In the digital economy, many jobs can be removed from the physical location of the firm. Does it matter when you order a product online where it physically comes from? Does it matter where the person who takes your customer query is physically located? The trend in the emerging economy is towards teleworking. Job roles in this context calls for skills in operating computer-based data, in dealing sensitively with people, in handling product queries.

For the north east of England, this 'new' economy has been embraced with enthusiasm. According to One North East, in 2003, there were 47,000 people employed in call centre work. Sunderland City College was said to be the first college in the country to run a college course that helped people gain the skills needed for call centre work. Yet today, many such jobs are under threat of relocation to India! In India, call centre workers earn as little as £2,000 per year, compared to the UK starting salary of £10,000.

e-Business insight — Call centre jobs

Call centre jobs go to India

Thousands of British banking staff could learn as soon as today that their jobs are being exported to India when Lloyds TSB and Barclays are expected to reveal the extent of their intentions to expand on the subcontinent.

Their plans for further expansion in India follow this month's announcement by HSBC that it is to move 4,000 jobs to India, Malaysia and China and shut five processing centres in Britain.

Lloyds TSB has already warned its 79,000 British-based staffs that it plans to move 1,500 jobs to Bangalore after a successful pilot project.

It is now thought to be making its final decisions about which UK operations will be most affected by the decision, with call centres in Glasgow, Newcastle, Sunderland, Newport, Bridgend and Swansea, all potentially vulnerable.

Many financial services companies have been attracted to using highly educated, English speaking staff in Asia to deal with back office and call centre roles, although HSBC has taken the most radical steps so far by admitting that processing centres will have to be closed.

Jill Treanor, *The Guardian*, October 30th 2003.
Source: Guardian Newspapers Ltd. 2003

Potential increase in e-business failures

Business units come in different shapes and sizes, but they are all capable of failure if they make the wrong decisions, or circumstances external to them – say within the industry in which they work – change. When a sole trader, (a one person business) or a partnership fails, the business can be declared 'bankrupt'. An Official Receiver is appointed and takes legal rights over all of the owner's property. Creditors (people owed money by the business) are allowed to discover what the owner intends to do to repay them. In the case of limited companies, 'liquidation' can be declared. An Official Receiver becomes a 'liquidator' and takes responsibility for selling off assets and repaying debts, or selling off the business itself.

Some economists have argued that the internet has introduced much more competition into markets and because competition has increased (firms from anywhere around the globe can enter markets, prices are much more competitive) some firms are failing as a result. This effect of course varies from industry to industry.

A *Timesonline* (www.timesonline.co.uk) article in November 2003 reported that businesses in the UK are 'going bust' (bankrupt) at a record level, with 36,557 businesses failing so far in 2003. The internet cannot be blamed for all of these failures and many other factors need to be taken into account. However, it is acknowledged that long term changes in the UK economy can certainly explain *some* of the rise in bankruptcies.

Potential for increase in internet crime

Tremendous amounts of money are swirling around in the digital economy. Where there is money, there is crime. Why else would people be worried about security, or data? What follows is merely a broad sweeping glance at some of the main flavours of internet crime.

Fraud

There are several types of internet fraud.

Internet auctions are popular among many people. However, internet fraudsters can place all sorts of property up for sale that he or she have never owned. Sometimes this is done after other items have been sold legitimately and a reliable reputation has been established. On receipt of your credit card details and cash or cheque has been received, the so called 'seller' disappears.

The same applies to non auction, selling websites. A website looks good and appears to be legitimately selling goods; it takes your credit card details then disappears from existence with your cash.

Confidence tricks on customers of financial institutions by requiring them to visit another site, asking them to confirm passwords and other confidential information and then stealing their money.

Packet reading – hackers locate patterns of data, such as credit card digits and intercept and copy them. This is a more sophisticated scam, involving some technical ability.

Cramming – charging a customer for extra services on top of what they have already ordered. The best known case of this was Xpics, which ran a network including various pornographic images; people were asked to offer up credit card details to prove they were over 18 years old then they found it impossible to cancel the subscription.

The Nigerian Letter Scam was typical of a method of *e-mail fraud*. Pleas for financial help are sent out from foreign governments asking for funds to be deposited in a foreign bank account, in return for large returns at a later date. Needless to say, no returns are ever made.

Investment fraud by promising 'get rich quick' schemes. Websites spring up with fantastic opportunities to 'invest' in something. Anyone sending money can kiss it goodbye, as the website disappears after a few days. If something looks too good to be true, it probably is!

PricewaterhouseCoopers believe that fraudulent e-commerce transactions make up half of the annual fraud total in the United States.

Cyber-terrorism

In a world affected by threats of dreadful physical terrorism, the danger of cyber-terrorism cannot be overlooked. Computer systems in key defence installations or government agencies could be vulnerable to malicious attack. In 1999 attacks were thought to have been made by terrorist hackers into the computer systems of the US Pentagon.

Illegal content

Microsoft Corp. has recently announced it is closing down chat rooms in 28 countries in efforts to stop the presence of sexual perverts getting in contact with children. Research from Internet Filter Review, found that the average age a child is first exposed to pornography online is 11 years old; nearly all, (90 percent) of children aged 8–16 have viewed pornography online, mostly while doing homework (source: CyberAtlas, 2003).

Rapid expansion of the web during the latter half of the 1990s led to growing public concern about illegal and offensive material on the internet. As a result of this, in the UK the governments Department of Trade and Industry, the Metropolitan Police, some ISPs (Internet Service Providers) and the Home Office got together to agree a new system of monitoring the content of the web. The result was the *Internet Watch Foundation*. (see www.IWF.org.uk).

The role of the IWF is to offer a hotline service so that people can report offensive or illegal internet content (particularly child pornography); secondly, the IWF – with other related organisations – promotes the voluntary rating of internet content and the use of filtering techniques, to protect children from gaining access to illegal or inappropriate material. Thirdly, the IWF provides an educational role, promoting awareness of the potential dangers of the internet.

e-Business insight — Paedophilia

1 Chat rooms

Paedophiles are individuals with a sexual interest in children. Chat rooms emerged as places on the internet where paedophiles could themselves masquerade as children and make contact with children. In 1997, the American FBI and other US government agencies secured convictions against 200 cases of 'sexual exploitation of minors'. Child sex offenders enter chat rooms and begin a process known as 'grooming'. Over time, he or she gains the child's confidence and develop a relationship. The next step is for the offender to arrange a face to face meeting or persuade the child to send or receive pornographic material.

2 The Wonderland Club

This was a paedophile network operating in 12 countries. Membership was restricted to people who had at least 10,000 images of child pornography – different from images held by existing members. For a monthly fee, members were allowed access to the club's pornography files and meeting grounds.

Over 1 million photographic images had been collected of children before 100 arrests were made by the police in 1998. Only 17 of the 1260 victims in the Wonderland archives have so far been identified. By 2001, 50 convictions had been achieved worldwide.

It's not to be recommended for anyone to participate in chat rooms where the *true* identity of the participants cannot be fully verified. It is particularly dangerous for children.

Chat room

1 In groups of no more than four, research the question of 'Policing the internet'. Prepare a poster display showing the various methods that have been employed so far, across the EU as well as within the UK.

2 Prepare a leaflet for parents of school children under 16, sensibly and sensitively advising them about the dangers of the internet and pointing them to other sources of help and assistance.

Potential for internet generated inequality

A global digital divide

We are living in a so called 'information age', a 'knowledge-based society' and the world is now an online global village; with fantastic opportunities for e-learning, for e-commerce, for e-entertainment, for indeed for e-everything. Yet, recent figures still showed that almost 90 percent of internet users are in industrialised countries, with the USA and Canada accounting for nearly 60 percent of the total (source: International Labour Organisation: World Employment Report 2001).

This is said to be a cause of a 'digital divide'. We meaning that some people can access the equipment, the telecommunication links, the software needed to access the internet, whilst others cannot. Consider the opportunities and the benefits afforded by the world wide web. Are these people less deserving of these than us? The physical world has evolved into an unequal one, must the digital one too?

Nation	Population	Internet users		ISPs
United States	280.5 million	165.7 million	(59 percent)	7,000
Canada	31.9 million	16.84 million	(53 percent)	760
United Kingdom	59.8 million	34.3. million	(57 percent)	<400
France	59.76 million	16.97 million	(28 percent)	62
Germany	83.2 million	32.1 million	(39 percent)	200
Ghana	20.2 million	200,000	(1 percent)	12
Kenya	31.1 million	500,000	(1.6 percent)	65
Pakistan	147.6 million	1.2 million	(0.8 percent)	30
Republic of Congo	55.2 million	6,000	(0.1 percent)	1

(Source: CyberAtlas November 2003)

Figure 6.4 Global internet inequality – a selection of nations

A digital gender divide

One of the most striking divides in the digital world relates to Internet usage differences between men and women. Recent investigations by Jupiter Research show that 52 percent of US online shoppers were women, compared to 42 percent of European online shoppers. Women are spending more online in the richer countries than men and unsurprisingly they are visiting different sites (women: clothing, bedding, household, children; men: electronics, financial – source: Nielsen/Netratings). In the poorer countries, men are outpacing women by a significant amount. In Latin America, only 38 percent of Internet users are female.

A national digital divide?

Figure 6.4 illustrates that the UK, being part of the wealthier group of industrialised nations, is relatively well off in terms of internet access. Within the United Kingdom, research by Professor Richard Rose, of the Oxford Internet Institute, shows that 59 percent of the population use the internet regularly and only 4 percent have absolutely no access to *somewhere* with an internet connection (source: BBC News, Nov 2003). The research also shows however, that access to the internet still varies with age; only 22 percent of retired people surf the internet, whilst 98 percent of school students and 67 percent of the working population go online.

So why do people *not* use the internet? We have spent a good deal of time analysing the benefits and opportunities from the internet, yet here we are discussing a significant group of our population who just do not seem to bother with it. According to the Rose report, (a survey of 2,000 individuals) people who don't access the web, just do not see how it can offer anything of benefit for them. They do not see the need. This is the most likely explanation for the age divide. Older people have lived and shopped all their lives without the internet, so why should they be concerned with it now? It is not a fear of the technology itself, or lack of education, just disinterest based on a sense of irrelevance.

The AMD Global Consumer Advisory Board (GCAB) reported in October 2003 that, within the UK, the overwhelming majority (89 percent) of the 16–24 age group were connected to the web in 2002, compared to only 14 percent of those aged over 65, thus confirming the Rose findings. Income was found to be the most important factor in determining connection and London and the South East of England were the most connected areas.

Impact on communities

If the creation of a digital economy is potentially having an effect on so many aspects of our lives, what can be the potential effect on our communities? Throughout the twentieth century we saw a movement away from close-knit, distinctive, communities based upon key industries. This was reinforced by the changing pattern of retail outlets. Instead of local shops and outlets being a reflection of *local* tastes and needs, all retail outlets began to take on *similar* characteristics. You could go anywhere and see the same shops, (Dixons, Next, Marks and Spencers, Boots, River Island...and more); have you ever noticed this? The question now is, will increasing internet shopping finally kill off the local shopping mall? Will shopping become yet another private (not social) activity?

A 'community' used to share similar characteristics; in terms of work and lifestyle. In the latter half of the twentieth century people gradually shrank back to their own homes. Fewer people shared similar work or social experiences. The differences between us became greater. The people next door were unlikely to go to work with you; you would have less and less in common. These things have without doubt changed the notion of 'community'.

The internet and civil liberties

In Britain, as in much of the western world, we live in a 'liberal-democratic' society. This has important meaning for each of us as individuals. We value certain freedoms that each of us tends to take for granted; e.g. the right to freedom of speech, of assembly, the right to privacy. These things are regarded as so important they are wrapped up in several international treaties; The United Nations Declaration of Human Rights and The European Convention on Human Rights both contain articles on freedom of expression and association. In short, we don't choose to be governed to such an extent that we lose our individual freedoms – government is *limited.*

This is very important when we consider the question of regulation of the internet. We have already seen many times that there is a need to regulate *some* aspects of the internet in the interests of us all. The UK Regulation of Investigatory Powers Act 2000 allows widespread monitoring of the internet and the decryption of encrypted data on demand. This means that the State (government) gets certain rights to interfere with our lives. Is it right or justified that government agencies, police etc. can monitor our use of the internet? The internet has the potential to liberate and extend freedoms of expression, of ideas, of taste. If the internet is *over*-regulated, is there a danger that our individual civil liberties will be affected?

Chat room

In groups, prepare supporting cases for *both* of the following positions:
- Regulation of the internet is a danger to civil liberties in the UK.
- Regulation of the internet is a necessary evil.

The internet and young people

As a twenty-first century person, how is the digital world going to affect you?

Adolescence is said to be a hard time – I can't remember myself! Teenagers have to assert their identity, discover who they are, experiment within a range of life roles and find their own path. Curiosity, feedback from others and acknowledgement of who you are, are vital in helping in this process. Some writers (Erikson 1991) have said that the internet allows much of this to be done anonymously by teenagers. Online, they can discuss problems more freely, share things and as a result perhaps become more tolerant and understanding of the differences between people.

Teenagers need to feel they belong and the internet can give this sense of belonging; it is known that teenagers primarily use the internet as a communication tool. In doing this they experience others and make genuine connections. Some individuals will benefit from this, especially those who may be more reserved. However, it is important to remember that 'cyberspace' is only a component of life, not life itself. Young people must be alert to the dangers of living too much of their lives online. There is no replacement for *real* social interaction.

Over to you Think about your own use of the internet. Prepare an individual written statement to present to the rest of your group, outlining the part it plays in your life. Do you think it is a force for good?

Outcome activity

Social implications
You work for a local SME (small to medium sized enterprise) which employs around 250 staff. It is an important firm in your locality. Senior management has recently taken a definite decision to move the business online in order to expand sales reach and compete more effectively. Work is well under way with the help of external consultants and the new channel of the business is likely to go live within a matter of weeks. Your manager has been asked to attend a meeting of the local Economic Development Team of the local Council. The topic is 'the social implications of e-business'. She has asked you to prepare for her a full briefing paper.

Task 1
To achieve a Pass grade:

Identify and summarise the major social implications of a significant growth in the volume of e-business.

Task 2
To achieve a Merit you must also:

Analyse the major social implications of a significant growth in the volume of e-business activity and identify sections of the national community likely to be both positively and adversely affected.

Task 3
To achieve a Distinction you must in addition:

Evaluate the social implications of significant growth in national e-business activity and consider the extent to which such growth requires careful management by national and local government.

Database systems

After completing Unit 7 you will be able to:

- investigate the *purpose and application* of databases in providing internet-based business solutions
- describe the general *structure* of databases and database systems and their features
- develop and model *entities and relationships* for a given business activity
- implement *a relational database application* for a given business activity.

Your understanding of this unit will be assessed by three internally marked assignments.

The World Wide Web in its entirety is in a sense one big 'database'. The problem is that on the web, the data that is carried is very randomly gathered. There is hardly any structure to it at all. Web pages are just files that link together, leading off into untold other avenues of even more 'data' held in all sorts of other files.

This unit deals with the *systems* and methods that help to create order in databases. You will first of all look at the general nature of a database, seeing its purpose within any online organisation and seeing how databases play a crucial role in delivering the sort of information that businesses and consumers need. From there, you will briefly survey some of the applications of databases.

You will look at the way databases can be structured and see the importance of proper planning in database design. You will become familiar with the terminology used in planning and designing an effective database through a worked example and finally you will illustrate a straightforward database implementation, for a specific business situation.

Databases are at the heart of e-business. The ordering of data and the creation of a meaningful body of useable data are crucial business functions in today's digital world.

7.1 Purpose and application

What is a database?

A database is a collection of data *items* held on a computer system. A data 'item' is an individual entry. So in an imaginary database holding all the details of your classmates, a data 'item' might be, *surname, first name,* or *street*. All the details relating to one classmate, (i.e. name, address, tel. no) is a **record**, the details of the whole class is known as a 'file'. All of the details about all of the class, held together are referred to collectively as 'data'. A database holds everything together and allows for new data entry, retrieval and amendment.

You have a basic database in the phonebook on your mobile phone. The Driver and Vehicle Licensing Agency (DVLA) in Swansea uses a (slightly bigger!) database, to hold all the data about every single vehicle registered in the UK and about every licensed driver.

The word 'information' means something other than data. Data is just a collection of individual details. But in business, data is of no real use unless intelligent sense can be made of it. Database systems (some examples are described in Section 7.2) help to do this by allowing the data to be presented to a user in a readable format. The DVLA database consists of a large bank of numerical codes representing car registration numbers and owner identity. The database system presents this to users in screen formats which allow *information* to be extracted.

The purpose of databases

We consider a database to be a collection of related data. To make use of this collection of data, businesses make use of a range of **database management systems (DBMS)**. These systems are the software that manages and controls access to the database (see Section 7.2). In what contexts are databases used?

Databases have become central to our existence, whether we are aware of it or not and virtually all of the illustrations of database uses that follow, represent some aspect of the work of an online e-business.

Supermarkets

We visit the supermarket and fill our basket or trolley, or we place orders online. When we go to the physical store, the assistant uses a bar code scanner to scan the bar code on each of our purchases. This is linked to a program that uses the bar code to find out the price of the product. The product is found in a 'product database'. This product database is accessed for a number of purposes within a business context, as shown in Figure 7.1.

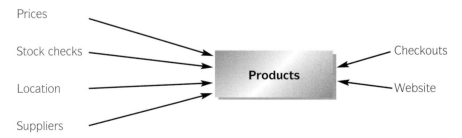

Figure 7.1 Uses for a product database

For each of the areas shown in Figure 7.1, different members of the supermarket staff, for different reasons and functions, will need to access the database.

Credit card purchases

Each time anyone makes a purchase using a credit card, a database is accessed that holds information about the purchases that have already been made using that card. A database application program looks at the number of the card, checks the price of the goods, checks purchases made so far, checks the card holder is within the limit, before details of this particular purchase are added to the database. The database is also accessed to check that the card is not on the list of those cards stolen or lost.

Booking a holiday

Each time a Travel Agent checks up on a holiday, they access a number of databases containing holiday and flight details. A database system has to make all necessary booking arrangements and make sure two people don't book the same holiday.

Web-based database applications

In a web context, the web browser acts as the 'interface' (the link) between the client/user and the database (or databases). This makes it possible for the database to function as the information source connecting e-businesses to multiple users, around – if necessary – the world.

The internet, as we know, is a 'client-server' model. Our individual PCs are 'clients' and web services are provided from web servers. This *two-tier* approach worked fine with 'clients' and 'database servers', until around the mid 1990s when the need for e-businesses to truly deliver masses of data, to potentially many thousands of end-users, proved too much for client-side computing resources.

In the two-tier model, shown in Figure 7.2, with growing web-based business needs, the client's computer resources could not keep up. Far greater CPU (central processing unit – the heart of a PC!) power, RAM (random access memory) and disk space (storage) were needed as well as considerable administration resources, to back up the processes.

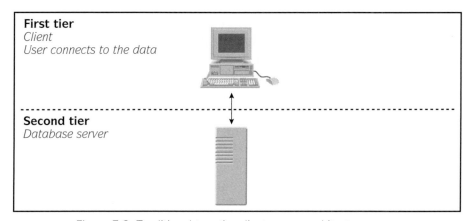

First tier
Client
User connects to the data

Second tier
Database server

Figure 7.2 Traditional two-tier client server architecture

Most of the websites doing e-commerce on the internet are based on database systems. If you visit Amazon.com to buy a book, the online store allows you to browse different categories such as American History or Classic Cars; alternatively you can browse by author. In whichever case, there is a database on the organisations web server that consists of book details, shipping, stock levels, availability. The 'book details' contains data on ISBN, author, price, sales history, publishers and reviews. The database – in line with the relational principle outlined before – allows cross referencing of categories so that if you buy say, a book about sports cars, Amazon's system can automatically offer you details of similar books you might like.

Remember the point made about personalisation in Unit 2? It is the database that allows Amazon, or any other web-based business, to identify who you are, from their database of previous purchases or registrations.

How do e-businesses successfully connect their databases to the web?

For modern e-businesses, a three-tier architecture is used. This architecture is shown in its basic form in Figure 7.3 below.

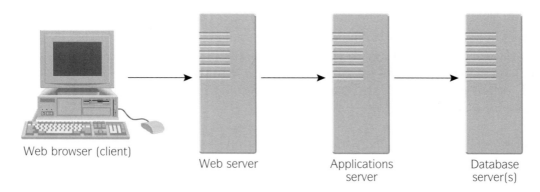

Web browser (client)   Web server   Applications   Database
                                       server   server(s)

Figure 7.3 Three-tier e-business server environment

A client runs a *web browser* on a desktop PC somewhere and accesses a website. This machine handles the display of the web pages and allows the visitor to interact with the content. A *web server* provides the internet services by managing http requests from clients and returning the web pages requested. Then an *applications server* handles the main business operations and content. What this is depends on the nature of the business, but could consist of many kinds of data or a range of images. Finally, one or more *database servers* offer data storage, data collection and data retrieval services. Again, depending on the nature of the e-business, there could be several content servers. These could include database servers for storage and access to catalogue content; for a information relating to a transactions and payments system, for storage of customer details, for maps, drawings, documents. See the *e-Business insight* panel relating to Leighton 4Projects for an illustration.

Dynamic website content

Think of a website that contains an online catalogue for selling clothes. The site contains a set of thumbnail images of all of the items in the catalogue. Selection of one of these renders a full sized image with supporting information about the item. The site allows for a 3D rendering of an item based upon what the customer specifies in terms of colour, size, fabric. The image can be modified based on light conditions, backdrop or occasion. Accessories can be selected to go with the item and there is a voiceover commentary, providing more details. While items are being viewed, a running total of any expenditure incurred is shown together with discounts. Purchases are made through a secure online transaction.

A database in this context is offering complex, advanced information based on customer selections. The website is *dynamically* customising what it presents to a user.

One of the most common means of doing this is by the use of '**cookies**'. A cookie is a piece of information that is sent to a client machine by a web server when it responds to a request for a web page. When the client next requests that web page, the browser also packages the cookie. The web server can now identify the user. Every time a user requests a web page, this happens and as a result a series of requests relating to a known user and the unique identifier contained in the cookie, allow the website to select customised information.

Outcome activity

e-Business database applications

You are the Assistant Training Manager for a local firm and you are devising an induction programme for new trainees. The firm has recently adopted an online strategy, incorporating an online product catalogue. It is felt that all staff should be fully aware of the background to the developing internet strategy. To your delight, you have been asked to contribute some straightforward guidance about databases.

Task 1
To achieve a Pass grade:

Describe the ways in which an online business might make use of databases that are accessed via the internet.

Task 2
To achieve a Merit you must also:

Investigate the information needs of a range of business processes that make use of internet based data applications.

Task 3
To achieve a Distinction you must in addition:

Analyse the impact on a selected e-business of the introduction of internet database applications and evaluate the contribution of such facilities to efficient business operation.

7.2 Database structure

Structure

Databases come in two types. Simple databases are called 'flat-file'. These are collections of data held within a single file. A very simple structuring of data is possible, such as a list of names and addresses, a list of student grades, or details of your CD collection. A spreadsheet can be used to build a flat file database with columns representing a field and a row a record. In old style systems in a business setting, different departments held different sets of data held in their own computer files; again, this led to lots of duplicated data.

Flat-file databases have limitations, especially in e-business situations. Imagine a business selling computer hardware and other electrical goods. If all data is held in a single file, the file needs to contain details of customers (name and address), products purchased, selling staff and the supplier of the product. The flat-file database would look like Figure 7.4 below.

ORDERSFILE

Order no.	Order date	Item no.	Description	Price	Supplier	Customer	Sales first name	Sales surname	Date employed
1	1/10/03	21145	CD player	179.00	Toshiba	Grimes	Carol	Martin	1/12/99
2	1/10/03	32178	Oven	399.00	Neff	Thomas	Steven	Brown	24/6/00
3	2/10/03	33344	Hairdryer	19.99	Philips	Burns	Sue	Rowley	11/11/01
4	2/10/03	32178	Oven	399.00	Neff	Akbar	Sue	Rowley	11/11/01
5	2/10/03	39281	Dishwasher	249.00	Bosch	Ferrell	Betty	Lloyd	18/3/91

Figure 7.4 Flat-file database

Just by looking at this small example, we can see that this flat-file database introduces some problems.

1 Imagine selling 250 ovens. The same data has to be entered 250 times, the price, Item no. and description. This is time consuming and wasteful.

2 Selling staff details have to be entered several times. This is wasting disk space.

3 Input errors are more likely. Every sale means new data input, so if Sue Rowley's name is mistakenly spelt Sue Rawley and she doesn't get her sales bonus, the business will have an upset member of staff.

4 Data has to be updated. If Carol Martin marries and becomes Carol Jarmolovic, every data item with her name in it has to be changed; her address changes, the same problem; her telephone number changes, and so on.

5 If data has to be modified, other problems occur. If Carol leaves to have a baby and her records are deleted, are all records of her sales also lost?

Flat-file databases are a useful method of data storage but they cause their own difficulties. One way of overcoming these problems is to introduce multiple tables. In the above example, the first step to improving things would be to have two tables, which we know as *files* – an EMPLOYEE table and an ORDER table.

Employee ID	Employee first name	Employee surname	Date employed
1	Carol	Martin	1/12/99
2	Steven	Brown	24/6/00
3	Sue	Rowley	11/11/01
4	Betty	Lloyd	18/3/91

Figure 7.5 File 1 – EMPLOYEE table

relationship

Order no.	Order date	Item no.	Description	Price	Supplier	Customer	Employee ID
1	1/10/03	21145	CD player	179.00	Toshiba	Grimes	1
2	1/10/03	32178	Oven	399.00	Neff	Thomas	2
3	2/10/03	33344	Hairdryer	19.99	Philips	Burns	3
4	2/10/03	32178	Oven	399.00	Neff	Akbar	3
5	2/10/03	39281	Dishwasher	249.00	Bosch	Ferrell	4

Figure 7.6 File 2 – ORDER table

field

record

In database terminology, each of the rows in the table, is known as a *record*, each of the columns is called a *field*.

By creating two separate databases in the form of simple tables, we have eliminated the problems mentioned earlier. We now don't need to keep repeating the input of staff data. All we need is to relate the employee ID to the sales.

This introduces an important principle about modern database systems. They enable *relationships* between data to be made. So in the above case, there is a relationship between the staff details and the orders that have been taken, because an Employee ID is included in the sales table. Now, there can be a relationship between the two sets of data. This is known as a **relational database**. Remember, data on its own has little meaning; however, link the two sets of information together and intelligent sense can be made of it. For instance, it is possible to see how many sales have been made by particular staff, or to calculate the value of the sales each has made. This kind of database uses logical relationships between data; the result is *information*.

For the purposes of an e-business, what is the significance of this? An e-business is a business that has digitised the way it operates and sells. The distinction between simple e-*commerce* and e-*business* is that the former refers just to the transaction process (i.e. selling online), whereas the latter refers *in addition* to all of the background processes that come together to support e-commerce. An e-business has not only got an online presence, it also employs a range of software applications in the background that feed into the website. Crucial among these will be a database. The whole of the enterprise will make use of the database and many of its systems will draw upon data from it.

Data dictionary

A **data dictionary** contains a list of all the tables in a database, the number of records in each table and the names and data types of each field. The data dictionary is an important part of any database management system (DBMS). It is an aspect of the database that is hidden from users. Its purpose is to allow the DBMS to know the definitions of all the data held in the database and through it, to access any data it needs.

Various frameworks for a data dictionary are possible. A simple data dictionary for a library database might be as shown in Figure 7.7.

BOOK table

Field	Data type	Other information
BookID	Text	Primary key
Dewey Number	Number	Max 10 characters
Title	Text	required
Author	Text	required
Publisher	Text	Field size 25
Date Published	Date/time	Short date format

BORROWER table

Field	Data type	Other information
BorrowerID	Text	Primary key
First name	Text	Field size 20
Surname	Text	Field size 20
AddressLine 1	Text	Field size 50
AddressLine 2	Text	Field size 50
County	Text	Field size 20
Postcode	Text	Field size 10
Date of birth	Date/time	Short date format

LOAN table

Field	Data type	Other information
LoanID	Text	Primary key
BorrowerID	Text	Foreign key
DateDue	Date/time	Required/Short date

Figure 7.7 Data dictionary for a library database

A data dictionary is information about the data within the database. The illustration given is at its simplest level. In large scale databases, data items can be referenced via numbering schemes or codes. Details about security settings can also be incorporated. When you are familiar with other elements of database design and construction that are offered later, come back to the data dictionary and you will be better able to see how it fits in to the overall database modelling process.

But what is a database management system?

Systems

Database management systems (DBMS)

Whereas a database stores all of the data, a database management system is a software application that interacts with users (clients) on the one hand and the database itself on the other. There are many types of DBMS. Some, such as Microsoft Access, are small scale and designed for desktop (PC based) applications. Others are huge systems that run on large powerful machines. Typical examples of the latter are:

- Computerised library systems
- Flight reservation systems
- Automatic teller machines.
- Parts inventory systems.

Because there are many variations in DBMS, what follows is a generalisation. However, a typical large scale DBMS will offer the following facilities:

- Data can be defined. Users can specify data types, structures and the constraints on accessing the database. These things are done through a Data Definition Language (DDL).
- Users can insert, delete, update or retrieve data from the database, usually through a Data Manipulation Language (DML). Because there is a central store for all data and data descriptions, the DML can offer a general enquiry facility to utilise the data; this is known as a query language. The most common query language is known as **Structured Query Language** or **SQL** (pronounced 'Sea-Quel').
- The DBMS provides for *controlled* access to the database, possibly offering:
- A security system, preventing unauthorised access
- An integrity system, maintaining consistency of stored data
- A concurrency control system, allowing shared access to the database
- A recovery control system, restoring the database to a previous state following hardware or software failure
- A user accessible catalogue, containing descriptions of all of the data in the database.

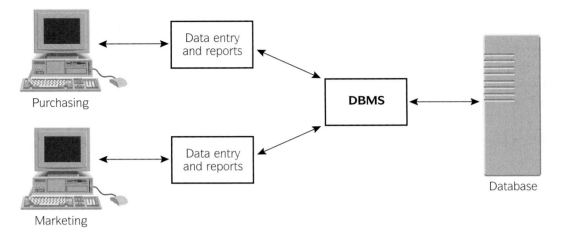

Figure 7.8 Typical business context for a database management system (DBMS)

In Figure 7.8 above, the database is accessed by various users via the DBMS. The purchasing staff need particular reports from the database, based upon specific data; the marketing people require other specific reports from the database. Each functional area within the business inputs and maintains data, based upon the design of the DBMS and the needs of the business. Each receives reports according to their function.

It will help to look at the Microsoft database application Access, a piece of software that makes database creation and use available to just about every business manager. Microsoft Access is an 'application development' program. By making use of Access, anyone can become familiar with key database concepts. What follows is NOT intended as a detailed walkthrough Microsoft Access. However, it should allow you at least to get started.

Features of Microsoft Access

Microsoft Access is a relational database management system which enables users (such as you) to *create* and *use* databases on a PC. All of the elements of a database are stored as one file on disk. This file must have a conventional filename in accordance with Windows naming standards and have the Windows file extension .MDB.

Creating a database

Microsoft Access allows a user to create the four basic components that give structure to a database, these are:

- tables
- forms
- queries
- reports.

In order to show the purposes of each of these, we will follow the creation of a basic database of library borrowers, loans and books. We want to be able to keep track of books in a library and who has them out on loan. A borrower can take out more than one book at a time.

The first thing we need to consider is what will our database hold data about? In this case we first of all have two obvious things, BOOK and BORROWER. In database terms, these are called **entities**. Each entity will be represented by a table in our database.

Step 1

Write down a list of the information that the database will need to keep about a book and its borrowers. These, remember, are called fields (see earlier examples).

You should have identified that the BOOK table could have the following fields:

BookID (a unique identifying code or **primary key**)
Dewey Number
Title
Author
Publisher
Date Published

In database standard notation, (table name upper case, primary key underlined) this is written down as:

BOOK (BookID, DeweyNumber, Title, Author, Publisher DatePublished,)

The BORROWER table could have the following fields:

BorrowerID (a unique identifier – or primary key)
Surname
Firstname
Title
Address Line 1
Address Line 2
County
Postcode
Date of Birth

Written down as...

BORROWER (BorrowerID, Surname,Firstname,Title,AddressLine1, AddressLine 2, County, Postcode, Date of Birth

These tables contain some useful data, probably other fields could be added to hold even more details. However, on their own they do not yet offer us the data we need, which is data about who has which books out on loan. How can we create this information? We have options here.

Choice 1 – we could add more fields to the BORROWER table, showing which books a borrower has out.

Problem – how many fields do we set aside? A borrower may borrow up to six books, he or she may borrow none. How much space will be wasted? Where will we query the database because so many fields might be empty?

Choice 2 – on the BOOK table, we add fields to show whether the book is out, who has it and when it is due back.

Problem – it's better than choice 1, but a library will have hundreds of books, lots of records will need to be searched in a query.

Choice 3 – Create a new table to hold the details of all books out on loan.

The solution – The new table needs only three fields:

- BookID (called a **foreign key** because it is also the primary key of the BOOK table)

- BorrowerID (also a foreign key because it is the primary key of another table)

- DateDue.

The table will be structured as follows:

> LOAN (BookID, BorrowerID, DateDue

Step 2

Create the tables in Microsoft Access (2000)

This is the component of Access that lets you create somewhere to store data.

- Choose file from the menu bar

- Choose **Blank Database** from the drop down menu on the right

- In the File New Database dialogue box, create a Library folder (to keep the database) and give the database a name

- Click create, to open up the table dialogue box

- Select **Create table** In Design View (see Figure 7.9).

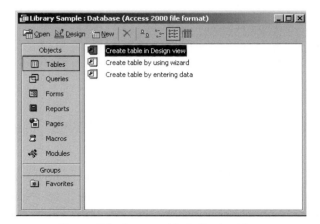

Figure 7.9 Create table in Design View

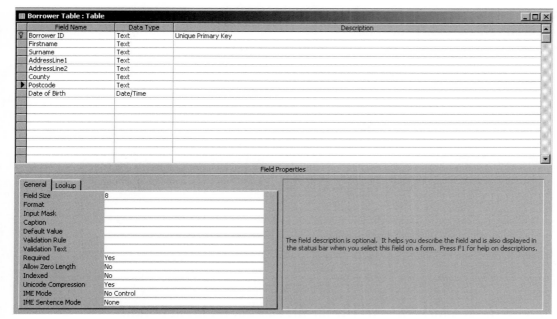

Figure 7.10 Table creation in Design View

Figure 7.10 shows the Table creation window. In here, enter the list of fields you have previously decided should be contained in your database. Figure 7.10, illustrating the BORROWER table, shows that the left hand column takes the Field Names. Each field name must be a particular *data type*. This is because Access needs to know what kind of data is to be entered in that field. For example, you want to store the date of birth of the borrower, (there may be organisational rules relating to this) by specifying a particular data type, Access can check the data entry is a date, rather than just text. Each field allows a choice of data types (as shown in the drop down menu shown here).

Figure 7.11 Drop-down menu of data types

Some of the *data types* available are:

Text – can contain any character on a normal keyboard. Thus you can use text for car registrations or postcodes.

Memo – the memo field can be used for storing unstructured information such as the description of a book.

Number – can contain only digits, plus or minus signs, a decimal point.

Date/Time – several different date or time formats can be selected.

Currency – monetary values in one of several formats.

Yes/No – here you can choose either yes or no.

AutoNumber – Access automatically enters a unique number for each record added to a table.

> **Over to you**   Open Microsoft Access.
>
> Create the database for the Library System as described above.
>
> Create three tables using Design View. BORROWER, BOOK and LOAN
>
> Before you start, discuss and note the various data types you need within each field of the three tables.

Step 3

Entering data into the library database

A database obviously needs data. Data is entered into the tables by using one of two methods; firstly a *datasheet* view can be used. The Datasheet view is available from the View drop down menu. The example for the BORROWER table is shown in Figure 7.12.

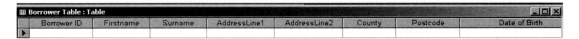

Figure 7.12 Datasheet View for the BORROWER table

The Datasheet view is not an especially user-friendly way of entering data. An alternative method is to use a *form* (see Figure 7.13).

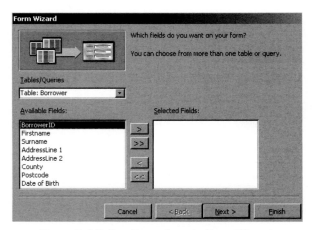

Figure 7.13 Creating a form in Form Wizard

The Form Wizard is activated by clicking on the Forms tab on the left panel of the Table design window. As you can see, the wizard has automatically offered a list of the data fields from the BORROWER table.

Assuming we need all of the fields we have designed into our BORROWER table, we will simply select all of them.

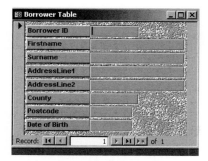

Figure 7.14 The borrower form

By selecting all of the fields according to our initial design and following the wizard's instructions and choosing the 'stone' look (a choice of form styles offered by Access), we get the form shown in Figure 7.14.

Why Forms?

A form is an optional choice. However, if you consider you are designing a database application for other people to use, then forms have advantages.

- They are more attractive to use.
- Fields can be placed in a convenient way for data entry.
- Some fields, say 'County' in above case, could be given a default value because the library is unlikely to move from where it is.
- Data validation can be done automatically, e.g. is the date in the correct format?
- Forms can contain fields from different tables.
- Several data entry forms can be created for different purposes, each just showing the relevant fields from the tables.

Step 4

Using a query.

If you have completed the activity, you will have already created the BOOK table according to the field choices made earlier (if not, do it now). Your probable design view is shown below.

Figure 7.15 BOOK table data types in Design View

Now, create the LOAN table, as follows...

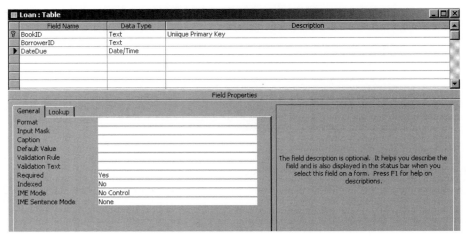

Figure 7.16 LOAN table data types in Design View

Now it's time to make use of one of the most powerful tools in a relational database, the **query**. Remember the point that was made earlier; on their own data tables mean little. However, when the data is intelligently combined, data becomes real *information.*

In our example here, a query can combine the data contained in the three tables, BORROWER, BOOK and LOAN. In the case of a library, obviously it helps to know if someone has exceeded the loan date.

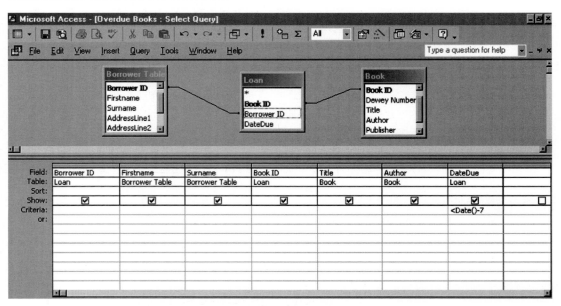

Figure 7.17 Overdue books query

The Query window shown in Figure 7.17 is split into two halves. The top half contains three objects representing the three tables of our library database. In the query we have created, we want to look at information based upon data from all three tables. The bottom half of the window contains a grid where you (among other things) tell Access which fields to include and in which order.

In this case, we are querying whether the DateDue has been exceeded.

How to create a Query

In the database window, select **Queries**. Select **Create Query in Design View** (Access 2000) and then **New**.

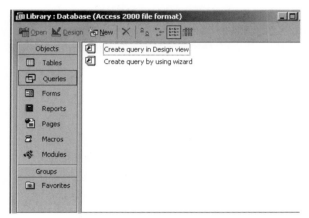

Figure 7.18 Creating a query

In the resulting New Query box, double click **Design View**, to bring up the following Show Table Dialogue Box.

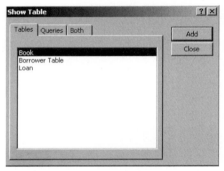

Figure 7.19 Show Table dialogue box

In our Library database, we have three tables as shown. Click on **Add** for each table, then close. The Query window shown at Figure 7.17 appears. The three tables from which we are querying data appear in the top section.

We now want to add the fields we need in the query, we will include details of the borrower, the book and the loan DateDue. We can include the fields in a number of ways:

- Drag and drop from the table into the field cell in the query

- Double-click the field name in the table object

- Click the down arrow in the field cell to display a list of all the field names to select from.

Selecting the criteria

What is the nature of our query? What do we want to know from the data we have in our database? These are the criteria for our query. There are several kinds of query. We could look for a range of values within data, we could check for certain dates, we could set 'and' or 'or' values. In our example we are looking for loans that have gone past the DateDue. So, what we have done is place an 'expression' in the criteria cell of the DateDue field.

An expression tells the table to work something out. In this case, we want the system to tell us if someone has a book which is 7 days beyond the DateDue. The expression is <Date()-7. This means in effect... OK, it is today, give us the name of anyone having a book where the DateDue was more than 7 days ago.

Reports

When we want to extract or retrieve information from the database query, we can ask for *reports*. Once again the database window allows the developer to use a report wizard. Figure 7.20 shows the opening window of the report wizard, allowing selection of the field to be included within the report. The report can then be customised to suit the style preferred.

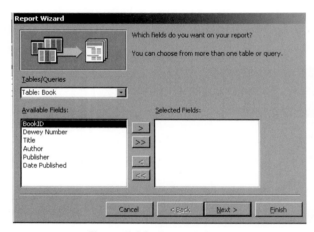

Figure 7.20 Report Wizard

Having selected the seven fields required in our report on overdue loans, we see the resulting report (Figure 7.21).

Overdue Loans

Surname	Firstname	Book ID	Title	Author	Borrower ID	Date Due

Figure 7.21 Overdue loans report

Based upon our initial query, drawing on data from our database containing the three tables BORROWER, BOOK and LOAN, we have been able to get a report giving us the information that borrowers Louise Duke and Sunil Patel have books 1001 and 1003 out on overdue loan. This small scale, desktop application development package, lets you create a usable database that can be of use in many business contexts; storage, presentation, retrieval and reporting all being made possible with just a little practice.

Outcome activity

The structure and design of databases

You are preparing Induction materials for people who will be working within an e-business context; many of the processes they will relate to involve aspects of the company database. Using Microsoft Access as an illustration, you are asked to do the following:

Task 1

For Pass grade award…

Describe the structure of databases using data types, fields, records, tables, queries, forms and reports.

Task 2

For Merit grade, work must also…

Select data types, fields, records, table queries, forms and reports that are appropriate to a range of business situations.

Task 3

For Distinction grade, work must also…

Justify the selection of database elements with reference to their features.

7.3 Database entities and relationships

Entities and relationships

To create a useful database requires a little planning. We are trying to create something that is a model of what really happens in data terms within an organisational environment. This is what was done in the library example.

What is happening in a real library? *Books* are being *borrowed*. Our database straight away therefore needed at least two things within it, to *represent* these things. These are called entities and they usually require tables to be created for them, as in our case.

Over to you Consider the following real world contexts. In each case, write down on paper the 'entities' you can identify.

1. Guest house renting rooms
2. Taxi firm
3. Cricket club
4. Mail order (B2C) firm selling range of domestic products
5. Used car sales business.

Let's take two of the above examples to illustrate what is meant by entities and relationships in database terms. What we are doing is called 'data modelling' because we are trying to reflect in terms of the data what happens in the real world.

In the guest house scenario, two things should immediately be obvious; firstly there are *rooms* and (hopefully) *guests*. The guest house exists to *book* these rooms out, for rent. This gives us three entities (see Figure 7.22).

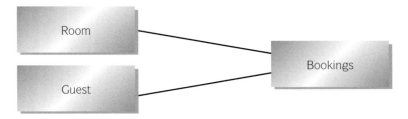

Figure 7.22 Guest house entity relationship model

Notice that there is no natural relationship between the room and a guest, until a booking is made. Entities are drawn as shown, as a box with a single line being used to show a direct and permanent relationship. Rooms have bookings and guests make bookings. In this case, the relationships shown are just straightforward, they are *One* to *One*, a room has a booking; a guest makes a booking; each booking relates to both a room and a guest. A database will have a permanent record of each individual booking. But, as we shall see later, perhaps we need to alter this.

However, in many cases there is a need to identify the specific kinds of relationship between entities.

Different types of relationship

These are drawn in an *entity-relationship diagram (ERD)*.

In some cases, relationships are *One* to *Many*. In the case of the cricket club, this kind of relationship could exist between a team and players. This is drawn as shown in Figure 7.23.

Figure 7.23 Entity-relationship diagram – one to many

The 2nd Eleven team has many players, a player belongs to only one team.

In other cases, relationships are *Many* to *Many* (see Figure 7.24).

Figure 7.24 Entity-relationship diagram – many to many

This relationship shows that each student can belong to many clubs and that each club has many students as members.

Now back to the guest house scenario. On reflection, each guest may make many bookings and over a period of time, each room can be booked on many occasions. This means that the entity relationship diagram for the guest house database needs to be changed.

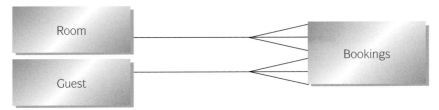

Figure 7.25 Modified entity relationship diagram for a guest house

In entity relationship modelling, it is also possible to *name* the relationship, in order to show the nature of it. For example, entity x could *own* entity y, or entity x *has* entity y. The names describing the relationship would simply be added above the linking line in a diagram.

Attributes

Each entity possesses certain *attributes*. These are characteristics or properties. Each room in the guest house for example has a number, a number of beds, a toilet, shower or bathroom; each guest has a name, address, tel. no and each booking a date. In Section 7.2 we saw how attributes are listed after the entity (table) name.

Each entity represents a table within a database and each attribute is a data item that fits within it. You may be wondering why bother with these different terms, when they are talking about the same thing? The way to think about it this; when you are *modelling* a database, the terms *entity* and *attribute* are used; when *implementing* a database, entities are located in *tables* and attributes are shown in *fields*. Tables representing entities are known as *base tables*. They are a permanent part of a database. Between them, the base tables should contain all the information needed by a system.

In the guest house situation, the entities have been shown as Room, Guest and Booking. Each room has attributes that you – as database designer – have to identify. These could be...
ROOM (Roomnumber, Roomtype, RoomRate).

For Guest, you could have...
GUEST (Forename, Surname. Title, addressline1,addressline2).

and, for Bookings ...
BOOKING (Datearrival; Nonights; DepositPaid; BalancePaid).

Primary keys

Each table has to have one field that *uniquely identifies* each record in the table. Often, the primary key stands out as obvious, for example, where there is a product number in a catalogue table, or a specific order number in a purchases table. If no obvious primary key stands out, then one must be created. In a table definition, at the modelling stage, the primary key must be <u>underlined</u>.

For the guest house...

ROOM (<u>Roomnumber</u>, Roomtype, Roomrate)

GUEST (<u>GuestID,</u> Forename, Surname, Title, addressline1, addressline 2)

BOOKING (<u>Bookingreference</u>, Datearrival, Nonights, Depositpaid, Balancepaid)

The Primary key tends to be placed at the start of the list of attributes but it can go anywhere.

Foreign keys

In a database that contains several tables, each representing an entity within the business, we know that the data must be related to other data to make sensible use of it. This is what relational databases are. But how do two tables relate to each other? We have already experienced this in our brief tour of Microsoft Access and the case of the library. A foreign key is a primary key in one table, that is added to another table, so that the two can relate with each other. Look back at the library example and you will see that the BOOK table was linked to the BORROWER table by adding a foreign key into the LOAN table. The foreign key was BorrowerID and this meant that LOAN was able to relate to BOOK on the one hand, and BORROWER on the other.

Business processes

What is meant by business *processes?* The whole purpose of computer-based information systems is to support key business processes. What these are depends upon what the business actually does. There is no generic description, other than to say that data is stored, exchanged and information retrieved. Take the following business contexts:

1 **Fish and chip shop**. The processes might be... Ordering (fish, potatoes, burgers, confectionery, vinegar, salt, fat), storing, selling, cooking, recording (sales, deliveries etc.)

2 **Newsagents**. Ordering (newspapers, magazines, confectionery, cigarettes, beers, wines, spirits), recording deliveries, customer records, invoicing.

3 **Garage**. Maintain customer records and service records, order parts, invoicing.

4 **Manufacturing organisation**. Staff records, stock records, equipment records, suppliers, customer relations, invoicing; health and safety; quality system.

5 **Service organisation**. Customer records, relate to customers, deliver service.

All businesses employ some process at an *operational* level, these are things that the business does on a day to day basis, so that its basic objectives can be achieved. At another level, other *strategic* processes support the general position of the business. These depend upon the size and status of a firm and could include things like marketing; developing a strategy; design, research.

The point is that processes need to be effectively managed. To manage anything requires information. This is the significance of the database in a business of today.

Database normalisation

Tables in a relational database need to be looked at carefully to cut down unnecessary data. If the same data appears several times in different tables then we have a problem known as 'data redundancy'. To avoid this, a systematic procedure called **normalisation** is employed. The idea is that a large relational database will operate much more efficiently in dealing with queries, once data has been normalised.

Normalisation involves checking the tables in a database against three rules; these are known as:

1   First normal form (1NF)

2   Second normal form (2NF)

3   Third normal form (3NF).

First normal form (1NF). This means that no table contains *repeating* attributes (i.e. fields). If there is a repeating attribute, then you must return to the entity-relationship diagram and create a new entity.

Second normal form (2NF). A table that is in second normal form (as well as being in first normal form), has no columns in it that are dependent on only part of the primary key. This mouthful just means do not include attributes in tables that are not needed.

Third normal form (3NF). A table is in third normal form if it contains no 'non-key dependencies'. Non-key fields are those that could not act as Primary keys; i.e. they contain data only. In a table definition, if two or more non-key fields are dependent on each other, then a new entity is probably required.

In the guest house scenario earlier, a ROOM table could contain roomnumber, roomtype and roomrate. Roomtype and roomrate are informational fields, neither could act as the primary key (i.e. *uniquely* identify a field) so they are both non-keys. They are also dependent upon each other, because all roomtypes are charged at the same roomrate. So, imagine these in a table of data about the rooms and you have a certain roomtype listing the same roomrate, duplicated several times. Refining the table structure to 3NF results in a new entity – Roomrate, with roomtype as the primary key.

Benefits of normalisation

A database which has been put into 3NF is likely to be more efficient than one which is not normalised. Each piece of data is entered and stored only once; data can be updated, amended or deleted easily; interrogation of the database will be quicker and memory space will be saved because redundant data is taken out.

Modelling techniques

The use of entity-relationship diagrams (ERD) is a 'top down' approach whereas normalisation is a 'bottom up' approach. Best results will be obtained if you use both of these modelling techniques together (integrated) to consider all the details of the database you are designing.

Testing a system

Testing is best carried out according to a well-defined plan. In database design, it is likely that important business systems are being affected. People's job roles are likely to feed into the processes and systems that surround the database. It is assumed therefore, that the design process has had significant input from managers or staff affected by the new information system.

Once a database system is past the conceptual design stage, various kinds of testing would begin. Firstly, component by component, various aspects of the system will be tested by the designer. Secondly, tests will be done to ensure that the new system integrates well with other aspects of the system. Thirdly, users will be asked to test the system to see that – within the real work environment – the system works using real data.

A test plan

Drawing up a test plan should be done thoughtfully and systematically. You must show that you have thought about how the system *should* operate, what its functions are to be and what potential faults there could be. Figure 7.26 shows a possible framework.

Test no.	Test data	Aim	Expected outcome	Comment
1	Enter 'New GuestID' into guest table.	Test 'Add new guest' function	New GuestID is added to database	
2	Enter 'GuestID xxy'	Testing invalid format	Incorrect format message 'Only GuestID yyx'	
3	Use incorrect password 'ABC'	Test password	'Not a valid password' message	

Figure 7.26 Framework for a test plan

All important parts of your new database system should be tested and where feasible, comments and verification of your testing should be added in the right hand column.

Outcome activity

Creating a model database

Employed in Human Resources, you have been asked to create a working database that is to be used for demonstration to a group of new staff. You can use any business processes you feel are appropriate.

Task 1

To achieve a Pass grade:

Develop an entity-relationship model for the processes you choose to illustrate and normalise the data structure to third normal form.

Build tables that conform to 3NF structure and build a query that can retrieve data from at least three tables.

Task 2

To achieve a Merit you must also:

Accurately identify entities, attributes, primary and foreign keys and draw an entity-relationship diagram that conforms to your 3NF structure.

Provide functions for the input, retrieval and presentation of relevant data.

Task 3

To achieve a Distinction you must in addition:

Prepare supporting training materials in which you:

Compare and contrast the two analysis techniques of normalisation and entity-relationship modelling.

Write an accurate data dictionary.

Devise and document an appropriate test plan.

After completing Unit 13 you will be able to:

1   describe the features of the *e-business planning process*

2   identify the *internal planning issues* to be considered

3   identify the *external planning issues* to be considered

4   *describe the resources* required to support the e-business planning process

5   draft a structured e-business plan.

> **Your understanding of this unit will be assessed by an internally marked assignment**.

Business planning is an ongoing process that applies to the management of every business enterprise; all businesses have to consider their strategic position and look ahead to where they want to be in the future. This unit will take you through the specific process of planning to do e-business. In the e-business field, planning processes can take place in one of two broad contexts:

○ within an existing business

○ from a **startup** position as a completely new enterprise.

An e-business plan created from within an *existing* business is only marginally different from a startup plan. Whereas a startup plan is a systematic statement designed to convince potential lenders or investors that profit can be made from a *new* business; a re-orientation strategy for an existing business tends to put all of the issues in an organisational and operational context. The business idea is already proven, what is required are justifications about why do e-business; how it will be done; what the implications will be, what is the new business mission?

The unit will look at what planning 'processes' are involved in these contexts. What are the intentions behind a plan to do e-business? What is the redefined business mission and goal? The perspectives of stakeholders will be examined in the case of an existing business and some consideration will be given to practical aspects of implementing an e-business strategy. However, you are NOT required to implement your plan.

The unit is designed in such a way that purely *descriptive* coverage of the planning processes and the various internal and external issues a business must face up to, will attract a Pass grade. However, to attain the higher grades you must actually *draft your own e-business plan*. One way of approaching this is to use an existing SME (small to medium sized enterprise, between 50 and 250 staff). By using an existing enterprise you may be able to acquire useful organisational data that will help you get started.

The unit is structured in such a way that you should be able to naturally move toward producing a good, sensible plan. However, you will not be able to produce a useful plan unless you know how one is structured. Therefore the preliminary section, Section 13.1, will give you a basic template you can use. Then the section (Section 13.2) on the general processes of planning will point out several of the issues that you must deal with in preparing to complete your plan. This will help you to devise your approach. Sections 13.3 and 13.4 will each look in turn at the internal and external issues any business must face up to. Many of these will help you to add detail into your plan and offer various analytical techniques that should be of help. Finally, Section 13.5 deals with resource implications, an important issue for any business considering an e-business strategy.

13.1 The framework for an e-business plan

What is a business plan?

A simple way to think of a business plan is to think of the route you take between your home and your school or college. Your home represents the business *as it is now* and your school or college represents the business *as you want it to be*. The roads, paths, crossings, alleys and directions you follow, represent the plan. A business plan, therefore, is a route map showing everyone where you, as a business, want to be and how you intend to get there.

In real terms a business plan is a written document that identifies a firm's goals and outlines how they will be achieved. In many cases, a business plan is produced by entrepreneurs who are looking to establish a new business. Such a plan is trying to attract partner investors or lenders to raise capital. Many of the banks try to assist new entrepreneurs by offering business plan templates; see for example www.barclays.co.uk , and follow the links to 'writing a business plan'.

In the developing e-business world, as we have discussed, many long established businesses are looking to move some aspect of their existing business online. This still calls for the creation of a new plan, designed to outline the new direction the business is going. The audience for such a plan may be financial backers such as banks or new investors. The plan therefore needs to be convincing both in terms of its content and its presentation. The plan also needs to show that you, as a major thinker and actor in the planning process, have considered the needs of all those who are affected by this change of direction.

Whatever the context, a business plan is likely to be carefully sectioned along the lines shown below.

The format of an e-business plan

The plan should be professionally presented with a *front cover* specifying the business name and address.

Inside, the plan should open with a brief 'executive summary' that concisely summarises the business idea and objectives that you will include in the sections suggested below. This is one of the most important parts of the plan. It will be the first part that is looked at and if it is not convincing, it will be the only thing that is read. Keep it clear and concise, but be sure to include some remarks about how you intend to make your 'e' business a success. For example, if your plan is for an e-commerce website, say how you intend to generate traffic and keep customers wanting to come back. In other words, what will be your Internet Value Proposition (see Unit 2). The executive summary should be no more than two sides of A4 in length.

The main body of your plan should be clearly sectioned under the following headings.

1 Business description and mission
2 Management of the business
3 Competition
4 The market and customers
5 Products and services
6 Marketing and sales
7 Operational plans
8 Financial plans and projections
9 Action plan
10 Track and evaluation

1 Business description and mission

The mission statement expresses the philosophy, the goals and the ideals held for a business. It may need to be reviewed as the plan unfolds.

The *description* of the business should be punchy and attention grabbing. It can include the following:

- Staff and management structure.
- Brief outline of products and services.
- Summary of the market being served.
- The website URL and outline of content.
- Company history summarised.
- Details of how the business will offer its unique IVP.

2 Management of the business

People who may financially back a business are very interested in the quality of the management and their ability to lead the business to success. Therefore this is an important section. Try to give good details in response to the following questions:

- Who are the managers? What are their responsibilities?
- What background skills/qualifications do they have that will help the business achieve its goals?
- How do the management team complement each other?
- What are the staffing requirements of the business? (including training)

- How does the organisational chart look?
- What, if any, outside advisors would be used.

3 Competition

An awareness of the industry a firm is in, or plans to be in, is a key indicator of realism and good foresight. The digital world is growing rapidly and there is lots of competition. It is wise to analyse the competition, even if they are not yet online (see Unit 2).

Research should include some examples of competitor promotional materials, or anything else that can be found about them. (if they are online this is easy!) When giving details about the competition, answering the following questions in as much detail as possible will be impressive.

- Name at least 3 direct competitors.
- Detail a further 3 indirect and potential competitors.
- Summarise what you have found about their business operations and promotional work.
- What do you consider to be their strengths and weaknesses.
- How does their product/service or web offering, differ from what your business intends to do?
- Once these things have been detailed, then go on to point out the ways in which your business will compete. Do this by trying to respond to the following questions:
- What do you have, or will have, that your customers don't?
- What will make customers come to you rather than competitors?

4 The market and customers

This section is designed to show that you understand who your customers will be and how your business will serve them. Your business must be 'market focused'. An e-business strategy will 'target' a market (described in Unit 2). However, do not define the market too narrowly, there must be a substantial base of customers to make the business profitable.

- Describe the customers and *target market*.
  - In internet terms a *potential* market for a website sales channel could be anyone, anywhere in the world, who had a credit card. Is this realistic?
  - An *addressable* market is a group of people (B2C) or firms (B2B) who are likely to have an interest in what the business offers.
  - A *target* market is a group within the addressable market who are more likely to buy from the website, because you know they share characteristics that will favour your product or service.
- Say how the customers currently communicate/make contact with the business. Do they telephone? Visit? Fax? E-mail? Walk in?
- How will products be 'moved' to the customers? What about returns?
- What are the growth prospects for this market?

Primary and secondary market research

To define and understand a target market often requires some primary research. Specific demographic characteristics (age, sex, income, education) could be given; how many individuals are in the market? What proportion uses the internet? How many buy online? here are several online services offering good statistical analyses of internet trends, although you may find that full access is restricted to registered users. You could nevertheless try:

www.Jup.com
www.CyberAtlas.com
www.emarketer.com
www.nua.ie/surveys/

For the purposes of your assignment, you need to attempt to show that you can identify a market and analyse its characteristics and trends. The data is available.

5 Products and services

Assuming the e-business plan refers to an e-commerce website, you need to outline persuasively how your site will attract visitors, make them an attractive offer and retain them. Try to respond to the following questions in completing this section:

- Describe the products/services in a way that is clear and easy to understand.

- How will customers benefit from your service/product?

- Describe in outline what a customer/visitor to your site will experience when they visit. Take the reader concisely through the Home page, navigation, customer service strategy, help & advice pages, delivery and transaction processes.

6 Marketing and sales

This section builds on what you said in section 4. What will be the methods you use to promote either your new e-business or the new 'e' aspect of an existing business? Offline promotion of a website URL can be effective (Diy.com promote their URL on all their leaflets and livery). Try to deal with some of the following issues:

- How will you address your target market? What will you do to attract them?

- What image are you aiming to project?

- What will be your pricing strategy?

- What features of your product/services are tailored to meet the needs of the target group?

7 Operational plans

It is necessary to show that you have thought not just about whether the business will work, but how it will work. Consider the case of Joe's Brew given earlier (in Unit 5, Section 5.2) it is very relevant to this. A business website may generate interest in your products/services but how will the business operate to deliver what it promises? The following things need to be looked into:

- Who will manage or update the website content?

- How will product or service offerings be fulfilled?

- What internal operations will be critical to business success? E.g.

  - E-mail

  - Technical support

  - Information systems

  - Advertising

  - Public relations

  - Human resources policies.

  - Security systems.

  - Internet service provision

  - Application service provision.

8 Financial plans and projections

A financial projection needs to be open and honest. Any over-exaggeration of financial potential will be seen. Any risks should be outlined clearly and honestly. This section should include as much of the following as possible:

- Income forecast – a profit and loss statement.

- Balance sheet – total assets, total liabilities, total owners equity.

- Monthly cash flow projection.

- Budget statements for personnel, advertising, public relations.

9 Action plan

You could present this in the form of a timeline, or a Gantt chart. Give the reader some sort of idea of the timescale for your e-business plan.

10 Track and evaluation

Consider:

- In what ways will you monitor and evaluate the success or progress of the plan?

- How will you measure the objectives you have set?

- How will you make adjustments if things go wrong?

Other information

Any additional charts, diagrams, or financial statements could be attached to your plan as Appendices. They should be clearly labelled and referred to in the main body of your plan.

13.2 The e-business planning process

This unit looks at some of the practicalities of e-business planning. Beginning with the basic processes of planning, to consideration of which stakeholders in the business will be affected, how implementation might take place and ending with an overview of previous failures in the dot.com world.

Processes of planning

Defining the mission

The process of either redefining a business, or indeed starting a business from scratch, can begin from an identification of a business mission. In most cases, this is enshrined within a **mission statement**. A mission statement declares what the business is trying to be, why it exists, who it serves and what it hopes to achieve in the future. Here are a couple of examples of mission statements.

J Sainsbury
Our mission is to serve customers the best quality and choice to meet their everyday shopping needs.

McDonalds
"McDonalds vision is to be the worlds best quick service restaurant experience. Being the best means providing outstanding quality, service, cleanliness, and value, so that we make every customer in every restaurant smile" (quoted on bized.ac.uk/compfact/mcdonalds/mc9.htm)

When a business is adopting a new online strategy, it is an opportune moment to look again at its mission. What does it hope to be in the digital world? How can its purpose and its goals be captured in one, clear, concise and motivational statement? A new mission should be based on what the business has historically been, it should try both to build on (hopefully) an existing sound reputation and yet capture the essence of its new direction.

One way of approaching the new mission statement is to draft a new version at the outset of creating the e-business plan. Then, once the plan is complete, revisit the draft and reconsider whether the statement fully captures the new target market and whether it fully embraces the 'value proposition' that the new e-business is seeking to offer to the market.

Developing the business on the internet

How can an e-business exploit the opportunities of the internet? At first glance it appears obvious that the World Wide Web offers global coverage and entry into any number of markets. It is easy to get carried away by thinking that this is a *guarantee* of vast profits. However there are strategic considerations to do with where costs have to be incurred in the business, where and when revenue can be expected. Some markets can safely be neglected in favour of those where your target groups are likely to be. Alternatively, efforts can be made in areas where you see a growth potential.

Take the example of a shoe manufacturer who spots a niche market for outsize (i.e. very big!) shoes. He/she may decide to *concentrate* manufacturing efforts, promotional efforts, website design, e-business processes, by sacrificing efforts elsewhere; these are all focused on exploiting the very large market for outsize footwear that undoubtedly exists worldwide. This opportunity does not exist in the local high street, only on the global web. However, there are costs involved with this strategy and these costs and opportunities have to be balanced and considered. Costs can be either monetary costs, the costs of new equipment for example; or they can be opportunity costs. These are those things that have to be sacrificed in order to achieve an alternative goal.

Influential stakeholder objectives

When a business has established itself and is operating profitably, there are a number of groups and individuals who could be described as 'stakeholders' in the business. These are people who have a 'stake' or an interest in how well or poorly it performs. Figure 13.1 shows the possible range of stakeholders that are possible in a business activity.

Figure 13.1 Business stakeholders

Some of the stakeholders are internal, some are external.

Internal stakeholders

Owners

In business terms, owners can either be sole traders who take all decisions and all profits; they can be private partners who share in decisions and risks together; they can be shareholders as members of a Limited Company of one sort or another. Owners have obviously got a major stake in what a business does. Often the role of owners can be identified from the size of the business. In medium to large enterprises it is probable that a Limited Company exists; this will be managed by Directors who will also be shareholders in the firm.

The likely response of owners to an e-business strategy will depend upon how convinced they are that such a direction will lead to profitability. In an SME context, owners are likely to remain close to strategic decision making. These matters will have been referred to them for consideration. They will have been a party to the planning process. It is hardly conceivable that a director/owner will agree to an e-business re-orientation that they do not consider feasible.

Managers

In larger firms, management is likely to be separated from ownership. However, managers are answerable to shareholders and will be held to account if major decisions go wrong. Managers are appointed to take on roles to do with planning and control. Most typically, managers in SMEs are responsible for operational (i.e. day to day running) matters.

In embarking upon an e-business strategy, a manager must accept new responsibilities, new pressures and perhaps be required to acquire new skills. He/she may well be required to meet with and work with, people who have unfamiliar skills and qualifications. For example, web designers, software analysts, systems analysts, technicians. It is in the interests of managers that they adapt to a new strategic 'e' direction. Their jobs are on the line if they fail to do so. How they respond will depend upon their individual level of involvement. It is human nature to be wary of change. Most managers will willingly adopt an e-business approach, particularly if they see an opportunity to be identified with success.

Employees

Employees sign contracts of employment agreeing to follow all reasonable instructions relating to their job. In return, they will receive payment and perhaps other forms of reward. Loyalty is expected from management and owners. As well as basic payment and reward for their skills, employees can expect to receive training and welfare care from an employer.

In recent years the role of employees has changed. The modern firm tries to view employees as a resource to be nurtured, to be looked after and valued. The more an employee is trained, given the chance to acquire new skills and aptitudes, the more valuable he/she becomes.

All human beings naturally tend to fear change. People get used to a settled order of things. The response of staff to a major change of direction for an organisation, my well at first be hostile. There may be fears about jobs and careers. Some staff will fear the new technology, they will worry they may be found wanting for new skills and ways of doing things. Careful and sensitive management is required.

External stakeholders

Customers

Business survival depends on being aware of customers and their requirements. This is at the heart of marketing. Success usually means that a business not only attracts customers but retains them. It is much more costly to acquire new customers than it is to keep existing ones. To do this means taking care of them, listening to them. Customers who are regular and loyal will feel that they have a stake in the business and a wise management policy will encourage such a feeling.

How might customers respond to a complete change in strategy and methods? The answer to this lies in the steps that management and owners are prepared to take to reassure customers or clients. Depending on the nature of the change to e-business, some clients will need help, some may need concrete support in terms of how to deal with the new method. It will be a positive marketing effort to assist loyal customers and to bear in mind their needs. Perhaps a consultation exercise *before* the change is implemented will be beneficial. A realistic business management will not expect to keep everyone loyal. Some customers will be lost.

Government

Of course the government is a stakeholder in an SME. We know already that much of government policy is aimed at encouraging and supporting firms in going 'e'. There is much advice and help available for the SME looking to innovate; often this can come from other firms that have already gone through the 'e' business barrier. The likely response of government to e-business innovation is likely to be positive and encouraging.

Suppliers

B2B relationships are crucial whether online or offline. A business considering going online must examine the industry within which it works. Suppliers are the lifeline of the business and work in partnership with the business in the supply chain. Suppliers, if they are to be in any way affected by a change in strategy, must be kept informed and involved in discussions. Sometimes it may be possible to work in collaboration with suppliers in an e-business venture. Increasingly, new business applications are facilitating online partnerships. Suppliers are likely to favour a move online just so long as their business profitability remains good. Those whose business may be affected negatively will be less impressed. However, although suppliers are important stakeholders, they do not have formal rights in a strategic decision. Consultation is all they can rightfully expect.

Community

A business has its place in a local community and the local people are major stakeholders in the business. Good management is aware of this and depending on the kind of business under consideration, they will always be conscious of the views and opinions of the local population. Good PR (public relations) is an important part of modern marketing. It is hard to generalise too much on the possible effects of a strategic decision to do e-business. Local people expect to know about major changes that might affect them. Planning major strategic changes must take into account any issues that may affect the local community, particularly in the unlikely event that an e-business change is to their disadvantage.

Implementation strategy

We have already seen in Unit 1 that an 'e' dimension can be built into a standard business plan. Whereas the standard plan begins from a blank sheet, an e-business re-orientation strategy begins from a situation in which business processes are already in place. This in some ways causes new difficulties and resistance. Often things become easier when a new fresh start is made. Old ways can stand in the way of new procedures.

D Chaffey, in *E-Business & E-Commerce Management* (Pearson Education 2002) refers to **Business Process Re-engineering (BPRE)** as finding radical new ways of carrying out existing business operations, assisted by IT systems. Chaffey quotes Davenport (1993) as suggesting a structured way of introducing new e-business processes.

According to Davenport, stages could be as follows:

- *Identify business processes that can be modified by innovation.* Select those that add most value to customers, or achieve the biggest efficiency gains for the business. Examples might include better ways of procurement (buying), better customer relationship management (CRM), better ways of organising the movement or shipping of products.

- *Identify factors that assist change.* Important among these are new innovative software applications or technology.

- *Develop the process vision.* This means communicate the reasons for the changes and what is hoped to be achieved.

- *Understand the existing processes.* Try to document the way things are currently done, measure them where possible so improvements can be judged.

- *Design and prototype the new processes.* Practical new methods should be introduced, firstly by simulation, then gradually into full operation, *consulting at all times with those affected.*

It is worth emphasising again that without restructuring business processes, an e-business strategy is highly likely to fail. There is no information system yet on the market that is capable of overcoming human carelessness, or hostility.

Finally, in implementing a new strategy, a business has always got the option of seeking advice from outside. The government website UKonlineforbusiness offers a network of advice and assistance.

Reasons for failure of dot.com strategies

The so called 'dot.com phenomenon' refers to the period during the late 1990s when many new, purely internet based companies, started up and subsequently failed. An important factor in judging any business' potential is to look closely at precisely how the business will generate revenue (cash). This is known as the 'revenue model'. The most straightforward model is to simply to sell tangible products, or offer some kind of service, for profit. Internet commerce is still based to a considerable extent upon this model, but there are many other models now evolving; digital application service provision is one (see the 4Projects *e-Business insight* in Unit 2), sale of advertising space is another and so called 'infomediaries' a further example.

Boo.com was a well known example of an internet start up that failed after lots of hype and promise. The Boo.com site was launched in 1999 after two significant delays. After a short period of trading, a quarter of its staff had been made redundant. The business simply found itself unable to generate the revenue required to finance its expensive site development costs and its promotional effort. Boo.com closed in 2000 and was eventually sold off. Over £70 million was raised in capital. The problem was that forecasts of demand were inaccurate, revenues were incapable of covering the ongoing costs and there had been an over estimation of the likely market for online clothes shopping at that time.

The lessons to be learned from the dot.com failures were considerable. The internet is not a guarantor of success. Merely because sales can potentially be generated, does not mean that they will be sufficient to carry the business forward for a considerable period of time. The dot.coms arose at a time of overly optimistic internet enthusiasm. With little or no understanding of the marketplace, or the costs of getting customers online, investors ploughed cash into companies simply *because* they were dot.com. Dot.coms were often vastly over-valued.

Desmet (2000) said that the critical factor to think about when considering the likelihood of success for a dot.com company was the **churn rate.** This is the proportion of customers (or subscribers) that *no longer* purchase a company's products in a specific period of time. The message is to get the basics right in terms of costs, then plan to acquire and retain customers.

13.3 Internal planning issues

Defining the strategy

In the modern business world, innovation relating to some aspect of e-business has become almost essential. It is also essential, however, that the planning process looks in a careful way at the various factors *within* the business organisation that have an influence on the success or failure of any new strategy. It is first of all necessary to consider the nature of the business. This will determine the level of e-business adoption that will help the business prosper.

As e-business gradually develops throughout advanced economies, there is said to be several levels of adoption that are available to firms, the so called 'e-business evolutionary cycle':

1 **Basic internet access**. Where the aim is primarily to communicate better with customers and partner firms; e-mail and research are used extensively.

2 **Web presence**. Online content is offered via a website, to improve marketing communications. The aim is to open up new markets and opportunities, increase public awareness.

3 **Online transactions**. The web is used to process sales transactions with customers, suppliers and partners. In the background, some parts of business processes are automated within an information system linked to the sales process.

4 **Mature e-business**. A web-based business that is based on extended internal and external (extranet) information systems and linked business processes; all integrating with customers, partners and suppliers. Employees are mobile and all resources are efficiently connected.

Chat room

Look at the following list of business activities. In groups, discuss which of these you feel are suited to various levels of e-business transformation. Draft short statements justifying your conclusions.

- Used car sales
- Printing
- Solicitor
- Component manufacturer
- Fish and chip shop
- Estate agency.

Give one example of your own, illustrating a business at some stage in the e-business evolutionary cycle.

The point to consider is what ways *will* a particular business benefit from an e-business approach? The business needs to carefully consider the strategy it feels applies to its activities. This is the 'innovation' the government is calling for from British SMEs.

e-Business insight — Card Corporation

Liz Grant, director of UK Online for Business (attached to the DTI), quotes the example of Card Corporation based in Leeds, a company that produces short runs of commercial stationery – business cards and the like.

"Their customers can now come online and design their own stuff. The company has actually transferred a function from within the business to customers. They've stripped out the costs of doing it, and it's much faster. On top of that they've been able to diversify – selling the technology they have developed to other companies"

(Quoted in *The Sunday Telegraph*)

Internal audit

An 'audit' is a systematic check of something. When a business is putting together an e-business plan, it is essential to consider the various aspects of the internal organisation that either lend themselves to, or be a barrier to, an e-business re-orientation. There are various methods of analysing these internal factors. Here we will look at two common approaches.

SWOT analysis

In many cases, this is the starting point for any development of a corporate strategy. A business must become intensely self-aware before embarking on a new course.

A SWOT analysis is a popular strategic planning tool that we first encountered in Unit 2. It involves an audit of the whole internal and external environment surrounding the business. Here, we look only at internal issues.

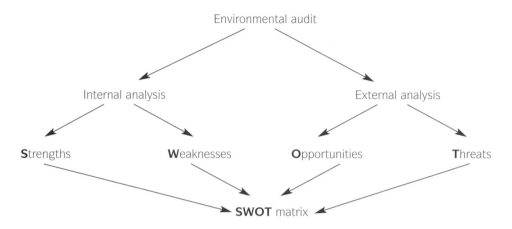

Figure 13.2 The SWOT framework

In this section we are considering *internal factors* that will affect the planning process. What does the business have within its organisation that could be labelled *strengths* in the planning of an e-strategy? Obviously this depends on the business itself, but *could* include:

- Management skills
- Management qualifications
- Management style
- Positive corporate culture
- Good staff skills
- Flexible working practices
- Good communications channels
- Well-established brand or image.

What factors internally does the business have that could be labelled weaknesses? Again, depending on the business:

- High staff turnover rate (many employees leaving)
- Cramped office accommodation
- Ageing hardware
- Mature product range
- Fragmented organisational structure.

The matrix is just a form of presentation that is easily read and the implications seen. Having identified internal factors, we have completed the SW aspect of the SWOT analysis. The OT factors are given in Section 13.4.

Value chain analysis

This form of analysis looks at a series of business activities (or internal processes) with a view to determining their capacity to 'add-value' to what the business is doing. These are broken down into primary activities and secondary activities.

Primary activities

Inbound **logistics** – activities to do with receiving and storing goods and materials that have been bought from outside sources.

Operations – The manufacture of products and services. Ways in which resource *inputs* (materials and parts) are converted to *outputs* as products.

Outbound **logistics** – activities to do with getting finished products to buyers.

Marketing and sales - informing buyers and consumers about the products and services the business provides.

Service – activities to do with maintaining a product performance once it has been sold.

These are supported by secondary activities.

Secondary activities

Procurement – activities to do with acquiring the goods services and materials a business needs. (includes negotiating with suppliers)

Human resource management – recruiting, developing, motivating and rewarding employees.

Technology development – managing information processes and protecting and securing 'knowledge' in a business.

Infrastructure – dealing with linking procedures to do with finance, planning, quality control and general senior management.

The process of carrying out a value chain analysis involves breaking every process and activity within the firm down and placing it under the above headings. Then they must each be assessed, as to their efficiency in relation to costs, or competitive advantage (i.e. in what ways do they contribute to the firm's mission?). Once a picture emerges in relation to this analysis, efforts should then be focused on areas where competitive advantage can be gained.

> **N.B. Neither a SWOT analysis, nor a value chain analysis, should be included *within* an e-business plan. However, the *facts and perspectives drawn from them*, will be important parts of the content of a plan.**

13.4 External planning issues

The e-business plan, as we have seen, must contain key sections and some of these must get their content from a systematic analysis of the external environment. A number of techniques can be used. These have the advantage of ensuring that business management look at the situation of the firm from a range of perspectives.

A wide ranging look at external factors can be derived from a PESTLE analysis.

PESTLE analysis

Political – *what political influences are likely to impact on the organisation's potential to deliver what they wish to?*

'Political' refers to those things that are connected to government policies and to the general level of political stability, here and overseas. A business needs to consider matters relating to taxation for instance, or anything that affects how particular markets operate.

Economic – *are there any factors to do with the economic situation that might affect the business?*

Is there likely to be a drop in trade? Is unemployment set to go up? Will there be new controls on consumer credit? Will interest rates go up or down? Is inflation set to rise?

Social – *how people live and work together in society is an important issue.*

Are any large scale population changes taking place? Is the working population prepared to move around? Are lifestyle changes taking place? What are people's attitudes to work and leisure.

Technological – *scientific and knowledge about technologies develop rapidly and need to be monitored.*

Software developments, computer technology developments, new materials and refinements to the whole range of communications technology, are important considerations.

Legal – *changes in the law could have a major impact on the prospects for an e-business.*

As this text is being prepared, government policy is to ban the use of mobile phones whilst driving. A business whose primary product is hands free sets might wish to take note. Other legal issues may relate to health and safety, employment regulations, product safety regulations.

Environmental – *governments are increasingly conscious of the need to protect the natural environment.*

Controls on pollution, noise regulations, waste disposal and checks on manufacturing processes are all issues that management must be aware of in planning business changes.

Then, the plan needs to draw upon the remaining elements of the SWOT analysis, the opportunities and threats sections.

Completing the SWOT analysis

We saw in Section 13.3 that a SWOT analysis usually treats strengths and weaknesses as internal factors of an e-business and we discussed them on page 207.

Opportunities and threats are usually (but not always) regarded as *external factors* to a business. Clearly management will hope that there are real opportunities available from an e-business approach. Opportunities from adopting e-business tactics could include:

- Improved supply chain efficiencies (see Unit 1) improved partnerships.
- Improved market reach.
- Reducing costs of distribution. (disintermediation)
- Improved promotional impact. (e.g. virtual tours, digital images)
- Better customer relations (CRM software)
- Improved awareness of and sensitivity to, market changes.

Threats from the external environment include:

- Competition.
- Economic slowdown.
- Demographic changes.
- Changing consumer preferences.

How does a business begin to meet these challenges? As we are discussing these analytical techniques within a context of e-business planning, we assume that the whole planning exercise is based on preparing to face them. However, another analytical technique is available that builds on the SWOT analysis; this technique was developed by Michael Porter in 1980 and is known as Porter's Five Forces analysis.

Porter's five forces

This model is based on the insight that a business has to meet the opportunities and threats that are thrown up in their external environment. The business' strategy should be based on a sound understanding on the industry they work in. According to Porter, every industry and every market is shaped by five competitive forces. These, together, have the effect of generating the level of competition in an industry and therefore affect the chances of profitability.

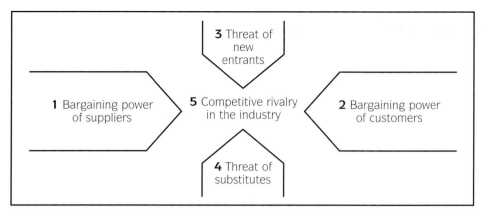

Figure 13.3 Porter's five forces

1 **The bargaining power of suppliers** is an important consideration and is especially high when a firm depends upon one, or a few large suppliers, with few alternatives. In such a situation, room for strategic manoeuvre is limited. However, a firm considering an e-business tactic may put itself in a favourable position in terms of its supplier relationship.

2 **The bargaining power of customers** has to be taken into account. Do they have alternatives? Do they purchase in large volumes? Are they sensitive to price changes? The firm must consider the effect of an e-business strategy on customers with these things in mind.

3 **Threat of new entrants** refers to the ease with which new firms can enter an industry and change customer loyalties. Each industry has barriers to entry that can prevent firms coming in and offering more competition; these include, high cost of initial investment, economies of scale (i.e. minimum volume requirements to be profitable), access to raw materials, existing relationships between partner firms in an industry.

4 **Threat of substitutes** comes from the existence of new alternative products with better performance and lower prices that serve the same purpose.

5 **Competitive rivalry between existing players in the market** How many firms are there in an industry doing similar things?

The PESTLE analysis, the SWOT analysis and the application of Porter's five forces analysis are tools that can be used to populate the e-business plan. The information and perspectives that are gained should be structured into the plan as shown in Section 13.1.

Chat room

In groups, take *one* of Porter's five forces and specify how an e-business strategy can improve a firm's competitive position.

Prepare set of notes explaining in full how an e-strategy can achieve this.

13.5 Resources of an e-business plan

No matter how thorough the planning, at the end of it all a plan needs to have resources allocated to it before it has any chance of being successful. Anyone could plan the most fantastic e-business, but it must be borne in mind that resources in terms of finance, people and technology need to be found.

Resources fall into a number of categories and many have them have already been mentioned earlier in this unit. Once again, the resource requirements will depend on the nature and degree of the e-business goals. However, we can say that the following resource investments are essential in any level of e-business change:

1   **Hardware infrastructure and software.** A serious attempt to transform business processes will require the purchase and installation of computer hardware and other ancillary pieces of equipment. The hardware infrastructure will probably need to be networked and utilise professionally produced software for a variety of applications. The tactical question will relate to the extent to which such installation and maintenance is sourced from outside the business. We know that an emerging pattern in e-business is for powerful applications to be externally developed and hosted (see for example www.leighton.com).

2   **Finance.** e-Business development can be a costly exercise and requires heavy initial expenditure. It is well known that Amazon.com – as an example – took over five years to reach break-even point. e-Business revenue models are notoriously slow to show return on investment, a cause of many of the dot.com crashes of the late nineties. For an e-Business to establish itself, finance is needed to support it through an initial loss-making period. This requires great faith in the idea in the first place (hence the need for careful planning!). How might a business source the funds it needs? Sources of funds for business investments can be either internal or external.

3   **Internal funding.** Retained profit (after tax) is a major source of internal funds. It is usual for a large proportion of funding to come from profit. Other sources of internal funds include depreciation (which is making financial provision for replacing old equipment or machinery) and the sale of assets (e.g. vans, equipment).

4   **External funding.** Funds from outside could be short term, from banks in the form of an overdraft or a loan. However, for a business that is capable of growing rapidly, **venture capital** is also an option. A 'venture capitalist' is someone with funds who is willing to invest money and often expertise into a business with the promise of fairly rapid profitable return. The venture capitalist will purchase shares and commit to the business long term if necessary.

Sourcing external funds from venture capital could have advantages for a business with real growth potential in a developing e-business market. The venture capitalist may invest considerably and does not in normal circumstances get involved in any way in the day to day running of the business. Banks, on the other hand, require regular repayments and charge interest on loans. The time scale involved is usually quite restricted and, quite often, a persisting overdraft facility is converted into a loan by a bank.

The long term financial stability of a firm can be seriously undermined if too much capital is sourced externally from loans, in relation to that raised from ordinary shareholders. This relationship is known as 'gearing'. When a firm has external debt that is higher than the capital invested by ordinary shareholders, the '**gearing ratio**' is said to be high. In this case, other potential investors, as well as the firm's creditors, are likely to see this as a signal that it may not be capable of meeting its commitments. Highly geared companies are viewed as risks; low geared companies have potential for growth.

Apart from finding the most appropriate sources of additional funds to invest in an e-business plan, a firm must calculate the return it is likely to get from a level of investment. Say a firm decides to spend £200,000 on a particular IT capital project, managers need to have some idea of when the investment will pay for itself. So let's say the following income is generated from a specific project.

Anticipated income from new IT investment

Year 1	Year 2	Year 3	Year 4	Year 5
£40,000	£54,000	£54,000	£55,000	£67,000

In this case it has taken four years for the IT investment to payback its capital cost. When planning investment, management will be looking to invest in equipment and software that has the quickest payback (note: all IT firms will claim that their particular systems will payback the quickest!).

When measuring the performance of a company from its accounts, people can look at the total assets, including the amount that a firm has invested in such things as IT systems, and then calculate a ratio known as Return on Capital Employed (ROCE). The higher the ROCE the better, it is therefore crucial that investment in an e-business project can give good returns within a reasonable time period.

The e-business plan

You are employed as a consult for a manufacturing SME that is considering its options for going online and adopting an 'e' approach, integrated throughout its operations. Managers want to have a sensible e-business plan that is well structured and considers all of the essential issues.

Task 1

To achieve a Pass grade:

a   Describe the features of a business plan for a selected SME that includes planning for an e-business strategy.

b   Identify the key internal issues likely to be faced by the business when it is planning an e-business strategy.

c   Identify the key external issues likely to be faced by the business when it is planning its e-business strategy.

d   Identify the key resource requirements of e-business planning for the business.

Task 2

To achieve a Merit you must also:

a   Draw up an outline business plan for a selected SME that includes planning for an e-business strategy.

b   Analyse the key internal issues likely to face management when they are planning an e-business strategy and comment on how you feel they might be successfully addressed.

c   Analyse the key external issues to be faced when planning an e-business strategy and comment on how you feel these might be addressed.

d   Explain in detail the likely resource requirements of a three year e-business plan for a selected SME.

Task 3

To achieve a Distinction you must in addition:

a   Draw up a detailed and comprehensive business plan for a selected SME that includes planning for an e-business strategy.

b   Evaluate the key internal issues likely to affect a successful e-business strategy and prepare a blueprint plan for a local Business Link partnership on how such issues might be addressed at SME level.

c   Evaluate the key internal issues likely to affect a successful e-business strategy and prepare a blueprint plan for a local Business Link partnership on how such issues might be addressed at SME level.

d   Assess the likely minimum resource requirements necessary to support a realistic three year e-business plan for a selected SME.

After completing Unit 14 you will be able to:

1   describe the key *features of e-business implementation* on selected organisations

2   outline a clear *marketing plan* as a part of an e-business implementation

3   outline the *organisational and customer service issues* that are associated with e-business implementation

4   outline *approaches to contingency planning and risk analysis* in implementing an e-business plan.

> *Your understanding of this unit will be assessed by an internally marked assignment*.

This unit looks at some of the important issues surrounding the implementation, i.e. putting into practice, of an e-business plan by established business organisations. We know that many businesses have established a new digital strategy from *within* an existing business. In fact this has been the main growth area in e-business. However, organisations that have been established for work in the physical world have to face up to many new forces in the digital world after they have put an e-business plan into action. The nature of these will be examined in Section 14.1.

The unit will then go on to analyse the way in which the new online business can create a systematic and effective *marketing plan*; by identifying and analysing its target market, establishing the new goals for an online presence and efficiently processing various kinds of customer feedback. Section 14.3 looks at the ways in which *organisational structures* and internal processes might be affected by a move to e-business, before going on to examine *customer service* factors in the online world. The closing section deals with risk assessment and some approaches to *contingency planning* for emergencies or difficulties if things go wrong. Finally, the unit goes on to look at some important matters relating to *security of data and system software* in e-business contexts.

Looking at the implementation of an e-business strategy is a useful exercise. It will help you to appreciate the general impact of this growing way of operating upon a range of organisations and brings together much of the content from other units. Of course, it follows from – and relates particularly closely to – Unit 13 *e-Business planning*. When you approach the unit it is best to start from a general perspective, dealing with the various issues in a way that will apply to *all* organisations that adopt an online strategy. Then, try to focus upon one specific business organisation to draw out the reality of what has (so far) occurred in that case. In this unit we will look closely at several issues as experienced by an innovative business in Sunderland, Save and Drive (at www.saveanddrive.co.uk).

The assignment given at the end of the unit asks you to examine the case of a fictitious small to medium sized manufacturing firm. You may be able to find a firm close to you that can be a useful source of information. As always in vocational work, you must try to place your work in a real business context. What you can find out from the real world, should be then reinforced by theoretical information.

As ever, each assignment task is offered in three levels. You may offer straightforward descriptive work and achieve a very commendable Pass award for the unit. However, work additionally offering appropriate detailed analysis will achieve. Merit and work containing full evaluation – i.e. intelligent comment and observations, pros and cons etc. – will achieve a Distinction. You have every incentive to go for the highest grades. Good luck.

14.1 Features of e-business implementation

'Implementation' means putting an e-business plan into action. As we saw in Unit 13, the kind of plans formulated will hinge very much upon the kind of business under consideration and the specific products' online potential. Some products simply don't lend themselves to e-commerce. What follows in this section assumes firstly that the business is already up and running and secondly, that it is going for a fully fledged e-business approach. Many businesses will have only modest ambitions for their e-business strategy and there is a range of levels of e-business implementation that can apply in different scenarios. However, there are several features about implementing *any* significant e-business plan and we can say these are characteristic of *any* serious web-based business.

Firstly, the change will have some kind of impact on the business; secondly, there will be aspects of global competition to face; thirdly, communication across the World Wide Web can have an effect on the business and finally, the digital world releases businesses from many physical constraints that affect firms selling in the high street. In this section we will look at these factors.

Impact of implementing an e-business plan

The planning process described in Unit 13 is designed to help business managers and owners be prepared for the likely impact that e-business can have upon an organisation. The impact can be considerable. In fact, if planning is effective and thorough, the impact *should* be considerable, as we will shortly see. There are several forces that can have a big impact upon a business once e-business implementation begins:

- Investment costs
- Volume of enquiries and transactions
- Enterprise resource planning (ERP)
- Reorganisation of internal functions
- Global competition
- Online discussions for products and services
- Equality of business website presence.

Investment costs

A crucial aspect of e-business planning involves calculating how much it will cost a business to implement an e-strategy. These costs will depend on what the plan involves. Is the business planning a complete re-orientation towards online work? If so, what internal 're-engineering' of processes will be involved? The degree of change determines the costs associated with buying or leasing equipment, with staff training, with promotion and marketing, with seeking and employing external help, with (possibly) hiring new staff.

Needless to say, the costs outlined above can be considerable. Historically, dot coms (i.e. purely web-based companies) that began as new internet startups in the nineties incurred very high initial costs. This means that their break-even point tended to be a fair way down the line, after launch. In other words they were working hard to catch up for a lengthy period of time. The most notable illustrations of this are Amazon, Yahoo and Ebay, all of whom finally announced substantial profit figures in 2003.

The dot.coms mentioned above should not however be taken as typical illustrations of all e-business ventures. The cost of the dot com start ups simply reinforces the point that even where an existing business is well established, the investment required to fully exploit e-business opportunities will be high.

Where do costs arise? New hardware is an essential investment because old hardware tends to be quickly out of date. Additionally, older hardware cannot easily be integrated with newer systems. No patchwork of upgrades will ever be as efficient as a completely new system. There is no cheap and effective way to digitise a business.

To invest in new hardware and new systems is not a one-off expenditure either. Once a computer system has been installed it needs to be maintained. The argument is that just as you are wise to maintain a car and avoid running it until it stops, so a business must do the same with its computer systems. A regular system maintenance contract costs money. Once a computer system is installed it becomes an asset; however, in a relatively short space of time this asset starts to decline in value. The speed of change and development in ICT (as we all know) guarantees this.

Investment in new software at the outset is obviously essential too. Sometimes smaller businesses may buy a number of packages to accomplish different things. Accounting software, customer database software, e-mail and communications software, stock management software; then at some later point they find that these separate programs do not fit well together as an *integrated* system. Businesses need to think long and hard about the kind of information they, their staff and their customers require.

Issues surrounding investment in hardware and software, as well as ongoing system maintenance, mean that the business must decide on is whether or not to **'outsource'** the necessary work involved in implementing an e-business plan. This means buying in from outside the knowledge, the skills, the equipment and software required to move a business online. Once again this expenditure will be considerable and ongoing. So, the benefits that might be gained from investing in e-business have to be considerable (the knowledge and assurance gained from effective planning). What will be the return on the investment?

A move to digitise a whole business should help to *cut the administrative costs of the business*. Electronic payments systems can be implemented to pay staff wages, to pay supplier bills, generate and issue invoices and do bank transfers. This can save a lot of administrative time. The creation of an intranet (an internal website run wholly within the business) can save money on forms, on copying and printing. The whole process of communication within the business becomes more streamlined and efficient.

Finally, the fully digitised business can tap a worldwide network for supplies and materials. This process, known as **e-procurement**, means the business can seek out the best marketplaces online and obtain the best deals. So, from at least three angles, doing e-business is a cost saving venture once the initial capital investment has been made.

Chat room

In groups of four and acting as a team, create an effective presentation detailing the main costs generally involved in moving to a full blown e-business approach.

Take a specific SME in your area and outline and evaluate the impact of an e-business implementation.

Volume of enquiries and transactions

By placing a business up on the internet you are likely to get greatly increased volumes of enquiries and potential transactions. The story of Joe's Brew in Unit 2, showed that this can sometimes take a business by surprise. Joe took two enquiries one week, 2,500 the next and by the third week of his 'home brew' website he was receiving 500 enquiries a day. Other websites started putting links to his without his knowledge. The internet is a wild and uncontrollable beast if someone like Joe has insufficiently planned or invested.

A case study given by Microsoft bCentral (www.bcentral.co.uk) tells of a lawyer in the USA who followed, in a somewhat more sophisticated way, the example of Joe and his home brew. The lawyer – correctly – looked at the internet as a way of generating more business. He decided to set up a website that contained downloadable forms, such as basic wills and contracts. Clients would complete them at home, then e-mail them back and they would be checked over by the lawyer. In this case the site was professionally designed, credit card transactions could be taken and the site had comprehensive and lawful disclaimers. The lawyer felt he had every chance of a great e-(legal) business.

The legal service website was launched on a Friday. The lawyer went to his office on the Monday morning and found he had 2,200 hits and 1,800 purchases. By the Wednesday of the same week he had another 6,600 hits and 900 further purchases. This was $50,000 in orders waiting to be processed but he didn't feel ecstatic about it. The lawyer couldn't cope with the volume of work and was faced with the choice of employing more staff or shut the site down. He chose to shut the site down and refund the money.

What went wrong? As in Joe's case, an intelligent idea was bravely implemented but was overwhelmed by the capacity of the internet to generate business. The lawyer calculated that he would mainly get business from his home state. In fact, orders were received from all over the USA and well beyond.

Over to you   Referring back to Unit 13, what aspects of e-business planning could have avoided the problems experienced by the two businesses described above?

Enterprise Resource Planning (ERP)

Moving a business into a digital mode in order to fully do e-business means more than merely creating a website and sitting back and waiting for orders to flow; the illustrations given in the previous section show this clearly. The full blown e-business possibly has to change all of its internal business processes in order to sell successfully on the internet. Why? Because old methods and systems often do not fit with e-business.

There may be an answer to this problem. Whilst 'computerisation' has been around a long time and many long established businesses have made very good use of electronic data interchange (EDI), modern software can integrate all business processes within an Enterprise Resource Planning (ERP) system. A firm involved in manufacturing, as an example, needs to have processes to:

- Plan products
- Buy parts or materials
- Manage stock (inventory)
- Relate to suppliers
- Offer customer service
- Track orders taken or received.

By digitising these important processes, the firm achieves a much speedier, more efficient, contribution to the supply chain. The firm's costs can be lowered, reliability improved and relationships with both suppliers and customers improved. Because data is more reliable, coordinated and integrated, the firm can offer just in time production. This means that instead of production being based on *anticipated* demand, (what you think might happen) it is based on *actual* requirement and produced and shipped to a customer when needed. An ERP system of course *must* these days be internet connected. In this way, firms can truly act in partnership within a supply chain context and relevant data can be shared and exchanged securely.

Reorganisation of internal functions

A business organisation by definition is structured in order to achieve something. Classically, an organisation is represented by a pyramid type structure with a single boss at the top, then two perhaps more subordinate seniors, then branching out into functional areas such as Finance, Marketing, Sales, Production or Buying. The nature of these functions in an organisation depends on what the business does. Doing e-business can affect the structure.

Classic business structures like this tended to develop separate blocks of information within each functional area because managers within them perceived they had different needs. Each department or function tended to develop its own system. This meant that often different computer systems would be installed within different functional areas. The functional areas themselves, created to help the business achieve its aims and objectives, become *barriers* to useful information exchange. By implementing e-business principles, an ERP system draws from all the data in separate functions and makes it available in an integrated and integrating fashion. This in itself helps to enable the reorganisation of functions (see Section 14.4).

As the e-business develops, the organisation will need to consider the best way to restructure itself to accommodate new e-processes. We have seen elsewhere that there are several options, including even setting up a separate e-company or alternatively setting up a separate e-commerce department within the existing organisation. In the early stages of implementation a business may simply rely on a senior management steering group and allow e-business to permeate the organisation naturally, as new work patterns develop.

Global competition

Once a business has an online presence, it has global visibility. This means that a firm can potentially extend its 'market reach' across the entire globe. In planning an e-business strategy, a sensible firm will have an awareness of its target market. It will be aware of its potential market and its accessible market; these are the customers more likely to access and use the website. The planning process should have considered who – and where – customers are likely to be.

Once the business has implemented its e-strategy it is open to comparison with other similar internet offers. Customers have an increasing range of choices open to them on the web. Prices can be compared easily, offers, product features and after sales services can all be contrasted. The newly online e-business must be aware of competitor offers and keep in touch with the depth of internet consumer knowledge, which is growing fast.

One way to secure a market position and fight off competition is for a B2B company to create lasting and useful *relationships* online. For instance, technical people in one firm may relate online very closely with similar technical people in another. Using the ERP software described earlier, and adopting the fully fledged e-business strategy, a business can entrench itself within fruitful online marketplaces and become an important participant within a supply chain. In this way the firm can become more secure. However, the openness of the internet will always exert pressures upon the firm to respond to consumer comparisons; remember there is a downward pressure on prices and an upward pressure on customer services. An e-business must be prepared for this.

Because of the openness of the internet, there is always room for new entrants into a marketplace. This has already been described, as one of the several 'threats' the new e-business has to confront.

Online discussions for products and services

Because the web is an open forum (it was always intended to be), when a business is online, people are free (within the legal parameters that are in place) to express views or to discuss products and services they have experienced. We saw in an earlier unit how the Ford Motor Company in America was faced with hostile web-based information because of an alleged fault with one of their cars.

There are several kinds of open forum on the web, where individuals can post their opinions, form groups of like-minded people and discuss the issues they commonly experience. In 2001, one of the longest established 'Usenet' groups, Deja, was taken over by Google. Text based chat, e-mail, discussion groups, can all be used to generate a groundswell of opinion. The online business needs to beware of unhappy customers who can easily spread word of their discontent. The high street business that upsets one customer may find he or she informs another half a dozen people in casual conversation. On the web, thousands can get to know within hours. Customer expectations on the internet are high.

Because consumers can easily compare product prices as well as performance there is always pressure to lower prices. Increasingly web based businesses are taking advantage of internet technology by setting prices dynamically. This means that prices change automatically according to market demand. When demand is high, price is set higher and when demand is low, price automatically falls. The fact that such technology exists and is increasingly being employed means that a new e-business must keep an eye on its pricing in order to constantly check that it remains competitive, if its e-strategy is to compete on price.

The need to compete online, given the pressures on price and the potentially high costs involved in doing an e-business implementation, mean that online products need to be constantly reviewed. A website offers content first of all. There is always a need to modify the content and keep it up to date. If a business offers an e-service, then it needs to always listen to customers and if necessary change the product offer. If a firm is involved in manufacturing, the increased level of communication along the supply chain will help to increase the rate of product development. Changes can more easily be discussed, plans and resources shared, key people consulted and designs accessed by all partners. These factors all contribute to a speeding up of the pace of product development.

Over to you   Consider three contrasting online businesses that have adopted an e-strategy from within an existing business. Explain in general terms the impact you feel implementing the e-strategy will have had on the business.

Equality of business website presence

It follows from all that is described so far in this section that on the internet businesses can be seen by consumers as of equal standing. There is no physical yardstick to measure the status or standing of a firm. By the nature of the web, private consumers may freely shop around for the best deals or for the most interesting 'value proposition'. In B2B markets relationships can become more set; contracts and deals are established and trust is built up. As ERP systems, extranets and secure systems become established in marketplaces, the volume of web based communication between businesses increases, as does the interaction between business and government and business and private consumer.

The business that successfully implements an e-strategy will see an increasing volume of revenue being achieved from online sales. In this case such a business may feel that relocation – at least of e-operations such as call centre work – is a feasible option. Geographical location of customers becomes an irrelevance so long as the logistical issue has been sorted. DIY.com operate from Follingsby Park, near Washington in Tyne and Wear, they employ five different carriers to fulfil product orders and web orders have high priority. Online businesses, in theory at least, can locate anywhere.

Chat room

Discuss in pairs the question of e-business location. Do you agree that a business selling online can relocate easily? What factors do you think can prevent an e-business from doing so? Prepare an organised set of notes to back up your conclusions and try to include illustrations from real businesses.

14.2 Marketing plan

A marketing plan for an e-business is central to its implementation; it gives a foundation for the whole e-strategy and justifies the online marketing tactics that are to be employed by the business. Unit 2 details the principles and tactics of internet marketing and it will be worthwhile referring to that unit in this context too. There is any number of formats for a marketing plan, here we will focus on a four part structure, consisting of:

1 Identification of target markets
2 Establishing the goals of a web presence
3 Assessing market volumes
4 Processing feedback from customers.

Identify target markets

It is often said that marketing begins with market research, 'find out what customers want'. However in the fast moving digital age this is hardly adequate or realistic in itself. In 1997 an American airlines company sought out customer opinions on what they wanted from transatlantic flights. Many respondents replied about the services they would like to see available on flights. However, not a single customer said they would like access to individual power connections to plug in notebook computers. Why? because technology at the time didn't seem to call for it. Consumers are good at saying what they would like *now*, but not what they might need in the future. B2C businesses in the digital age need to be looking ahead, much further ahead than many, if not all, of their customers.

Having pointed that out, there does need to be a different level of research in the digital age. Not just research about customer requirements now, but research into future online trends, accessibility, and global as well as local markets. Clearly, there needs to be technical research and an eye needs to be kept on the developing marketplace but the identification of a target market must draw from the experiences of the existing business. The *e-Business insight* panel below describes how one Sunderland based Save and Drive, adopted its e-business plan.

e-Business insight   Save and Drive

In 1977 Dave Robson began a discount auto spares business in Silksworth, near Sunderland. At the time, the market for car accessories was huge. Anyone who owned a car more than two years old would need spares. Car maintenance and customisation had become a big leisure activity; people would often pop into the local auto spares shop just for a look round.

By the 1990s the market for spares was beginning to change. Cars were being built to much higher quality standards and, more importantly, they were becoming much less easy to 'self maintain'. The traditional internal combustion engine was increasingly being replaced by an inaccessible computer-managed 'black box'.

Dave Robson was joined in the business by his son Martin. A SWOT analysis told Dave and Martin Robson that new and wider markets were needed. A new customer base had to be found and a way of building on Save and Drive's well-established reputation for excellent customer support.

Martin Robson was internet-wise and computer literate. He and Dave were ready to innovate. Together they decided on an e-strategy. Their strengths were an excellent reputation, a good network of suppliers, great experience in the accessories trade and knowledge of the market. The Save and Drive website was launched. The new e-strategy was to open up a niche but nevertheless far wider market, for load-carrying equipment.

The rest, as they say, is history. Save and Drive is a classic story of how e-business is re-creating and re-energising many businesses. The website attracts a different, broader and more diverse customer base. The physical retail outlet still operates but has become a lesser aspect of the total business.

Save and Drive is a good illustration of planning and developing an e-strategy from within an existing business. In this scenario, the target market was realistically identified within the UK. The Robson's idea was to use web technology firstly to extend market reach beyond the local area, to then to offer a distinctive internet proposition from the site.

In pairs, visit www.saveanddrive.co.uk and prepare a brief joint presentation outlining to the rest of the group the distinct selling points of the Save and Drive website.

So an online business needs to do *online* research and look beyond traditional market surveys. Various organisations – already listed in Unit 13 – offer published information about who is online and why they are online. Some of these organisations offer detailed reports into web trends (e.g. CyberAtlas). The essence of any form of marketing is to *target* your segment of the market.

For Save and Drive, the whole world of the internet is a *potential* market, the UK however is the more realistic addressable market; then – much more focused – is a possible *target* of (say) men over 35 years of age in full time employment. Research shows that this particular group represent almost fifty percent of UK internet users in 2003 – a very sizeable group indeed. Further research shows that of all those who are online in the UK, forty-two percent do so from work and thirty-eight percent from home (BRMB International Research).

The goals of a web presence

Placing a website on the internet will be based upon any number of corporate goals depending on the level of e-business implementation. A great number of businesses, in all manner of industries, are seeing the benefits of merely having a basic presence on the web. If we take Save and Drive as an illustration, let's try to identify the goals of their particular internet presence.

Attracting visitors to the site

The Robsons' primary aim in going online was to increase business revenue (income). Business management had seen that the spares market was declining. The aim therefore, from the start, was to generate sales through the new online channel. To succeed in this, the site not only must attract visitors but seek to retain them. Save and Drive are obviously sensitive to many people's fears about credit card fraud (based on research?) and offer several alternative methods of payment.

Connect

Visit www.saveanddrive.co.uk. Prepare a presentation outlining the ways in which you feel the site:

a attracts visitors

b retains their interest

c encourages them to return to the site.

In a short paragraph, how would you sum up the image that Save and Drive are looking to create from their website?

In order to encourage return customers Save and Drive need to ensure that the website content is kept fresh, accurate and up to date. Perhaps Martin Robson may periodically review the overall 'mood' of the website and look to change the style and image. He will be hoping to create a 'web brand' for the site, making the Save and Drive name synonymous with excellence in customer focused web trading. All in all, the site has to offer an Internet Value Proposition.

Apart from the site content, several other methods are open to the e-business to build traffic to the site. Using the web itself, portals are websites that open up into other websites. It may be helpful for a business such as Save and Drive to be represented on them. Some of these are known as **'horizontal' portals**, e.g. Yahoo. These offer a wide range of services from e-mail to classified ads and attract many general private users. Vertical portals are specialist sites that tend to target a particular industry. Save and Drive operates in a B2C market.

Finally, search engine registration will be crucial. Save and Drive site will have been designed to include 'meta tags' within it that attract as many search engines as possible. Search engine software seeks out keywords within a web page's code. Someone searching, say for 'roof boxes' will be offered the Save and Drive site so long as the words 'roof boxes' have been included as keywords within the HTML code in the site header.

Market awareness

Online markets have increased not only in number but in volume of sales and type. The industry portal www.verticalnet.com lists over fifty different online communities dealing with various dimensions of industry. Some markets are peculiar to the internet age.

Save and Drive must build an online reputation with this in mind, knowing that lots of competition exists, that there are alternative suppliers of their specialist products and more and more of these are going online. Their site must offer value consistently. Value not just in terms of price, although this is crucial, it must offer a valuable online *service.* This service offer may be based on information, on image, on reliability, on technical expertise, on relationships. Preferably, it will be based on all of these things.

Martin and Dave Robson appear to be willing to exploit internet technology as far as they can. They have shown an awareness of market changes by their online presence and represent an excellent example of an innovative small business.

Customer feedback

The convenience of home shopping or – in the B2B context – of online buying, is matched by the equal convenience of passing on feedback. For the newly online business it is wise to build into a website the facility for customers to provide feedback about the site. The result is likely to be that the volume of feedback comment will increase significantly.

In an ideal scenario, all of the comment will be positive. Some sites sell themselves by offering a page on their site simply listing positive comment. In reality, if traffic building efforts have been successful, some feedback will be negative. Business leaders must pay heed to negative feedback. For example, if Save and Drive received many complaints about the speed of downloading important images, or of the lack of clarity of certain aspects of their site, they must set in place some internal method of looking into a potentially damaging problem. Save and Drives site encourages customers to make contact. The firm has set out to create a 'brand' and by monitoring returning feedback from site users and drawing appropriate conclusions, management may hope to raise the site's popularity. Indeed, it is always worth remembering that to *successfully* deal with a customer complaint can turn a potential problem into a PR triumph.

In the B2B context the question of feedback takes on a different form. Whereas the private client expects efficient, helpful, friendly and reliable service on a potentially 'one-off' sale, the business client is more likely to be in an ongoing relationship. Save and Drive will no doubt seek to nurture good relationships and acquire a reputation for rapid response to any issues. Web technology of course helps in this. A marketing plan drawn up by Save and Drive may well have thought about supply chain relationships for some product ranges. This could have looked at how to deal with design changes and information sharing along the supply chain; a topic that has been covered several times in earlier units.

Over to you What do you consider to be the importance of customer feedback to an online firm? How do you feel Save and Drive will have planned for feedback in their e-strategy?

14.3 Organisational and customer service issues

To implement an e-business plan has a number of repercussions on a business, both in terms of internal structures and processes and its relationships with external customers. Many of these have been dealt with elsewhere, so here we will offer a summary of the crucial issues.

Organisational issues

The organisation may find that the traditional hierarchy, where levels of authority are distributed vertically from top to bottom and functions are separated across horizontal lines, no longer retains its relevance in a digital organisation. Sometimes this change is referred to as '*from hierarchy to hyperarchy*' (Evans & Wurster – Harvard Business Review 1997).

The hyperarchy does not rely on horizontal levels of authority, or specialist vertical divisions. In a hyperarchy, communication is a network and information is much more evenly spread around it. The organisation is alive with interactivity and interconnectedness. In a sense, this mirrors the web itself. Information is removed from some sort of central depository and made available to many (subject to security restrictions).

Functional areas, for example specialisms such as marketing, or human resource management, tend to become more interdependent as they access and share common data. The well designed enterprise system has a tendency to draw everyone together. The well organised e-business must of course have a powerful central mission and share common goals. Electronic communication helps in this. In the e-business, new internal relationships can develop and new understanding can grow, as previously closed functions – each with their own *internal* agenda – re-emerge to approach corporate goals based on common understanding.

Over to you Take the example of Save and Drive (or any other appropriate SME). Look at the following job roles and complete the table designed to show how each role might have been redefined in an e-business context. To help you on your way, the first job role has been completed for you.

Role	e-Business re-definition
Managing Director	Co-ordinates and monitors e-strategy. Steers and leads website development. Monitors performance of e-commerce aspect of business.
Finance Manager	
Marketing Manager	
Human Resources Manager	
Shop Manager	
Storekeeper	

The human resources required to implement an e-business strategy will clearly need to be considered. Will existing staff be retrained in order to implement new processes or will external recruitment take place? There are advantages in either approach. On the one hand, internal recruits may well know the business and can be relied upon to employ new tactics to the benefit of the business. On the other hand, new recruits come with fresh ideas. Skilful employment of human resources will also include dealing with employee representatives. If job roles are to change, what will be new working conditions? How will job descriptions change? How will change be managed bearing in mind change is always stressful for staff?

All in all, a large scale alteration of business practices may call for the adoption of an entirely new **organisational culture**. This refers to the whole 'way of working' of an organisation. People become set in their ways, used to doing things a particular way. A new culture may enforce a new attitude of *positive* responsiveness to change. What might have been the 'culture' within Save and Drive? Recall the point made in Unit 1 at the outset?

> **Cultural Attitude 1** *"At Save and Drive we offer the best in auto accessories. Our products have stood the test of time and if we don't stock it, we'll get it.*
>
> **Cultural Attitude 2** *"The world is getting smaller and changing quickly. We at Save and Drive are ready to play a growing part in motor leisure with our first rate online service. We will offer the best and be the best"*

Don't the above sentences sound like mission statements? In fact, they offer a good illustration of how the mission of a business should run through everything it does, by becoming part of the culture of the business. Each statement betrays the attitudes and methods that are likely to run through everything the business does and all the attitudes management wishes to encourage.

Customer service issues

The average internet customer expects and demands high quality service. If you walked into a shop in the High Street and saw an item you wanted to buy, you would ask about it, check the price, possibly try it, hand over your cash and leave with the item. You would have hopefully achieved immediate *satisfaction* in your exchange, otherwise you would probably have a complaint to make.

The internet does not demand a much higher level of expectation than this. Internet shoppers merely want a fair exchange for their money. The difference is that online businesses have to offer something *other* than the mere product itself. The business needs to offer the entire website as a service of value. Everything about a selling site needs to offer first rate customer service, if not, customers will leave and go to a site that does and before they leave they will complain.

What does excellent customer service mean?

There are a number of aspects to this:

- The site does what it says it will do
- Handling negative publicity
- Dealing with channel conflict
- Manage fluctuating demand
- Customer enquiries will be well handled.

The site does what it says it will do

Delivery of goods ordered will be as specified; goods will be as described; payment methods and terms will be clear, as well as secure. Customer details will be private and respected and there will be no unsolicited subsequent mailing or passing on of details.

Customer enquiries will be well handled

The best way to lose customers after they have made an initial purchase is to make sure that any subsequent calls they make are handled by a slow, automated, system (Ever tried to talk with a series of menus?). The next best way to lose customers is to refer them to a remote offsite call centre, where the staff on call have no knowledge at all of the products. Call centres must ideally be well integrated with the core business. Online businesses must make the customer experience of both online and offline content as efficient and satisfying as possible.

Manage fluctuating demand

The online business needs to be capable of dealing with changes in short term demand for products or services. Some websites have gone down in the past because they just unable to cope with surges in demand (e.g. E*Trade in 1997 couldn't handle a one hundred and seventy-five percent increase in subscriptions caused by market changes!). If an e-commerce site is to be an effective part of a business' revenue stream, it must be available when customers want it.

Because the web helps to smooth communications between partners in the supply chain, production and necessary operational changes can be made early. The lead time from shop floor to market can be shortened. Customers at all stages in a supply chain will expect partner firms to respond quickly and flexibly.

Dealing with channel conflict

When Save and Drive began planning an online sales channel they were setting up something that could potentially take business away from their physical store in Sunderland. This is a form of 'channel conflict'. Save and Drive strategy could have been to closely link the two forms of business. In fact, Save and Drive appear to have succeeded in following an online strategy in such a way that the Sunderland store has retained (at least) its local customers. Other forms of channel conflict can occur where an online business damages a long standing offline relationship with a partner firm, because it has opened up the online business.

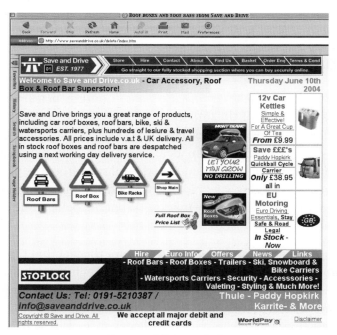

Save and Drive website

Handling negative publicity

Daniel Amor recommends that businesses adopting an e-strategy need to consider developing a 'dark site', i.e. one that is ready to counter balance negative online campaigning in the event of a major problem such as Ford's alleged flaming car. On a more mundane level there are potentially disastrous PR problems around the corner for e-businesses that fail to deliver a quality service online. Business planners need to be prepared for managing bad PR issues and hope in the event to turn these into positives.

Over to you As an e-business advisor, draft a report for the management of an SME giving your best advice on setting up quality customer service.

14.4 Approaches to contingency planning and risk analysis

A business that makes extensive plans and invests considerable capital and resources in order to establish itself online, must be aware that there are serious risks involved. Every experienced director or manager of an SME that has been involved in e-business implementation will have considered these. How an e-business responds to these risks depends upon the level and nature of the particular business, but there are three general approaches that we can identify:

- Contingency planning
- Risk analysis
- Securing data and system software.

Contingency planning

The first approach is to make *contingency plans*. 'Contingencies' are those things that *might* happen, but are not part of the intentions or goals of the business. Save and Drive for instance could be said to have made brave and forward looking decisions in developing the e-commerce side of their firm. In an ideal world, they have planned for growing sales from a wider geographical reach, yet retain good local sales from the physical shop. What happens if there is a serious safety issue with one of their main products? What happens if a major new competitor enters the market? What happens if one of their main suppliers goes out of business?

Contingency planning means taking into account the fact that these unwelcome events *could* happen (what if?). To take one of the above imaginary scenarios; *an important supplier goes out of business.* Dave and Martin Robson may look at their supplier firms and decide which ones are critical to their business. For these suppliers, a contingency plan may involve studying market and financial intelligence. The aim is to discover the strength of the supplier and estimate the likelihood of failure. An assessment needs to be made of the impact of a potential failure of various suppliers. Contract terms need to be checked. When all of these things have been established, the contingency plan needs to be drawn up.

For any e-business, the process of contingency planning must involve consultation among senior management. There needs to be common agreement based on the various areas of expertise within the firm. One of the most basic contingencies for an e-business is to prepare for a failure of their website, known as 'downtime'. Various unforeseen circumstances could cause a site to go down through no fault of the firm. Accusations of unreliability can be disastrous for an e-business. Daniel Amor (*Proactive Contingency Planning*, Advisor.com October 2000) suggests that managers could adopt a 'high availability' strategy designed to minimise downtime. This is an expensive option, but if the e-business is highly dependent on revenue from internet connection, then it has two servers not one. In this way, downtime is minimised and customer needs can be met more reliably.

The *essential components* of a contingency planning framework will be:

1   Anticipate what the risks will be.

2   Budget for 'worst case' scenarios.

3   PLAN what action to take.

4   Test the systems; test the website.

5   Communicate early (with staff, with customers, with external stakeholders) in the event of the worst happening.

Risk analysis

The contingency planning process described above will be complemented by a process of risk analysis. This means closely looking at what the business does and determining those areas where risks of error or omission are present. There are a number of ways of doing this.

An e-commerce site is dependent upon content. There is a risk involved in the provision and input of content to a website, or indeed any other aspect of an information system. There is a well known term, GIGO (garbage in, garbage out), referring to a computers capacity to trot out rubbish if that is what someone has input. In e-business, several departments can be responsible for providing content to a website. Careful risk analysis is designed to identify where mistakes can happen as a start in preventing their impact.

We know that *technology* changes all the time. Long before a system is implemented, managers can be sure that someone somewhere is working to make it totally redundant. On the other hand, sometimes the latest technology is the most vulnerable to problems. How does a business know which technology to employ? Making sure that information systems work, integrate with each other, and will last, involves a good deal of risk. The important thing for the e-business is to ensure that they are capable of staying in touch with ongoing technological developments and planning ahead.

There are other risks that the e-business must face up to. There is a risk that the business may run out of **physical** space to operate its e-commerce site effectively. Save and Drive, or any other SME adopting an e-commerce strategy, may face mounting orders and a need to operate a demanding level of storage or shipping. This might involve a number of delicate relationships with carriers. There may be internal problems with *human resources* as staff may not have the necessary skills to efficiently operate the information systems linked to the e-commerce function. Any internal IT staff might become overloaded, or the business becomes hugely over-dependent on a few skilled staff. External to the business, there are always political and social questions that might damage the business (see PESTLE analysis in Unit 13).

People who run businesses are used to facing up to risk. By their nature, entrepreneurs are risk takers. However, they only take risks when they those risks have been carefully considered and placed into context. This is in the nature of e-business success; face up to potential problems and risks and plan, organise and manage to overcome them.

Securing data and system software

One of the major risks in conducting e-business on the internet is that data or software will be insecure and open to damage or attack from external sources. The internet is by its nature open and uncontrolled. The potential for lucrative business must be balanced with a concern for security.

Daniel Amor in his book *The e-business (r)evolution* (2002) argues that e-businesses need to concentrate on five areas relating to information security:

- **Confidentiality** – control who gets access to certain information and restrict access to others.
- **Integrity** – information and programs are changed only in a specific and authorised manner.
- **Availability** – authorised users have continuous access to data resources.
- **Legitimate** use – resources must be used in an authorised way.
- **Non-repudiation** – a binding agreement between two parties in a transaction cannot be refused if there is 'irrefutable' evidence it exists.

An e-business, it seems, requires an information policy to *systematically* set these things out and it needs to employ technology where possible to enforce them.
The *risks to data* can be classified (according to Amor) as:

1   Loss of data integrity. Information is changed by an intruder.

2   Loss of data privacy. Information made available to unauthorised persons.

3   Loss of internet service. Downtime due to outside factors.

4   Loss of control. Data is used by people in an unauthorised way.

There are a number of steps that the e-business can take to practically minimise the risks to the company's data. Strict internal policies to do with data access and authorisation is one approach; another is to employ a carefully thought out system using encrypted communication. In this, all communications are encrypted, meaning they are coded and thereby hidden from third party, unauthorised, viewing. An encrypted message cannot be read without a 'key' and this is given only to strictly authorised personnel.

Outcome activity

Implementing an e-business

You are acting as a consultant to a medium sized manufacturing company (OR a local company of your choice) which is about to implement an e-business strategy involving a good deal of internet commerce. The strategy has, with your help, been very well planned and management feel they are well placed to make a success of this new sales channel. You are now required to produce a full report at this final implementation stage, giving your closing advice before the company takes further practical steps.

Tasks marked **1** attract Pass grade; Merit and Distinction require further work.

Your report should be structured into four *sections:*

Section one

1   Describe the key features of e-business implementation on the business.

To achieve a Merit you must also:

2   Explain the likely impact of e-business implementation on the business.

To achieve a Distinction you must in addition:

3   Evaluate the likely impact of e-business implementation on the business.

Section two

1   Outline a possible marketing plan for the business.

To achieve a Merit you must also:

2   Explain how the marketing plan you have outlined will help the business and contribute to its e-business strategy.

To achieve a Distinction you must in addition:

3   Evaluate the strengths and weaknesses of the marketing plan you suggest for the business.

Section three

1   Outline the likely impact on customers and staff of the firm, of the issues that are known to be associated with e-business implementation.

To achieve a Merit you must also:

2   Analyse the likely impact on customers and staff of the issues known to be associated with e-business implementation.

To achieve a Distinction you must in addition:

3   Evaluate the likely impact on customers and staff of the issues known to be associated with e-business implementation.

Section four

1   Outline the process of contingency planning and risk analysis likely to apply to the business as it implements an e-business strategy.

To achieve a Merit you must also:

2   Analyse the process of contingency planning and risk analysis likely to apply to the business as it implements an e-business strategy.

To achieve a Distinction you must in addition:

3   Evaluate the importance of contingency planning and risk analysis likely to apply to the business as it implements an e-business strategy.

Glossary of terms

Affiliate program	A method of placing links from one website to another based on collaborative agreement.
ASP (Application Service Provider)	A business offering software applications, or services, to meet particular business requirements.
Authoring tool	A software package that allows for the creation of web pages without any understanding of **HTML**.
B2C	Online transactions from business to (private) consumer.
B2B	Online transactions from business to business.
Bandwidth	A measure of the maximum amount of information that can be sent through a connection at a given time. Measured in bits per second (bps).
Banner ad	A rectangular promotional advert running horizontally across the top of a web page, often animated.
BPRE (Business Process Re-engineering)	Looking at the entire set of internal processes of a business with a view to finding new ways, often assisted by **ICT**.
Break-even point	The point at which total revenue from sales is equal to total costs.
Bricks and mortar	A business which is largely an offline physical operation, but with a limited online presence.
Broadband	A faster internet connection achieved through greater **bandwidth** measured in bits per second, (bps) capable of carrying a greater variety of data types (images, audio, video).
Browser	A software application that permits internet resources to be read on screen.
CBI (Confederation of British Industry)	A representative body offering the combined views of private industry in the UK.
Channel conflict	Tension or aggravation caused between businesses when an internet channel is opened up in direct competition with a long established *existing* channel; typically when a retailer is bypassed in favour of direct internet sales.
Churn rate	The rate at which customers stop using a product or service.
Clicks and mortar	A business combining an offline and an online presence.
Click-through	The rate at which users click on a link to another web page.
Contingency planning	Planning for unforeseen events, just in case.
Contract	A binding agreement between two parties.
Conversion rate	The percentage of visitors to a website that are persuaded to make a purchase or take other desirable action.
Cookie	A small file placed in a browser by a web server, that can later be used to identify a user.
CRM (Customer Relationship Management)	Usually referring to sophisticated software packages that hold customer databases and automatic response systems.
CSS (Cascading Style Sheet)	A method of creating blocks of **HTML** code that affects the styles of web pages across an entire site. Style sheets 'cascade' because several style sheets can apply to a single page.
Customisation	The ability to make what is offered from a website meet personal requirements; to alter web content to suit. (similar, but different to **personalisation**)
Data dictionary	A simple store of all data types and relationships to be found in a particular database
DBMS (Database Management System)	A computerised system to access a database, to store data, retrieve data, change data, add data or delete data. Microsoft Access is an example.
Deep linking	The process of pointing to links from one web page to documents within other websites, *other than the Home page.*
Digital signature	A method of electronically authenticating that a document originates from a particular party, by creating a unique identifier in the form of a sequence of bits.
Disintermediation	Bypassing the 'middle-man' (such as wholesaler or retailer) and distributing products directly to the internet purchaser.
DNS (Domain Name System)	A computer holding a database of all internet protocol addresses and domain names.

Domain name	The part of the internet web address that refers to the server and country code of a website – often the same as a company name.
Dot.com	A business created for purely internet operation.
DTD (Document Type Definition)	Included within a web page header code and specifies the type of web document that follows.
DTI (The Department for Trade and Industry)	A government department dealing with matters to do with private trade.
Dynamic content	Web page content that changes to suit the visitor.
Dynamic pricing	Techniques of altering web prices automatically to suit market conditions.
e-Envoy	A government office responsible for promoting e-business practices and encouraging the take up of e-government initiatives.
e-Minister	A government office responsible for promoting the 'e-agenda' in cabinet.
Encryption	A method of encoding digital data so that it cannot be read by a third party not possessing a 'key'.
Entity	A particular component in a relational database usually represented as a table, e.g. owner.
e-procurement	Digitising the entire purchasing process for a business so that initial requisition, ordering, delivery acknowledgement and payment are all computerised and web enabled.
ERP (Enterprise Resource Planning)	Complex computerised systems for planning all resources needed for production. Includes human resources, raw materials, components and finance.
e-strategy	A business strategy aimed at exploiting digital and web based opportunities.
e-tailer	An online retailing operation.
Extranet	An extended network of computers based on internet technology, going beyond particular organisations but restricted in access.
Five forces analysis	Based on an approach made famous by Michael Porter, a structured way of looking at forces at work within particular industries.
Fixed costs	Costs that are incurred irrespective of what is produced.
Foreign key	A unique identifier that acts as a **primary key** in one table but is foreign to another.
Free market	A market in which goods and services are bought and sold according to fluctuations in supply and demand.
FTP server	A computer providing facilities for file transfer protocols to be used allowing movement of files from one internet site to another.
Gantt Chart	A chart used for project planning allowing for timing and sequencing of a series of related activities.
Gearing ratio	The relationship between external capital and ordinary shareholder capital
GIF (Graphic Interchange Format)	An alternative file format for images in web pages.
Horizontal portal	A **portal** that leads to other sites from firms in different industrial sectors.
HTML (HyperText Markup Language)	The language of the web that is read by browsers to display web page content.
HTTP (HyperText Transfer Protocol)	The agreed way of transporting files from a web server to a browser.
Hypertext	Text that allows a **click-through** to another web document, fundamental to the entire World Wide Web.
ICT (Information and Communications Technology)	A collective term for all computer hardware and software used in a variety of commercial and public contexts.
Infomediary	A third party web-based service, operating for profit, offering consumer information of use to online businesses.
Innovation	Finding new ways of doing something, often assisted by **ICT**.
Intranet	A private, restricted network of computers based on internet technology; usually confined to particular organisations.
ISP (Internet Service Provider)	A company that owns computer equipment and telecommunication line access, allowing it to offer internet access services to individuals and firms.
IVP (Internet Value Proposition)	The notion of value offered from a website designed to attract and retain a potential user.

JPEG (Joint Photographics Experts Group)	A bitmap file format, based on colour pixels, often used for photographic images within web pages.
Jurisdiction	The formal power to decide on a question of dispute.
Logistics	The art of efficiently moving and storing goods.
Market share	The ratio of total sales in a market, to the sales of a particular product.
Marketing mix	A set of marketing tactics based on a number of features of a businesses activities; such as product, price, place and promotion.
Marketing remix	Altering or modifying the ingredients of the **marketing mix** to suit the internet.
Market-led approach	A business attitude that favours a responsiveness to market changes and developments.
Mission statement	An attempt made by business management to create a catch all sentence saying what the business aims to achieve.
MRO (Maintenance, repair and operation)	Shorthand terminology for all things a business often needs to buy in so that it can continue to function.
Normalisation	A systematic process of ordering and isolating data in such a way that repetition is avoided and efficient relationships can be created in designing a database.
Opt-in mail	Emails that are sent because a user has opted to receive them.
Organisational culture	The pattern of accepted attitudes and practices within a particular organisation.
PDA (Personal Digital Assistant)	A handheld computer.
Personalisation	The technique of making website content relate to a particular individual, based on knowledge of past purchases or history (similar, but different to **customisation**).
PERT (Programme Evaluation and Review Technique)	A way of systematically planning a project by timing the activities.
Portal	A website that acts as a gateway site leading to others.
POP (Point of Presence)	On the internet, the local access to the services of an **ISP (Internet Service Provider)**
Price elasticity of demand	The sensitivity of demand to alterations in price.
Primary key	A unique identifier within a table such as an order number.
Primary research	Original or new research, discovering new facts.
Primary sector	Part of an economy that works with raw materials in their original form, e.g. mining or agriculture.
Product fulfilment	Actual supply of a product once it is ordered.
Product-led approach	A business attitude (leading to inertia) towards marketing, based on views about products on offer.
Prosumer	A term created by Alvin Toffler. A person who actively participates in creating desired products rather than passively accepting those on offer to mass markets.
Protocol	Accepted rules specifying how computers or other devices communicate with each other.
Prototype	A test version of something used to find out if it works as it should.
Psychographic	Methods of identifying target groups within a market based upon various combinations of lifestyle or income characteristics.
Public sector	Organisations that are government funded.
Qualitative data	Data based upon opinion and feelings.
Quantitative data	Data based upon numerical analysis.
Query	A request to a database for information from relational tables.
Record	A single row in a table in a database.
Reintermediation	The introduction of new forms of 'middle-man' on the internet, e.g. websites giving shopping advice.
Relational database	A database that is created with a number of related tables and in which links are created as and when a user requests them, e.g. vehicles owners and registration numbers.
Relationship marketing	A marketing strategy that is based on establishing close relationships and understanding between firms and their customers.
Rule of law	The constitutional convention that stresses that the law applies equally to all.

Search engine	A website offering a service based on spiders or robots that search other registered websites and index the contents.
Secondary research	Research drawing on data already gathered.
Secondary sector	Part of an economy that uses raw materials in order to manufacture goods or services.
Segmentation	Breaking a market into smaller segments to better identify needs or requirements.
Server	A computer or device that provides services to other 'client' computers or devices.
SME (Small to medium sized enterprise)	A firm with no fewer than 50 and no more than 250 staff.
Stakeholder	An individual or a group with a particular interest in the success or survival of a business; can be internal or external to the business.
SQL (Structured Query Language)	A programming language for communicating with databases.
SSL (Secure sockets layer)	A method used to scramble data as it is sent across the web so that it cannot be read by a third party.
SPAM (Sending persistent annoying mail)	Junk e-mails that were not requested.
Startup business	A business just set up, starting out for the first time.
Static ad	An advertisement that is not animated on a web page.
Static content	Web pages where the content stays the same.
SMTP (Simple mail transfer protocol)	The rules by which e-mail is sent over the internet.
Superstitial ad	An advertisement that pops up between web pages as they load.
SWOT analysis	A structured way of looking at a business' current situation according to strengths, weaknesses, opportunities and threats.
Tag	A piece of **HTML** telling a browser that what follows should be rendered in a certain way; e.g. the tag **<B>** surrounding text, instructs a browser to render it in bold.
Targeting	Focusing a marketing effort towards a specific group.
TCP/IP (Transmission control protocol/ internet protocol)	An agreed set of rules by which packets of data are sent across the internet and reassembled by the receiver.
Tertiary sector	Part of an economy providing services such as banking, transport, leisure or retail.
Trading bloc	A continental group of nations combining together to form a unified economic power; e.g. the USA, Europe.
URL (Uniform resource locator)	More commonly known as the 'web address' and consisting of a set format often showing a server/directory/filename/document title. (e.g. www.heinemann.co.uk)
USP (Unique selling proposition)	An aspect, or aspects, of a tangible product designed to appeal to potential purchasers.
Value chain	A way of looking at how supply chain activities add extra value to products or services.
Variable costs	Costs that are associated with each unit of production.
Venture capital	Money found from interested investors who are seeking a profitable return in the future.
Vertical portal	A **portal** that leads off to other sites within the same industrial sector.
Viral marketing	Marketing that depends on e-mail or other electronic messages spreading around many users.
VLE (Virtual learning environment)	A software package that creates an online environment containing resources and communication tools between learners and teachers, e.g. www.Blackboard.com).
W3C	The World Wide Web Consortium. A group of neutral web experts – supported by a small team of full time staff – drawn from the worldwide pool of web developers, researchers and users. The W3C is charged with *leading* the World Wide Web into the future.
WAP (Wireless application protocol)	A specified set of communication protocols allowing wireless devices such as mobile phones to access the web.
Webographics	Statistical studies of web use and trends.
Web server	A computer that provides World Wide Web services onto the internet or an intranet.
WYSIWYG (What you see is what you get)	What you see on a computer screen will be the same as either what is printed out, or the same as that rendered by a browser.
XML (Extensible markup language)	A flexible method (unlike **HTML**) of creating web data and formats that apply to specific contexts, thereby making them understood and applicable in partner business relationships.

Index